ADVANCED PROJECT MANAGEMENT

Advanced Project Management

F L HARRISON

Gower

Published by
Gower Publishing Company Limited,
Gower House, Croft Road, Aldershot,
Hants, England

 British Library Cataloguing in Publication Data

Harrison, F. L.
   Advanced project management.
   1. Industrial project management
   I. Title
   658.4'04   HD69.P75

ISBN 0-566-02249-4

Printed and bound in Great Britain by
Biddles Ltd, Guildford and King's Lynn

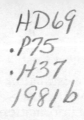

Contents

Illustrations

Preface

Project management is a highly professional branch of management which is used in all areas of industry, commerce and government. It involves the application of many specialist concepts and techniques, but all too often people working on projects receive little or no education or training in project management. As a result, the same mistakes are made over and over again, and projects cost more, and take longer, than necessary.

This book aims to bridge the gap between introductory books on project management, planning and control, and advanced professional practice. There are light-years of difference between, say, a training in simple critical path analysis adequate to plan and control a small project, and the training and experience required to handle the problems encountered in the management, planning and control of the typical manufacturing or construction project. Thus, this book is intended to be:-

- a professional level guide to the management, planning and control for engineers, accountants, managers, architects, chartered surveyors and others involved in project work.
- an advanced text-book for senior undergraduates and post-graduate students taking the courses in project and construction management which have been, or are being, introduced in many universities, business schools and colleges.

Over the last ten years, our knowledge and experience of project management, planning and control have increased considerably, and methods have been developed to overcome many of the problems encountered. This book describes how these modern concepts and techniques can save time and money. It draws on many years' experience of project management, planning and control, developments on North Sea Oil related projects and the US aerospace/weapons industries, experience with modern computer-based information systems, and organisation and human behaviour theories.

The book begins by describing the different forms of organisation structure used in project work, and enlarges on the 'matrix' form for single and multi-company project organisations.

The next three chapters deal with how to organise the planning process. They discuss who should do the planning, the role of the planner in 'real-time' planning, and the common misapplications of planning techniques, and describe the characteristic evolutionary life cycle of project planning, the various stages and levels of planning.

This part of the book also looks at the importance of manpower planning, critically reviews and compares the basic planning techniques and outlines the difficulties involved in applying these techniques to the larger project. It outlines the requirements of modern project computing systems and planning packages and describes how these systems can be used in conjunction with such techniques as milestone charting and S charts. The use of planning library modules, multi-project planning and control, and the Line of Balance technique are all explored in detail.

Chapters 5 to 10 contain a thorough treatment of estimating, budgeting and cost control. They outline the modern approach to project control, involving an integrated project management information system based on the use of the work breakdown structure, the work package concept, and forward-looking performance analysis integrating schedule and cost control.

The final chapter examines the all-important problems of human relations in the context of project management, including the basis for the 'authority' of the project manager, methods of coping with 'we-they' attitudes and conflict, and how to develop teamwork.

Acknowledgements

Many people have contributed, directly or indirectly, to this book. In particular I would like to thank:

Sally and Maureen for the typing and retyping of my manuscript without a grumble;

all those from the following companies, who have helped me alone the way to learn my trade, and encouraged me to try out the concepts and techniques outlines in the book – N.C.B., Cementation, I.C.I., Imperial Oil (Canada), Anderson Strathclyde and the Defense Systems Management College, Virginia;

my long suffering family for their patience, sacrifice and support.

F. L. Harrison
January 1981

1 Introduction

A project can be defined as a non-routine, non-repetitive, one-off undertaking, normally with discrete time, financial and technical performance goals. Since the late 1950s the terms project engineer, project co-ordinator, programme or project manager have become common and are signs of the increasing use of projects in all areas of industry, commerce and government.

Organisations using projects are, knowingly or unknowingly, involved in a relatively new concept of management, namely, project management. The management of projects is very different from the normal management of operations, and involves specialised forms of organisation and methods of planning and control. Training and experience in general management, or even in construction management, are not sufficient for effective project management, which has grown to become a separate, highly sophisticated area of management. The definition of the project management concept as a specialist area of management came about initially in the US Aerospace Weapons Research and Development Industries. The Manhattan Project during World War II was an early example, but it was not until the 1950s that project management began to crystallise into its present form. The problems of taking an aircraft, or weapons system from early research through technical development, design and manufacture are fraught with complexity, uncertainties and difficulties. This is particularly so when working on the frontiers of technology. Planning and cost control in these kinds of projects are very difficult, and different organisation structures, authority and responsibility patterns, and specialist

1

techniques are necessary. Other important users of the project management concept, from its earliest days, are the oil and chemical industries, with the engineering contractors involved in these industries. The management of engineering, design and construction projects in these process industries involves many of the same difficulties as in aerospace weapons projects.

These two industries are today probably the most professional in the application of the project management concept, and make widespread use of the most sophisticated techniques. Professional project managers in the large oil and chemical design and construction contractors are employed on an international, worldwide basis.

Large civil engineering contractors have also implicitly employed the project manager concept in contract management for centuries. However, in the past their projects tended to be not as complex as the aerospace/weapons and oil/chemical industry projects, and specialised organisation structures, planning and control techniques were not explicitly recognised or used. Today this has changed, and project management concepts and techniques are in common use in the civil engineering industry.

The project concept is also used in high technology research and development, in the engineering and manufacturing industries for new product development and manufacture, and in the design and construction of new plant and equipment. Building a new steel plant, manufacturing a boiler for a power station, adding a plant extension, developing and beginning the manufacture of a new product, designing, manufacturing and installing a heating and ventilation system are all projects, with similar problems and require similar management and techniques.

The design and introduction of computer systems, and the development and introduction of new suites of computer program also uses the project management concept. Thus the computing industry and the computing function within companies, both employ project management.

Outside the engineering field we find that the concept of product management in marketing is very similar to that of project management; the organisational forms, managerial

2

problems, planning and control techniques are almost identical. Similarly, the introduction of new products, the feasibility study for a company take-over, and the improvement of industrial relations in a company can all be treated as projects, and can benefit from the use of the project management concepts and techniques.

Many firms who have traditionally not been involved in project work are being forced to adopt project management concepts. This is partly because of the benefits obtained, but principally because customers, particularly foreign customers, are insisting on one firm taking overall responsibility for all the work involved in manufacturing, supplying and, or, constructing large and complex orders or contracts.

Therefore, projects, and as a consequence (explicitly or implicitly) project management, are being increasingly used in all areas of engineering, construction, manufacturing, research and development. These projects have similar management needs and problems, and thus the concepts and techniques of project management transcend industry barriers and all areas of engineering.

Projects and project management are used in some form or other, on many small scale ventures with good results, but it is on large scale applications that good project management is a really significant factor. The problems of man-management, financial management, planning and control, where many firms are involved, with long time spans, large uncertainties and very large sums of money, can lead to inefficiency, delays in completion and wasted money, unless effective project management is used.

Why project management?

The principal reason for the development of the project management concept, organisation, and specialised, often highly sophisticated techniques, is that the traditional forms of organisation structure and management techniques do not handle project type work effectively. There is a need for different forms of organisation, specialised information systems, managers skilled in the techniques of project planning, financial management, control and the particular human problem arising in project work, because of the special characteristics of projects and the problems caused by them.

Projects are essentially temporary activities for those concerned, with typical lives of from six months to five years. Management, organisation and information systems have to be established anew for each project, and there can also be only a very limited learning curve for those involved. Perhaps a manager may only pass through each phase of a project once, every year to five years. In addition, decision making in project work tends not to be repetitive and bad decisions at any stage in a project affect a project throughout its life, and it is not generally possible to recover from early deficiencies in project management.

Normally, projects involve several departments of a company working together and in the majority of cases more than one company is involved in work on one project. Often these departments, or companies are working on several projects at the same time, each at different stages in the project life cycle. Project work is therefore necessarily complex with respect to interdependencies between the departments and companies involved. This involves, explicitly, a complex organisation, including people from many different professions, backgrounds, trades, departments and companies. Additionally, these relationships and interdependencies are dynamic and never static. Typically at the start of a project, work emphasis may be in research and development; it then changes to engineering design, to purchasing and procurement, to manufacturing and, or construction, to testing and commissioning, and finally to operation. No one functional department or company is the most important over the whole life of the project and thus no individual functional manager can assume the leading management role for the complete project.

Because projects are unique one-off undertakings, there are problems in defining work, organisation, allocating responsibility, budgeting, planning, control, communication and co-ordination. Many projects have suffered difficulties because of a lack of clear definition of organisation structure, which in turn compounds these problems. Great emphasis must be given in project work to the planning and control activities, and many projects have suffered delays and over-expenditure because of inadequate planning and control systems. Special project orientated information systems are also required for effective project communication, co-ordination and control, and these systems are different from, and generally have to be separate from, the information systems in the normal traditional management organisation. There are also particular difficulties involved in achieving effective communication and co-ordination with several different organisations involved in a project, and as projects get larger and more complex, communication and co-ordination become more and more difficult, and yet more vital to the success of project work.

Usually, project work involves large capital expenditures, and the financial management and control of projects is thus extremely important, to minimise the overall cost of the project.

Finally, the temporary, complex and often loose nature of the relationships and authority patterns involved in project work, combined with the number of different departments and companies involved in any one project, whose objectives and management styles may differ, leads to human behaviour problems and a tendency for conflict between groups and individuals. Thus the traditional management theory and organisational structures have to be modified in project management.

Traditional management theory and project management

The traditional model of an organisational structure is based upon three organisational concepts, which are all violated in the management of projects, namely

1. The functional division of management.
2. The hierarchical concept of superior — subordinate relationships.
3. A number of so-called principles of management.

The conventional form of company organisation divides the

people in the company into groups of similar skills, interest, training and occupational specialisation. Therefore one normally finds a company organised into departments, such as engineering design, construction, plant operations, purchasing, marketing and finance. Such an organisation used in project work permits the efficient use of labour on several projects, as more or less people can be allocated to projects as required. It also increases the rate of development of professional skills by constant contact and interaction with colleagues in the same specialism. It permits the division of labour by specialism, for example, it is possible to have electronics, electrical and an instrument engineers in the same department. They can then be allocated to each project in turn as required, but retain their departmental base. Thus the functional organisation permits the efficient use and development of resources on multi-project work.

The functional organisation thus gives the organisation a horizontal dimension, into which it is divided by departments, and added to this there is a vertical dimension, with different levels, which represent varying degrees of authority. This hierarchical structure is the basic framework of the organisation and the superior — subordinate relationships are the lines in which authority flows from the top management to the lowest levels. Grafted on to this, in all but the smallest company, is a division of organisational elements into line and staff groups. Line managers have a direct responsibility for achieving the goals of the organisation, decision making and exercising authority. Staff members advise and counsel the line managers and have no legal authority, except within their own functional department, and are typically professional specialists. This structure forms the traditional management pyramid, with the only focal point of power binding the organisation together being the top management of the company, or division. This organisation is best suited to the handling of a continuous flow of basically repetitive work, with each department working on its own function. This is the situation in the typical factory department, or office and leads to stable interpersonnel and departmental relationships.

Unfortunately this traditional form of organisation does not handle projects efficiently, tends not to meet schedules and is operations orientated and not project or goal orientated. There are severe difficulties involved in achieving effective communication, collaboration, co-ordination and control with several different functional departments involved in a project with this form of organisation. The differences in activity, philosophy, education, training and personal values also tend to increase the likelihood of conflict and misunderstanding between functions, when engaged in project work under time and cost pressures.

In addition this traditional form of managerial organisation just cannot handle the dynamic, everchanging relationship and the complexities involved in project work. In large projects and in those industries where development, design, procurement and construction or manufacture must often overlap to achieve the shortest possible project time this is a particular problem. Effective communication and co-ordination of effort among departments and companies are very difficult to achieve with the standard functional organisations in project work, and yet lack of these functions is one of the routes to failure, especially where several companies, for example owner, contractors and sub-contractors, are involved in one project. The traditional organisation has no means of managing or co-ordinating their efforts through all stages of the work. It has no means of integrating different departments, at levels below top management, customers, contractors, sub-contractors, material and equipment suppliers into one organisation. Thus a special project form of organisation is required to tie together these separate organisations into one global organisation.

A different form of organisation is required from the traditional pyramid, which can transcend the individual department, division or company, with, in the extreme case, hundreds of companies involved. A form of organisation is required that ties together these separate organisations into one global organisation. To back up this, a project management information system is required for each individual project, which is normally separate from the normal operational management information system of a company. This form of organisation has come to be called the project, or 'matrix' organisation.

Even with this form of project organisation, there is the need for a separate management function to manage projects. The senior general management of a company cannot give the concentrated attention required for the effective management of any individual project. This is particularly so, when a stream of projects is being handled, each in a different stage of the project life cycle, for example, development, design, manufacture or construction. With the traditional departmental form of organisation, no one manager is entirely responsible for, and manages a project throughout its life. Emphasis by functional managers is often given more to the technical success of the project, rather than to the time or financial success. Functional departmental managers tend to concentrate their efforts and understanding within their own departments. This often leads to tunnel vision, that is, they can only view a project within the narrow scope of their own function and cannot exercise judgement on the overall project.

There is thus a need for vesting in one individual or group, responsibility for integrating all the management functions and activities of the many sub-organisations involved in the project undertaking. The man responsible for a project may be called a project manager, have complete control over all aspects of his project and manage a large organisation. At the other end of the scale, he may be called a project engineer or co-ordinator, with only part of his time spent in management duties, have very little authority and no staff. Both these people have the same responsibilities, and their management duties cover the same critical areas of management.

The project manager concept has thus evolved to be a general management and integrationist activity, below the level of top management. It provides the individual responsibility, management and co-ordination for any one project, which is essential for the success of any such undertaking. The project manager is responsible for the success of his project in terms of time, cost and technical performance. He must provide the management and leadership necessary to bind the people and groups from different department and companies working on the project, into one managerial organisation and team, and provide the drive necessary to ensure completion on time and within cost.

Thus the project management concept endeavours to provide at the minimum, the co-ordination of the work of the different groups involved and, at the maximum, the integration of all the groups involved into one effective organisation.

The characteristics of project management, which also cause it to differ from conventional management theory and which clash with the conventional principles of management theory, are that the project manager must manage people in his own company functional departments, and outside companies, from a position sometimes junior to department heads, and normally outside the traditional pyramid structure of authority. He deals vertically, horizontally and diagonally with peers and associates as well as their superiors and subordinates. No matter how necessary the horizontal and diagonal activities are, relationships are difficult to formally define, and the project manager usually has indefinite, or little direct authority over all the people working on the project.

Because of the distinctive characteristics of projects and work on them, these project personnel must also have specialised skills and knowledge of the techniques used in project planning, financial management, and control. In addition, they must have skills in handling the human problems which arise because of the characteristics of projects and also because of the particular problems associated with the project organisation. In this, several of the so-called principles of management, such as authority must equal responsibility and a subordinate must only have one superior, must be disregarded, with consequential problems in human relations.

The project manager has to have some knowledge of, and judgement of, the functions and disciplines contributing to a project, but above all he has to be a skilled manager. Unfortunately, the education and training of engineers is generally confined to technical functions and does not normally encompass organisation structure, management information systems, communication and co-ordination, specialised planning, financial management and control techniques, and the human relation skills required. These functions are essential to the success of project work, and it is in these areas a project manager must be a specialist.

Thus the management of projects is a difficult form of management and many projects have suffered in the past from inefficient project management, resulting in increased cost, delays in completion and managerial conflict. Recent experience, with particular emphasis on North Sea Oil related projects, has shown that the principal areas in which shortcomings in project management contribute to cost escalation and delays in the completion of projects are as follows.

1. The general management and logistics problems arising from the complex interactive nature of project work.
2. Lack of clear definition of organisation structure, which causes problems of authority, responsibility, communication and co-ordination.
3. Inadequate planning, budgeting and control systems, not integrated with the management structure.
4. The intergroup, interpersonal problems and conflicts that arise in the flexible and complex organisation of projects.

However, effective project management has been successful in handling the many planning, communication and co-ordination problems involved in project work. It has proved capable of integrating the various personnel and groups into one organisation and, due to the nature of project work, developing effective team work and commitment to the project objectives. It is now widely accepted, implicitly or explicitly, that some form of project management is necessary where large and complex undertakings are involved, and that its effectiveness can significantly influence the cost of a project and the time taken to complete a project.

2 Project Organisation

The form of organisation used to manage projects is often indefinite, or informal. Yet recognition of what organisational form is to be used, and its particular characteristics, are critical to the success of project work. Many failures are due to the lack of a clear definition of the organisation structure for the project, who is responsible for what and how much authority the project manager has or does not have. In addition, it is also critical for good performance that the organisation structure be related to the work to be done on the project, and that it be integrated with the planning and control systems.

Many projects are large and complex, and involve several contributing organisations, some of which are normally separate companies. In such projects, the organisation structure must, in turn, also inevitably be complex, and it is useful to look at the structure of the project organisation on two scales; namely, the project organisation within a single company, that is, in-company project organisation, and the global project organisation tieing several organisations into one project organisation.

In-company project organisation

There are three forms of project organisation in use today, with the underlying basic difference between then being the amount of authority that is given to the person responsible for the project, namely,

1. A line and staff organisation, i.e. a project co-ordinator.
2. A divisional organisation.
3. The 'matrix' organisation.

Project co-ordinator

The first stage of evolution to some form of project orientated organisation is to appoint someone, whose prime responsibility is the project, to co-ordinate the work on the project of the people in the functional departments. In this form of project organisation, the person responsible for the project acts essentially in a staff position to support line management in the functional department, and retains the traditional line and staff functional organisation essentially unchanged. This form of project organisation exists in three variations, where the person responsible:

1. Is a staff assistant to a senior general manager, and co-ordinates work on the project.
2. Is a project engineer, for example, in a factory, responsible for works projects, carried out by in-company personnel and sub-contractors.
3. Is a functional member of a group of people working on a project, and is given the additional responsibility of co-ordinating the work of the group.

The emphasis in this form of project organisation structure is on co-ordination, communication, planning and control. The project co-ordinator acts as a focal point for information on the project and is seen as in an advisory staff position, with the ear of the general manager, but not having line management authority and direct responsibility for the project.

This position generally has little status, and is normally occupied by a relatively junior engineer, with little authority or experience and training in specialist project management, planning and control techniques. Thus the project is not managed, it is co-ordinated. The project co-ordinator can only monitor progress, practice a weak form of co-ordination, given the goodwill of the functional personnel involved, and is in the position of a suppliant to the managers of the functional departments. He cannot effectively bring pressure to bear, or exert authority to obtain action. He must persuade others, from a position of weakness, and feels very insecure and frustrated, and is generally unsure of his role.

He finds it very difficult to manage, or exert leadership on the project, and control is normally weak. When evidence of an early trend is slight and inconclusive, he cannot normally get action. It is only when adverse trends are patently obvious, that he can get change implemented, and this is normally too late. Thus, this form of organisation can achieve the co-ordination of project work, but loses many of the advantages of the project management concept, and is normally only suitable for small projects.

Divisional project organisation

At the other end of the spectrum is the Divisional Project Organisation, which is the strongest form of project organisation. Personnel are allocated completely to the project organisation for the life of the project and the project manager has full line management authority, at least over people from his own company. This is in effect, setting up a separate goal-oriented division of the company, with its own functional departments. The project manager still has the problem of managing and co-ordinating the other companies contributing to his project, but he is the complete master of his own company organisation.

This goal-orientated organisation makes the management of projects, and their planning and control easier. With it, there is better integration of those involved, communication, both formal and informal is more frequent and there is more commitment to the project objectives. It thus tends to maximise the probability of completing the project on time and to budget.

Unfortunately it tends to use the scarce resources of a company less efficiently. It is necessary in this form of project organisation to duplicate the specialists in each project, and allocate them in total to each project, more or less for the life of the project. It is also difficult, or very expensive to have a division of labour within a speciality, and a divisional

13

organised project may have to make do with one electrical engineer instead of three specialists.

Therefore, though the separate divisional form of project organisation enables projects to be managed more effectively than the functional and project co-ordinator forms, and it avoids some of the problems of the more complex forms of organisation, it can only generally be used when a company is handling a single important project, or where one project is so very much more important than others, that it justifies setting up a completely separate company division. It cannot normally be used where a company is handling several projects on a continuous basis, as it splinters up the functional and specialist departments. This splintering reduces the number of projects that a company can handle, and it inhibits the transfer of personnel from one project to another as required. There are good reasons for retaining the functional departments intact, not the least of these are that the heads of functional departments are probably long established, exert considerable political power and do not wish to see their departments splintered among projects. In addition, it is an advantage to have these intact functional departments form a pool, from which specialist support can be drawn when required, and which permits the training and development of functional expertise to develop much faster in them, than if they were splintered up.

Thus the functional form of organisation is more efficient in the use of resources, but less effective in meeting project objectives, whereas the divisional form of project organisation is less efficient in the use of resources, but more effective in meeting project objectives. What is required in project work is an organisation which is both efficient in the use of resources and effective in meeting project objectives, and this is what the third form of project organisation, the matrix organisation, endeavours to do, although at the expense of organisational complexity.

Matrix organisation

The organisational form, which predominates in the in-company project organisation, and is used almost exclusively for the global project organisation, has come to be called the 'matrix' organisation. This recognises that lines of authority and responsibility, communication and co-ordination can exist horizontally and diagonally, as well as in a traditional vertical pyramid form. In this form, personnel working on the project have in addition to their responsibility to their own functional superior and, or separate company, a responsibility, or loyalty, to the project and to the man or group appointed to manage the project. There may be several such groups involved in any one project, for example, for the client or owner, contractors, sub-contractor, consultant and equipment suppliers.

In this matrix form of organisation, authority is shared between the project manager and functional managers. The project manager is not the complete master of decisions affecting his project, but operates in a decision-making matrix. His authority or influence cuts across traditional vertical line and staff authority patterns and leads to both horizontal and vertical lines of command.

A typical organisation chart for a matrix project organisation is shown in Figure 2.1. It is essentially a supplementary organisation which integrates people from the primary functional organisation for the purposes of goal achievement. The project manager in the matrix form acts as a junior general manager, and the in-company work is done by the various functional departments, for example, design, purchasing, accounting, construction or manufacturing and operations. It maintains these functional departments intact and permits the development of functional expertise, specialisation and the transfer of staff between projects. Department members can be allocated to a project for its life, or part of its life, on a full-time or part-time basis, but still remain part of the functional department. At the same time, the project relationship integrates them on the other dimension, provides a means of communication and co-ordination, management and leadership, facilitates planning and control, and gains their involvement in the project and their commitment to meeting the project objectives. By making the individual a member of both a functional and goal-oriented organisation it endeavours to obtain the advantages of both.

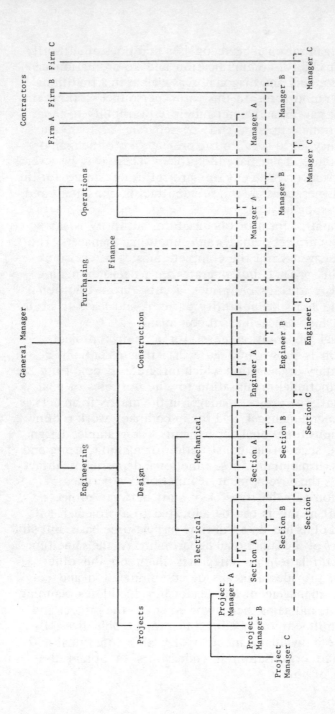

Figure 2.1 Matrix organisation

The project manager must rely on support and services from these functional departments. He determines, in consultation with their managers, what is required and by when, and the functional manager controls how and by whom. The functional line managers can do a better job of allocating their own departmental personnel to the various projects they are working on, than the project manager, as they know the capabilities of their own men and the resources available. The functional manager also has the responsibility for technical decisions within his department, and the project manager cannot compete with them in their own area of specialisation. He can bring pressure to bear regarding schedules and budgets, and ask for a re-evaluation or assessment of alternatives, when there are problems. Nevertheless, responsibility for specific technical decisions in the functional line managers, as they know their own work best, are doing it, and are responsible for it.

This matrix form of project organisation conflicts with traditional organisation theory in many ways. It has inherent in it, dual subordination, division of authority, responsibility without corresponding authority and a disregard for hierarchical principles.

These basic principles of organisation, with which it conflicts, are no more than generalisations about what has been observed to work in practice, based on past organisational experience. Being derived from experience, they are subject to revision in the light of new experiences and circumstances. It is as foolish to be totally bound by past experience, as to ignore it.

Disregard for these principles does mean that the matrix organisation has organisational complexity and an inherent conflict situation, but in large projects, involving different departments, organisations and companies, there is a new set of circumstances. In order to bind all these diverse elements into one organisation, committed to complete a project to its time, cost and performance objectives, and to effectively manage it, a new set of ground rules have had to be evolved.

Global Project Organisation

There is no real alternative to a form of matrix organisation for the global project organisation, as no other organisational concept is applicable, and can tie together all the separate organisation involved, into one organisation. This viewpoint, that all involved, client, contractor, consultant, architect, manufacturing manager, sub-contractor, material and equipment supplier, belong to one organisation is critical to the success of project work. If the performance, or lack of it, of any group or company involved in the project, can influence the overall project's success, then the principal project managers involved must consider them as belonging to the project organisation. Thus project management, communication, co-ordination, planning and control must be extended to embrace all these contributing organisations and integrate them into one global organisation.

These organisations are tied together by lines of authority, or influence, which are sometimes very weak, and often based merely on contractual and purchase order agreements. Thus the form of contract and conditions of purchase orders are lines of influence which determine how the global organisation operates.

This global organisation structure is therefore of necessity complex, often loose, and full of 'dotted' lines. The organisation chart for any particular project differs, depending on the number of principal contractors, who does what, consultants involved, and also differs on the point of view, that is, from the client's project manager, or principal contractors' project manager. One example is shown in Figure 2.2. This shows the principal lines of the project relationships only, and ignores the functional, departmental and company lines of command.

In addition to these project hierarchical relationships, there are normally relationships between similar functional groups in the different sub-organisations, or company. For example, the client's design engineers will communicate, and perhaps supervise the contractor's design work, and the client's construction group will similarly be involved with the contractor's construction group.

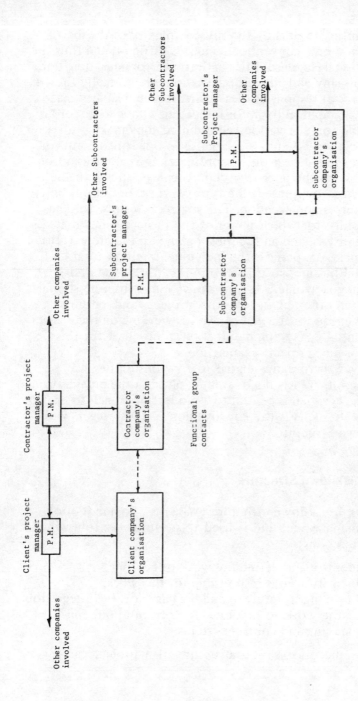

Figure 2.2 Global project organisation

19

Attempting to portray the full complexity of the matrix organisation on a conventional chart is difficult, and thus the organisational responsibilities in the matrix organisation, both for in-company and global organisation, are normally shown in a 'matrix of responsibilities' chart. A responsibility matrix is simply a graphical form for indicating who is to do, or be responsible for, the various component jobs making up a project. Figure 2.3 shows a large scale quadruled form, on which jobs are shown on the ordinate, and people, and or companies, on the abcissa. Symbols can be drawn in the co-ordinates, to represent the type of work, or responsibility, of each person, on each job. This matrix can show who has responsibility for which phase of the project, what that responsibility is, and all the jobs making up the project. It is easy to make up, permits the individual to check what his responsibilities are, so that nothing is overlooked and job overlapping is avoided. It also shows him whom he should consult on other phases of the project, and permits management to see at a glance, who is working on the project. It is essentially, the complex organisation chart for this matrix form of project organisation.

However, before the matrix of responsibilities can be established, there is a major step involved in the organisation of a project, which is central to a modern approach to project management. This is the construction in the project 'Work Breakdown Structure.'

Work Breakdown Structure

The work breakdown structure (WBS) is a major tool of project management and is used to perform the following critical functions:

1. Identify and define the work to be done.
2. Identify who is responsible for this work.
3. Form the structure of and the basis for, the integration of the work to be done, the organisation, and the planning and control systems.

Before the organisation structure of a project can be

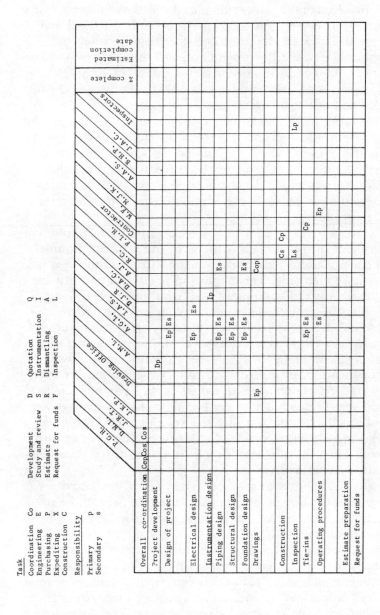

Figure 2.3 Matrix of responsibilities (with initials of those responsible)

formalised and a matrix of responsibilities established, the work involved in the project must be defined and responsibility allocated. The work breakdown structure is a formal and systematic way of defining and identifying what the component parts of the project are, and the work to be done on them. This is an important function, as in a complex project, items of work can be overlooked, that is, slip down cracks, and others duplicated.

This term, work breakdown structure, is simply a name for an end-item oriented family tree subdivision of the projects, products, or item to be built, components, work tasks and services required to complete the project. It defines the project, the work to be done, the organisation, and graphically displays the project. It is very similar to the Bill of Materials used in production planning.

The work breakdown structure is constructed by exploding the project into its component parts and services required, with each of these components, being further subdivided into lower level elements. This explosion is continued until the project is fully defined in terms of 'what' is to be done to complete the project, described as work breakdown structure 'elements'. Large or complex tasks may require numerous subdivisions. Other tasks of lesser complexity, or size, may require substantially fewer levels of work breakdown. Although primarily oriented towards discrete end products, software, services and functional tasks may also be included, provided each element is a meaningful product of management-oriented subdivision of a higher level element. This work breakdown structure divides the work on the project into manageable units of work, for which individual responsibility can then be defined.

Figure 2.4 shows in arrow diagram form, the activities involved in the design and manufacture of a project. Figure 2.5 shows one way of constructing a work breakdown structure for this contract.

In this example, the first level breaks down the overall project into the mechanical subassembly, the electrical and instrument subassembly, basic design, final assembly, general administration and overheads, and project management. In the next level the electrical assembly is broken down into

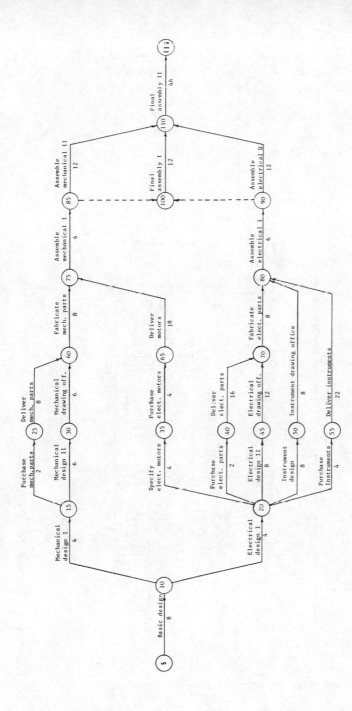

Figure 2.4 Arrow diagram

23

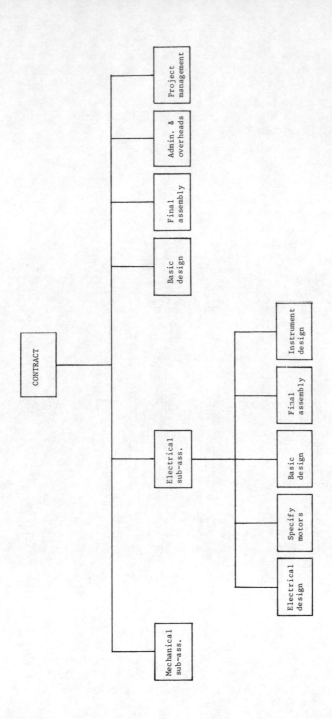

Figure 2.5   Work breakdown structure

24

the electrical components, instrument components, basic design and the integration into the subassembly. This then gives the lowest level of the work breakdown structure of the project, that is, the work breakdown structure elements.

It is often possible to construct a WBS for a project in several different ways, just as with a bill-of-materials for a product, with a different number of levels of breakdown and numbers of elements in each level. It is thus useful for a firm to specify a standard format for the characteristic type of projects it handles. One example of this is the 'Military Standard, Work breakdown Structures for Defence Material Items' used by the US Department of Defence. This covers the first three levels of breakdown for commonly procured items and leaves the contractor to define the further breakdown of the project. Figure 2.6 shows part of the work breakdown structure for a ship system based on this standard.

Thus the work breakdown structure is a formal method for identifying the work to be carried out in a project. However, the project's global organisation structure is also a formal structure which shows how the people and companies involved are going to carry out the work. Integration of the work breakdown structure and organisation structure is necessary in order to assign responsibility for the tasks to be performed. This interrelationship can occur at any level of work breakdown, but it is critical that this integration exists at the level where work is actually carried out.

Thus there is a second stage to the establishment of a project's WBS and this involves identifying the various functional activities required to complete the work on the lowest levels of the WBS elements. This relates to the responsibilities of each department or organisation involved, that is, who does what. Figure 2.7 shows this integration of organisation and work breakdown structure.

The functional work represented by this intersection can be considered an external subcontract or an internal pseudo subcontract, and can be described as a 'cost account' with an organisation and an identifiable person responsible for it, a planned start and finish time, resource requirements and budgeted cost. Just as these factors are defined for the overall project contract, so they must be defined for these key

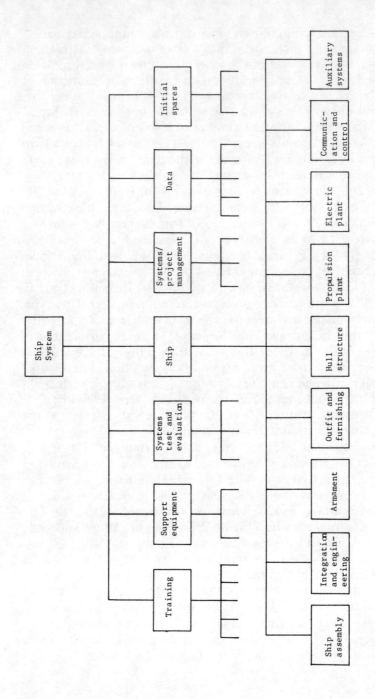

Figure 2.6 WBS for ship system

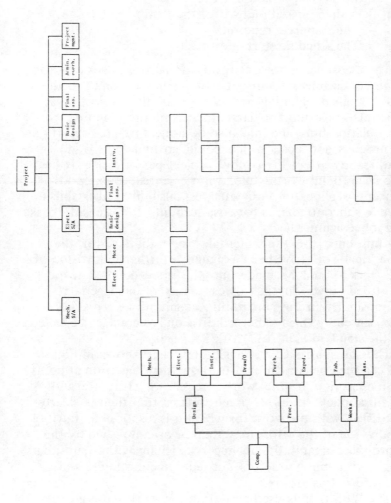

Figure 2.7 Integration of work breakdown structure and organisation. (Showing cost account structure)

27

intersection points, which are essentially subcontracts. Thus each must have formally assigned to it:

1. A description of the work to be performed.
2. Who is responsible for the work.
3. A time phased budget for the work.
4. The resources required.
5. The schedule start and finish.

These cost accounts, or organisational work packages, can represent sizable amounts of work. When it comes to the more detailed planning and control of the project, cost accounts are often too large to permit the planning of interrelationships, and may also be subject to large deviations of progress and cost, which could go undetected and significantly affect the overall project performance. It has also been found worthwhile, if not essential, to extend the concepts of allocating individual responsibility and establishing pseudo subcontracts, as for cost accounts, to lower level tasks and job assignments.

Thus once the fundamental responsibilities for the functional work have been assigned, a further subdivision of the work should be made and the more detailed work identified down to the lowest levels of management responsibility in the performing organisations. This work represented by this further subdivision has come to be called by the standard name of 'Work Packages'.

Thus the matrix of responsibilities chart shown in Figure 2.3 can then be constructed to show the integration at point of intersection of the work breakdown structure and organisational structures. Each organisation then is clearly identified, with the work for which it is responsible. Further subdivision of the effort may then be accomplished by the appropriate organisation managers assigning work to subsidiary units, with subcontractors and equipment suppliers also included in this matrix.

The WBS is thus used to define the work required to complete a project and allocate responsibility for this work to individuals and organisations. However, in addition to this important function, the WBS performs another function, no less critical to the success of modern project management, which is to establish the structure or framework of an Integrated Project Management Information System. It can be used to integrate the work to be performed, the organisation structure, individual responsibility for the work, together with the subsystems for planning, estimating, budgeting, information, analysis, control and reporting into one logical integrated project management system. This type of integrated system is essential to the management of large scale or complex projects and without it, this type of project will inevitably cost more or take longer to complete.

The intersection of the work breakdown structure and organisation structure at the lowest level of the WBS, is a convenient and logical point to integrate all these systems. The assignment of lower level WBS elements to responsible lower level functional managers, provides a key automatic integration point for all these subsystems and for the management, planning and control of the project. The expansion of these 'cost accounts' into work packages, extends this to more detailed work and these work packages form the basic elementary building blocks of the project management information system. The WBS then provides a framework for consolidation of these systems for planning, analysis and control for both project performance and organisational performances.

Thus a modern approach to project management planning and control requires that the work, organisation and the project management systems must be integrated and this involves:

1. *A work breakdown structure.* The explosion of a project into its component parts and all the work involved on these parts defined.
2. *Organisation structure.* The organisations and people involved in working on the lowest level of the work structure, must be identified and the organisation structure integrated with the work breakdown structure. Responsibility can be shown in a matrix of responsibility chart.
3. *Cost accounts/Work packages.* The intersection of the organisation structure and work breakdown structure

are key points for the integration of the project management systems. This intersection can be termed a cost account or organisational work package, and can be consolidated into both WBS elements and functional organisation subcontracts for performance reporting and control. They can also be broken down into discrete tasks termed work packages on which the whole control system is based. All the WBS elements, functional subcontracts and work packages can be identified in the information system as cost or information centres for planning and control. Each must be considered as a contract with identifiable responsibility, scheduled start and finish, budget and information system to monitor progress, cost and changes.

4. *Planning.* One level of planning must be integrated with these work packages, so that the plan is integrated with all other systems.
5. *Budget.* Time phased expenditure budgets must be established for each cost account and work package.
6. *Information system.* An information system must be established based on these cost accounts and work packages to channel information on progress, cost and changes.
7. *Analysis.* Analysis of progress, cost variances and trends must be carried out for the package, cost account, WBS element and functional sub-contract to monitor performance and relate it to individual responsibilities.
8. *Reporting.* Project reports must be based on this structure.
9. *Management action.* Corrective action should also follow this structure.

These concepts will be covered in more detail in the chapters on control, but they can be taken to be an underlying thread affecting organisation, planning, control and man-management of a project.

3 The Art of Planning

In the management of operations, work normally follows a well-oiled routine; people know their job and carry out basically the same job, week in, week out. Relationships and information flows are more or less permanent, and there is an effective learning curve brought about by work repetition. Monthly budgets are straight forward measurements of variables, that change only slightly from period to period. Operational management can thus be viewed in the short term as a relatively static situation.

None of this applies to project work! A project is by its very definition a non-routine undertaking; thus in all but the simplest project, the people, the companies, the work, the management information system, and many other factors require to be organised uniquely in temporary but ever changing relationships. Thus in project work, planning, that is, in this case, deciding who does what, when, how and why, is an essential aid to organising the companies, the departments and the people involved, and to executing, managing and controlling the work on a project. Without effective planning in project work, there is chaos.

Thus planning is an essential part of managing a project and is a means of

(a)   organising the work of the project;
(b)   deciding who does what, when, how and why;
(c)   determining the resources required;
(d)   allocating these resources on a time phased basis;
(e)   allocating and defining responsibility;
(f)   integrating the work of all the organisations involved;

(g) communicating between all those involved in the project;
(h) co-ordinating all the activities and people involved;
(i) controlling progress;
(j) estimating time to completion?
(k) handling unexpected events and changes.

It is also

(a) a basis for the authority of the Project Manager;
(b) a basis for the budgeting and financial control of a project;
(c) a basis for self-analysis and learning;
(d) a means of orientating people to look ahead;
(e) a way of initiating and maintaining a sense of urgency, that is time consciousness.

Finally, and above all, effective planning should help to complete the project in less time and money than would otherwise be the case.

In small projects, all activities, resources required, constraints and interrelationships can be envisaged by the human mind and planning done informally in the head, or on the back of an envelope. In addition, even on large projects, sometimes the various stages of the work have a simple, logical sequence which must be followed, and planning can be done informally. However, when a project gets over a low threshold in size or complexity, it is impossible for the human brain to take it all in, and some formal planning system is necessary to ensure efficient working. As projects get bigger and more complex, this planning and control get more difficult, but much more essential to their efficiency and success. In recent years such planning has often been associated with the use of advanced techniques. These techniques have not only made planning very fashionable, but they have also made it possible to effectively plan and control large and complex projects.

Unfortunately, the development of sophisticated techniques, that have made it possible to effectively plan and control large and complex projects, has also led to a concentration on these techniques and an inadequate recognition of the human factors involved. As a result, project planning systems often fail, many people have become disillusioned with formal planning, and a great many firms do not use planning as effectively as they should. In many firms no formal planning is done, and in many others, the plans produced are not used to organise and control the work. Advanced planning techniques are used as sales factors, or because the head office or client insisted on them. Complicated looking plans are produced, which are not used to manage the work on the project, and which serve only to impress the uninitiated and decorate walls. It is most important to realise that for the application of any form of planning to be fully effective, the plan itself is nothing more than information written on paper. Unless the people responsible for executing the work operate in accordance with this information, nothing will be achieved by this form of planning. In addition, many managers tend to take a short term view of planning and basically plan only for the immediate future. They cannot see the overall situation, problems and constraints involved, and how what they are, or are not doing today, will affect other areas on the project, and the project itself in three months, or three years time. Thus unfortunately, many unrealistic plans are produced which are not used by the key personnel involved, but almost just as importantly, cause the whole concept of formal planning to be held in disrespect. There are two reasons for this; one is the misapplication of the techniques of planning, that is, the 'Science' of planning and the other consists of several factors more concerned with how these techniques are used and which could be termed the 'Art' of planning. In the 1960s and early 1970s project planning came to be associated with the use of the Critical Path Method (CPM) and Project Evaluation and Review Technique (PERT). For a number of years it was fashionable to introduce these relatively sophisticated techniques into project planning and they did contribute much to the more effective planning of projects. It was thought that in all but the smallest project CPM/PERT had to be used, as no other method, including bar charts, could cope with the number of activities involved and the complex interrelationship.

Unfortunately many people have experienced difficulties with the use of these techniques and some have rejected them and returned to the use of the older and simpler bar chart method for project planning. This was principally because the effective use of CPM/PERT needs much more than a straightforward implementation of the technique, but also because of a lack of appreciation of the art of planning. Not only is training and practice required in the essentially numerical implementation of the technique, but also in its use in conjunction with other techniques on large projects and an appreciation of the problems encountered in its use, as discussed in Chapter 4. In practice, in all but the simpler project, no one technique is completely effective on its own. Each has disadvantages and limitations, and normally several or even all, of these common techniques are used in parallel to compliment each other. Essentially the project manager or planner should use a contingency approach to planning. That is, use the technique or techniques which work best for those involved, and which are appropriate to the job in hand. Just as it depends on the size and complexity of a calculation, whether a manager would use a slide rule, a calculator, or a computer so the size and complexity of the project should determine which technique or techniques he should use to plan it. However, there is little use in using sophisticated techniques, which are not understood by the managers and engineers involved, and thus will be used wrongly, or not used at all. Thus the techniques used must take into account their acceptability by the people concerned.

However, the decision as to which technique should be used, must be based upon knowledge, and the project manager or project planner should have a familiarity with all the common techniques used in project planning. All the other managers and supervisors involved, must also have some familiarity with the technique actually used to plan the project. Thus, all levels of management from foreman to managing director should have some training in the methodology and techniques of planning used in the project.

The advantages, disadvantages and limitations of the various techniques of project planning are covered more fully in the next chapter, whereas those factors described as the Art of Planning will be outlined in this chapter.

Knowledge and application of the techniques of planning are not sufficient by themselves to ensure the effective planning and management of projects. Just as important if not more so, irrespective of the techniques used, are: the adoption of a managerial philosophy, which accepts that planning is an integral part of the function of all those concerned in the project; gaining the understanding of those involved of how, and when to apply the various planning techniques and just what they can and cannot achieve; and how to build and use a plan to manage a project. Those factors will be covered under the following topic headings:

1. Managerial philosophy of planning.
2. Level of detail in a plan.
3. Real time planning.
4. Planning the planning process. (a) Project objectives and strategy. (b) An evolutionary life cycle of project planning. (c) A hierarchy of project plans.

Managerial philosophy of planning

Formal project planning is very difficult! Planning requires systematic analysis, the ability to look ahead, and understanding of all the activities that go into a project and their interrelationships. It also increasingly involves a knowledge of the ability to use modern quantitative and computer-based techniques of planning. Finally, it requires above all imagination, creative ability and thinking about intangibles. Thus for many people to use planning effectively, it implies a change in philosophy. Planning is a philosophy, not so much in the literal sense of the word, but as an attitude, or way of life. Planning necessitates a determination to look ahead constantly and systematically as an integral part of the management process, and to take decisions and allocate resources based on an integrated plan of action. Thus effective project planning is difficult to carry out and puts much more emphasis on a manager's conceptual skills, than does the normal day to day management of operations.

Resistance to formal planning often occurs because many managers have little experience of it, and find it difficult to do the necessary thinking through required. They are far more at home managing routine operations, than in thinking systematically about the future. Some are also reluctant to be involved in planning, as they dislike having to display their plans, or lack of them, to senior management. They prefer to work by the seat of their pants, in a 'laissez-faire' situation, and not to be subject to control action, or post mortem analysis of their planned work.

Thus, as a result of this, and many manager's lack of experience in formal planning, together with the time, effort and knowledge of techniques required for it, many firms employ planning specialists, or set up separate planning departments to carry out this function. Unfortunately, this in itself is insufficient to achieve effective planning. It is not possible to just 'graft' on formal planning to an organisation; there has to be a change in attitude, philosophy and knowledge of everyone concerned with the project. A separate planning department often leads to a concentration on techniques, inadequate recognition of the human factors involved and the adoption of an incorrect attitude towards how plans should be used.

Unless the people responsible for preparing the plan have done a thorough and logical analysis, the plan will not be realistic. Similarly, unless the people responsible for executing the plan, work in accordance with the information outlined in it, nothing will have been achieved by planning. Advanced techniques are probably necessary for the effective planning of all but the smaller project, but they are in no way sufficient to ensure the success of planning. The human factors are as important, or more important than the techniques involved.

Thus one of the main reasons for many plans failing, is that they have not been made by the correct people. The introduction of the staff planner and a separate planning department has meant that often, either planning is left in the specialist's hands, or that he can only get limited co-operation from line managers.

When plans are made by a staff planner acting on his own, the plans will have a high probability of being unrealistic, as it is just not possible for the planner to be fully informed, and able to exercise critical judgement on what is said to him in the many areas and functions of a project. More importantly, his plans will be unlikely to be carried out, as human nature being what it is, most managers have their own way of doing their job, and dislike being told in detail how to do it.

Effective planning requires the involvement of all those concerned, both to ensure the correctness of the plan and to obtain their commitment to it. If this participation and commitment is not achieved, plans will not be realistic and they will not be used.

A prerequisite for this participation is that the line manager himself, wants to and is able to plan. Therefore, one of the major problems encountered in formal planning is getting the functional line manager to accept planning as an integral part of their job, and to do the planning for their area of responsibility. This in turn requires top management support for planning, and an understanding of just what planning can, and cannot do, and a correct philosophy on how to use a plan.

It is thus essential to the success of planning, that on no account must it be left entirely in the hands of a separate planning department or planner. The planning specialist should only have staff responsibility for planning, and functional managers should be responsible for the development of their own plans, as planning is a basic function of any manager. The staff planner should only assist the manager by expressing his plans and thoughts with the most appropriate planning techniques, and to integrate them into the overall project plan. The manager in charge must do the actual planning for his area of responsibility. He is the only one who has the knowledge, the power to implement the plan and in the end, the one who is responsible for and must live with the outcome.

The project manager, or planning department's role is the exertion of leadership in establishing the project plan and in the co-ordination of every manager's planning effort; the provisions of hands and techniques to express the plans, and the provision of information to base plans on, the integration of the planning effort, and the education of management in both planning philosophy and planning techniques, that is, the art and science of planning. The specialist planner should act as a 'catalyst' in the planning process.

The use of sophisticated methods in planning does require specialist assistance and knowledge. It is difficult for a functional manager to develop all the skills and techniques of advance methods of planning, and probably more importantly, to have the time to apply them. Nevertheless, the functional manager should be aware of the broad principles of the methods, which are used by planning personnel on his behalf. Although the detailed work of planning might be taken out of the manager's hands, he is still ultimately responsible for it, and it must be 'his' plan.

That is to say, the project manager with or without specialised planning assistance will provide the framework, and the motivation for the overall project plan, and the managers in charge of each sub-organisation must do the planning for their responsibilities. The project management group can provide some of the necessary inputs, inter-relationships, technical assistance and carry out the necessary paper and quantitative work.

Level of detail

One of the major ways in which planning techniques can be mis-applied is in using them with an inappropriate level of detail. Many project plans have proved worse than useless, due to them being constructed, either in too great a detail, or in having the activities too aggregated. Thus a major problem facing a planner is what level of detail should he make the project plans in.

If plans are constructed in great detail, they will be large and complex, involve considerable work and take a great deal of time to complete. This means that they will not be completed in time to influence the early stages of the project, which requires effective planning and control just as much, if not more so, than later stages. When unexpected events occur and the logic of the plan may have to be changed, this will involve considerable time and effort. Also up-dating the plan, monitoring progress and re-assessing resource requirements will be major jobs. This makes it difficult to use the plan as a management tool in decision making, that is, 'real time' planning. By the time the plan is re-assessed, decisions will have had to be made, and it is too late to do anything about it, and planning will not be capable of keeping up with the pace of work and decision making.

Very detailed plans also necessitate vast amounts of paper work, both in issuing instructions to work supervisors and in reporting on work carried out. In project conditions, the more paper work produced, the less likely is it to be accurate. Supervisors will spend more time on paper work than in supervising and directing work, and thus morale and work efficiency will be affected. There are limits to how much detail managers, supervisors and project management information systems will deal with, before the mere volume of paper work itself breaks the system down, and the information loses touch with reality.

In addition, attempting to carry detail down to activities measured in hours, or even days on large projects, is counter-productive. It can be done with success for a limited number of critical activities on a project, and perhaps is necessary on maintenance shutdowns. Even on these jobs, frequent up-dating is required, delays and upsets occur, and the plan almost inevitably loses any pretence of mirroring what is actually going on.

In addition, if junior managers and supervisors are competent people, they quite justifiably object to being told to do things in great detail, for example, being essentially told 'to lift your left hand before your right hand'. They must be given discretion in their day-to-day work, and in practical circumstances, there is no question but that they need it to deal with constantly changing circumstances.

On project work the actual working situation changes rapidly at the point of work, as regards information, material, work available, manpower available, break downs of equipment, changes and delays. The supervisory level of management must handle all these factors and yet follow the logic of the planned outline of work with skill, adaptability, experience and judgement. No planning system can match the competent supervisor in planning and scheduling effectively the hour to hour and day to day work to cope with continually changing circumstances.

Finally, a very detailed plan will be very difficult to

understand, inevitably there will be mistakes, information will be out of date and unreliable, and there is a great danger that the plan will very quickly be shown to be wrong, confidence in the plan will be lost and it will not be used.

If activities are planned in too great detail, then the plan will not fulfil its functions of organising, co-ordinating and controlling the work on the project. People and organisations will not know what they have to do, and when they have to do it by. Important interrelationships between activities will be lost, and manpower planning will be difficult. Control will be next to impossible, as major deviations in time and cost could occur within single activities, which would detrimentally affect the complete project, and yet would not be picked up by the control system. A project is a complex set of activities, which involves many interrelationships, co-ordination difficulties and control problems, and project plans have to be built in some detail to permit project management to manage and control the project.

The basic factors which determine how detailed a plan should be is what function is it to carry out and how useful this detail is. If it is for reporting to top management, then it should be very coarse scaled indeed; if it is for use by work supervisors, it should show the work in great detail; if it is to be used for management decision and control then it need not be as detailed as the works supervisors level, but certainly a lot more detailed than that used for top management reporting. Thus the detail of the plan should vary with its purpose, the size and complexity of the project. For example, a large civil engineering project may be relatively straight forward, with a few very large activities, necessitating only a coarse scale plan. Alternatively, a small project involving the tieing in of a new plant extension to a refinery, during a refinery shutdown, may require finely detailed planning to complete the project satisfactorily. Thus, highly critical jobs with many interrelationships may necessitate very detailed planning.

The planning at work supervisors level should provide him with a guide to carry out his work, with some flexibility within an overall framework, which is in effect the plan. For example, the supervisor on the construction of an oil platform module may be responsible for the completing of two hundred welds by a certain date. If the sequence of doing each of these welds is critical and interrelated with steel erection, cranes, riggers, and others, then each weld and the work on it must be individually scheduled. However, in such a complex situation, lots can go wrong, and there is a high probability of the supervisor having to change the sequence, for good reasons and sometimes also, for bad reasons. It is very difficult for a planning system to keep up with such changes and be of much use. It can produce the initial plan, but this soon gets out of date. If it is necessary to plan the sequence of each weld, then this should be the supervisor's job and he should construct his own plan, within the overall framework. Working together with the steel erectors and riggers, he decides who does what and when, and it is his plan for his part of the work. If it is not necessary to have each of these welds done in a particular sequence, then there is no need to schedule each weld, one single activity or a handful of them to monitor progress, is often sufficient to cover them, instead of two hundred, or more activities.

Activities in a plan should be of a size that where responsibility changes, resource requirements change and interrelationships occur, then these can be shown. They should be of a size that permits close monitoring and control of progress and cost, without excessive paper work, so that things cannot go badly wrong, without being picked up by the control system. They should be of a size that permits some flexibility for work supervisors within activities, yet enforces rigidity of work sequence and scheduling where it is necessary. In large projects the problems of how much detail to construct a plan is partly overcome by using a hierarchy of plans of differing levels of detail, as outlined later.

Real time planning

One of the great fallacies held by many managers is expecting events to work out as planned! The only instances where this is likely to occur is in the short term, or where almost every pertinent factor about the future is known, or where there is

41

inevitable, straightforward, simple sequence of events with known resource requirements. Even with the best of planning, very few projects are completed to their original plan.

This is because there is never sufficient information available at the start of a project to plan accurately. Indeed, normally the only time that the complete information is available, is when the project is more or less complete.

It is not possible to forecast all the activities involved, to estimate accurately the resources and time required for these activities and to foresee every eventuality. In fact the activities being estimated are generally not constants. For example, the time taken to pour a batch of concrete, obtain delivery of a piece of equipment, get delivery of a batch of components through a factory, or to get a decision from the main board, are affected by many uncontrollable variables.

There is always considerable uncertainty about events in the future, and conditions and relationships are always changing. If any one activity is not completed to plan, then this may affect in some way all subsequent activities. With good management and co-ordination throughout the project and everyone following exactly the plan, then deviations from the plan may be limited, but how often does this happen?

Strikes may occur, equipment may break down, and labour productivity may be lower than expected. There may also be problems in management efficiency in handling complex projects, leading to a lack of co-operation and integration. Remembering also that two of the common causes of delay and cost escalation on projects, are design changes and delays in equipment delivery. These must effect future work on the project and necessitate replanning.

The concept that once having constructed a plan for a project, a planner can stand back and say to those involved 'carry on, its up to you', is a complete misconception of the function of planning and how a plan should be used.

Planning is an integral part of the management process, and cannot be separated from it. A plan on the other hand is a management tool, which a planner can build or assist to build, and this tool should be used by managers involved to assist them in making decisions, allocating resources, in organising, directing and controlling the work on the project; that is, a plan should be used by the manager to help him manage. It is a tool that is used, not only to assist him in the initial organisation of the project, but also to assist him in its on-going management throughout the life of the project.

In practice the only definite commitments from a plan are the initial decisions and resource commitments. Every further planned action and resource allocation is changeable in the light of future events. A plan must be looked on as a means of outlining the future work on a project so that initially the best decisions and resource allocations can be made to achieve the project's objectives. It enables the manager to examine the chain of cause and effect likely to arise from these current decisions, in the light of possible future events and consequent reactions, and to examine the effects of change.

Even though changes almost always occur to disrupt the original plan a plan is still required to quickly evaluate the effect of these changes on decisions and actions already taken, and on future resource commitments and actions. These changes which will always arise in the future, form new information inputs to a plan, which when combined with logical analysis, may dictate alternative future actions to those originally conceived. Without a plan, it is difficult to quickly see what the effect of changed circumstances have on present and future actions. With a plan, it is much easier and faster to re-evaluate the situation in the light of the change, to determine what corrective action or redeployment of resources are required to minimise the disruptive effects of such change.

Thus a plan must be looked on as a dynamic moving model of the project, and not be 'cast in stone'. It must be used adaptively and flexibly as a management tool to assist the manager to make the best decision and allocative of resources, both now and in the future, to effectively achieve his objectives. Planning must not be considered a failure if the original plan does not work out, but only if planning throughout the project has not assisted management to manage effectively.

If planning and plans are to be used as management tools, the planning and control process must be able to react quickly to unexpected crises and events. In order for a plan to be used adaptively and as a dynamic model, it cannot be looked on as a side line or staff activity. Plans must be used by project management much more integrally and quickly than previously, and planning must thus be a 'real time' activity. For planning to be real time, the speed of the planning activity must match the pace of the project work, or managers will take decisions on a judgemental basis without waiting for planning analysis, and plans will be unrealistic. The planning activity must also be sensitive to the unexpected nature of changes that occur. One way this can be achieved is by use of the modern interactive computer-based planning systems.

Thus planning cannot be considered as a one-off activity. It is not sufficient to construct a plan, pin it on the wall and then stand back, pleased with oneself. Planning and control are continuous processes, integral with the management of the project. Planning must always be considered in terms of a continuous planning and control cycle. It is difficult to separate planning and control, each is dependent on the other. Thus, it is useless to make a plan without having informative feedback, managerial analysis and control action. Within a short time any plan is usually out of date and both continuous and periodic reviews are necessary. Without these, a plan is merely a piece of paper which belongs on the wall as a decoration to impress the uninformed, or more realistically, soon after its completion, in the wastepaper basket.

Planning the planning process

Planning for a complex project is rarely a matter of sitting down and making a single plan before work starts. The planning process itself needs to be planned and organised. For example, consider how to go about planning the design, building and installation of an oil platform and pipeline in the North Sea. One could not just sit down and do it from scratch, even if one had done it before.

Given a target date by the company of three years hence, one needs to evaluate can it be done in the time and how should the work be carried out — do all the design, building and construction ourselves, contract out parts, perhaps contract the whole area of project management? One of the first cries would be 'I don't have enough information to plan it in detail'. It might be possible to plan the initial design work in detail, but it would not be possible to plan the rest until information came from design and procurement. The full detailed plan of the project could involve from 4,000 to 75,000 activities, all levels of management are not interested in such a large plan, and nobody could find their work and see how it interacts.

At the start of all but the smaller projects, sufficient information is not available to plan the project in detail. Its full scope may not have been finalised, delivery dates are not yet available, key dates such as contract award are not known, and a host of other factors are uncertain. Even when this information is available, there is often a need on large projects for project plans with two or more levels of detail. A plan which is used for scheduling and control of individual activities will be too detailed for management review and decision making. Plans made will vary in detail, depending on the information available, and the usefulness of the level of detail to the managers involved.

In addition, the greater the detail, the longer it takes to produce a project plan. For maximum effectiveness in project planning, action must be taken very early in the project. Therefore, taking the time to produce a detailed plan for the whole project in the early stages, will detract from the effectiveness of the control in these stages.

Thus the planning of a project must itself be planned, and one of the first steps in the planning of a project is determining just what plans are needed, how they will be used, what detail they will be in, what techniques will be appropriate and when the plans will be prepared. Planning can be overdone, with some projects requiring less than others. There is little use in planning to a depth which will not be useful, or for which insufficient information is available, or for which the management and supervisors involved cannot understand or follow. Inappropriate planning emphasis leads to a reaction against planning and the attitude, 'let's stop this paper exercise and get down to real work'.

Project planning must take into account the following concepts:

1. Project objectives and strategies.
2. An evolutionary life cycle of project planning.
3. A hierarchy of project plans.

Project objectives and project strategy

All too often project planning is considered to be simply who does what, when. Preceding this operational stage of planning is a decision-making phase, which is unfortunately sometimes treated in an offhand manner, but which may 'set' the course of the project adversely, and no amount of operational planning may be able to change this. Thus, this pre-planning stage is one of the most important stages of the project's life and one with far reaching effects.

It is in effect the objectives and strategy setting stage of project planning, in which the overall objectives, in terms of technical and capacity performance, time and cost goals, are specifically outlined, and the major strategic decisions are taken on how to carry out the project.

This project strategy phase involves the analysis of the possible alternative ways of carrying out a project, and the probable results, before deciding on a definitive course of action. The kind of decisions taken at this stage, are whether to use a major contractor to design and construct the project, or to design it oneself and use subcontractors on construction. It also includes policy decisions on the form of contract, the number of direct contractors, their involvement in plant design, the way in which variations and design will be controlled and on penalties and incentives.

The importance of project objectives and policies cannot be overemphasised. Throughout the life of the project, the project manager must compromise between his conflicting and multiple objectives. He has to balance technical standards against the cost and effect on the completion date; cost against time and technical standard; and time against cost and technical standards. To do this logically, to be able to reason with and be able to stand up to conflicting interests, and to

46

justify decisions to senior management requires that he must know the real commercial significance of these factors. How important is the cost, the time and the technical performance, and how can he play off one against the other? Minimum time and cost, with the highest technical performance, are normally incompatible objectives. A clear understanding of policy is important for everyone involved. Is it speed at all costs; what is the real value of time saved; is final cost critical to overall profitability and thus should the plan be 'poor boy' with a 'tight' design and no spare capacity?

Completion date versus target date

The forecast project completion date is a highly emotive factor, that often causes problems and misunderstandings. It is impossible at the start of a project to accurately forecast the actual completion date, as there is simply not enough information available, and what is being forecast is in fact not a constant. Time to completion is highly variable, dependent on a thousand factors and decisions taken in the past, the present and the future. Generally, completion dates are set with 'rose coloured spectacles' and are rarely met. Occasionally, completion dates are set loosely by old hands and when they are met, or beaten, there are congratulations all round, all quite unjustified.

Completion dates cannot be set at the start of the project; target dates can. A target date is an objective and a motivational factor, which may or may not bear any relation to a realistic completion date. The term 'a project is two years behind schedule', need not be a reflection on its managements' efficiency, but may be more a reflection on man's unbelievable optimism. A target date influences the project's strategy and how the work is to be carried out. For example, because of a tight target date a firm may have to go on a cost plus basis to several contractors, rather than complete the design and agree a fixed price with a single contractor after competitive tendering. A target date is thus a date to which project management will endeavour to plan to finish the project, and it will influence the decisions taken, the resources required and the resource allocation. It may or may not be realistic.

The actual completion date can only be forecast with any degree of reliability after considerable work has been carried out on a project.

In planning to meet a target date, it is always advisable to allow a 10–20 per cent contingency time allowance. It is common practice to allow a budget contingency, and it is illogical not to also allow a time contingency. Thus if desired target date is three years hence, the date to be used for planning purposes should be two years and six to nine months, depending on the stage of definition of the project.

The evolutionary life cycle of projects

Projects and project planning, in any industry, have a characteristic evolutionary pattern and a distinct life cycle. Project planning should be a continuous function which starts, in some form, at the conception of the project and extends until the project is in satisfactory operation, or is fully complete.

The following stages can be identified in a project life cycle:

1. Project development and preliminary engineering.
2. Bidding and contract negotiation.
3. Engineering design.
4. Purchasing and procurement.
5. Construction and, or manufacture.
6. Commissioning.

Contract negotiation and engineering design can vary in sequence, depending on which stage of the development of a project that the client, or owner, goes out to bid, and the type of contract involved.

If the planning is started in the project development phase, a summary plan would cover all six stages of the project and a detailed plan would be developed to cover the preliminary engineering and contract negotiation, followed by the planning of the engineering design work. As work actually moved into engineering and design, so would detailed planning move forward to procurement and construction or manufacture, and as work moved into construction, so would detailed planning of the commissioning work proceed, following what is termed the 'rolling wave' concept.

Though detailed planning must of necessity follow this rolling wave, because this is how the information becomes available, the planning for all stages must be integrated. The work done in any one stage interacts with the work done in the other stages, and they cannot be considered in isolation. Traditionally the planning and control of work in each stage was done more or less independently, with little or no interchange between stages; each department or company planning its work, as if in a vacuum. This may have been satisfactory when the engineering and design work and purchasing could be completed, materials and equipment delivered, before the manufacturing or construction stages were started. Unfortunately, many present day projects have to be completed in the minimum possible time, and thus the work in all stages must overlap and, or be integrated to achieve the shortest possible project duration. In today's competitive business world, and with the high cost of capital, new plant projects must be completed as quickly as possible to get an economic return.

Thus planning must extend to cover every aspect of the project from start to finish, and include planning for those contingencies that can be foreseen. Planning should cover from project organisation through development, design, purchasing, manufacturing, construction, to start up and initial operations. In fact special emphasis must be given to those later stages as no matter how the design, manufacturing and, or construction has been handled, one organisation or company is handing over to another, and any delay is expensive, as almost all the capital funds will have been expended and are unproductive, until the unit is successfully commissioned.

Thus despite the difficulties in information, planning must be integrated over the project life cycle. In particular there is a logical way of doing both engineering design, manufacture and, or construction, and they interact with each other to determine how the job is done. Any inefficiency or lack of integration in the overall project only becomes apparent at the final stages, that is, in manufacture or construction, and it is too late to change things there.

The balancing of design, purchasing, manufacture and construction, often involves pressures or restraints, brought about by the resources available at the manufacturing or construction stages. On large projects there are often insufficient numbers of key professionals or trades to meet the peak demands. The overall project plan may have to be modified to take this into account, or manufacturing and construction will continue as planned, only until the shortage of key trades begins to bite. From then on, the manufacturing or construction phases will be resource limited and very little can then be done at that stage to avoid a delay in completion.

In this situation the theoretical relationship between the cost of crashing a job, bears little relation to the practical. Regular overtime reduces productivity very quickly, and is very expensive. It is often simply worked to enable higher wages to be paid. This reduction in productivity is not so marked where work is machine based. Regular overtime may thus be required to attract labour, but great care has to be taken to maintain productivity. Short periods of overtime for specific visible objectives can often achieve this.

In general, a well-run manufacturing or construction project is difficult to expedite, and at best only a marginal improvement can be made, at considerable extra cost.

If the shortage of key trades, or long, or uncertain delivery on key equipment, is anticipated at the planning stage, the project can be planned to spread the work of these key trades over a longer period and so reduce the peak numbers required. This can be done by staging the manufacture or construction of the various parts, expediting certain areas of the project through the design and purchasing stages, to give efficient manufacture or construction. It requires difficult planning and cross planning between units, and intelligent anticipation to see that the work is continuous in each area, and continuity of trades and operations is maintained.

Planning the 'other' stages

Most people are familiar and conscious of the need to plan and control manufacturing or construction. Often less emphasis is given to other stages of the project and this is fatal to the project's chance of success. Planning must cover all stages of the project from start to finish and particular emphasis must be given to:

1. Project development stage.
2. Design stage.
3. Completion and commissioning stage.
4. Procurement.

In fact the planning and control of procurement is so important that it should be given as much attention as the planning of design, manufacturing or construction. Very few projects are not delayed, or do not have the sequence of work disrupted, by unexpected late delivery of equipment. This topic is covered in detail in a later chapter.

Project development stage

The project evolution or development phase may stretch for years or may only be recognisable as a phase for a very short period. The project may originate from top company planning, marketing, engineering, research and development or production. Basically the need for, or opportunity requiring capital investment is recognised by some function or person in the organisation. As a result a project proposal is prepared for and discussed by senior management, and either rejected, held for consideration, returned for further development or passed to the next phase for further study and development into a concrete project.

The evolutionary phase falls more into the corporate planning area of business than that of project management. It is only at, or near the end of it, that the project can be said to be born, and work on it falls in to the executive functional areas.

Where competitive forces exist in industry, particularly with new or significantly improved products, the time from project conception to actual production can materially alter the overall profitability of the project. Sometimes the time taken in research and development, if unduly prolonged, enables the competitor to get in ahead and pre-empt the whole project.

Thus it is just as important that the research, development and preliminary design stages of industrial projects be planned and controlled, as it is for the other more labour and capital intensive stages. There may not be the spur of invested capital obtaining no return, but there is the competitive marketing spur of missing a market opportunity, reducing the time until competition becomes fierce, or not being able to meet market demands. Time wasted in the initial stages of the project, when few people are employed, can be just as important as in the later stages, where many people are employed. Many project and construction managers have been faced with the almost impossible task of expediting a project in its later stages, at a great cost for a small time saving, when they were aware of delays in earlier stages, which could have been easily and cheaply avoided.

Often the argument is put forward that it is impossible to plan the research and development stages. It is true that it is difficult to carry out detailed scheduling and that time estimates are very uncertain. Nevertheless, it is possible to define the WBS, cost accounts and work packages, allocate responsibility, and thus effectively plan these stages, to organise them better as a result, to set target dates, to react to delays faster and to control this development stage of a project.

Once a project is born it moves in to the preliminary engineering and study phases which cover both technical feasibility and financial evaluation of the project. The scope of the project is defined, size determined, methods, processes, equipments, costs, sites, etc. all estimated. Various alternatives are considered until a complete proposal is put forward for the approval of senior management. Many projects do not go beyond this stage, as the company does not really know if a project is feasible or worthwhile, until this stage is complete. The importance of the preliminary engineering and study phases cannot be overemphasised. Decisions made in it largely determine what comes after both during design, manufacturing and or construction. During this phase, which will cost only a small fraction of the overall project, decisions are made which determine 90 per cent or more of the cost of the project and largely determine its operating profitability; the wrong process chosen, whether to go ahead or not, the wrong size of plant, the wrong type of equipment, whether to contract the work out or not, the timing, the speed of the work, etc. Wrong decisions on these could lock the company in to unprofitable investment for many years.

Design engineering

Traditionally the main emphasis on planning and control has been on the manufacturing and construction stages of a project, but in recent years more and more emphasis has been given to the planning and control of the design function. In practice it is critical to the success of a project that just as much time and effort should be given to the planning and control of design as is given to the planning and control of manufacturing and construction.

Effective planning and control of design is difficult but not impossible. There are a great many complex interrelationships, particularly with information requirements and designers do not like to be made to commit themselves to task completion dates, or be put under time pressures. Nevertheless it is essential that work responsibilities should be clearly defined, information requirements between functions determined and that the design work be scheduled with work packages established with visible milestones identifying achievements along the way. There is often the need to break work packages into great detail and establish 'inchstones' to monitor progress. This is where the structuring of the design work using the project work breakdown structure and its extension to the establishment of cost accounts and work packages, acting as pseudo subcontracts can be of considerable benefit. Each designer would have his or her own work package commitments and each work package would have its milestones and inchstones to monitor progress. The responsibility matrix would then identify who is responsible for what. Using this method, design work can be planned and controlled.

Often the pattern of these design interrelationships is characteristic to the company or industry, and standard planning modules or outlines can be constructed as described in a later chapter. The design process for the characteristic project is studied and the interrelationships determined. This then given a format to build a plan of the engineering design for all projects of that type. For example, Figure 3.1 shows a summary of an intermediate scaled bar chart for the design of petrochemical plant which is characteristic of process plant projects. Figure 3.2 shows the S charts described in a later chapter, which give a measure of the rate of work on these activities.

The major part of the process design has probably been completed in the development and preliminary engineering phase prior to these figures, and the bulk of the detailed engineering design will start when the company gives the final go-ahead, or a contract is awarded, which is week 0 on this bar chart. The initial work in the design engineering phase will be on three main areas:

1. Completing the area layout for the plant.
2. Specifying and ordering all vessels and equipment (i.e., the bill of materials – BOM).
3. Completing the engineering, electrical and instrument flowsheets.

A key milestone in process plant design is the completion and acceptance by all concerned of the preliminary area layout. This is necessary before work can start in earnest on the other functional areas, that is, structures, foundations, underground and aboveground piping and before the rate of work can accelerate on instrumentation and electrical work. One of the critical activities which must be started as soon as possible is piping design. Piping drawings may represent 35–45 per cent of the total drawings required on a process plant, but work cannot reasonably start on piping design until 8 to 12 weeks after the start of detailed design, as is shown in the figures. Piping design cannot start until a preliminary layout is completed and vendor drawings are available showing details of equipment and vessels. Similarly it is inefficient to start work, prior to receipt of vendors' data, on such activities as the design of foundations or structural supports.

The area layout establishes firm locations for: – vessels

```
      ACTIVITY                    10        20        30        40        50        60        70
----------------------------------+---------+---------+---------+---------+---------+---------+---
  1   BOM-VESSELS          +XXXXXXXXXXXX----------
  2   BOM-TOWER            +XXXXXXXXXXXX---------
  3   BOM-TUBE EXCH.       +XXXXXXX---
  4   BOM-AIR EXCH.        +XXX---
  5   BOM-HEAT             +XXXXXXXXXXXXX---
  6   BOM-PUMPS            +XXXXXXXXX---------------
  7   BOM-PUMPS            +XXXXXX-----------------------
  8   AREA LAYOUTS         +XXXXXXXXXXX
  9   INST.ENGIN.1         +XXXXXXXXXXXXX---------
 10   ELECT.ENGIN.1        +XXXXXXXXXXXXXXXXXXXXXXX--------------------------
 11   U/G PIP.ENGIN.1      +         XXXX---
 12   C.S. FIELD PIP.E     +         XXXX--------
 13   COMP.AREA L/O        +         XXXXXXXXXXXX--------------------
 14   ALLOY F.PIP.EN.      +         XXXXXXXXX------
 15   C.S.SHOP PIP.E       +         XXXXXXXXXX--------
 16   ALLOY SHOP P.E       +         XXXXXXXXXXX------
 17   STUCT.STEEL ENG.     +         XXXXXXX
 18   FOUND.ENGIN.         +         XXXXXXX----
 19   BOM-INST/MATL1       +         XX-----------------
 20   INST.ENGIN.2         +         XXXXXXXXXXXXXXXXXX--------
 21   INST.PIP.DRAW.       +         XXXXXXXXXXXXXXXXXXXXXXXXXX-----------------------------
 22   INST.WIR.DRAW.       +         XXXXXXXXXXXXXXXXXXXXXXXXXXXXXXXX-----------------------
 23   U/G PIP.ENGIN.2      +           XXXXXXXXXXXX---
 24   BOM/U/G PIP&MAT      +           XX------------------
 25   BOM-C.S.P&A 1        +           XX----------------------
 26   C.S.F/FAR.PIP.E      +           XXXXXXXXXXXXXXXXXXXXXXXXXXXXXXXXXXXXXX--------
 27   BOM-PLAT&LADD.       +            XX------------
 28   BOM STRUCT A.        +            XXX
 29   BOM STRUCT B         +            XX----------------
 30   BOM-EXCH.STRUCT.     +            XXXXXX
 31   BOM-PIPE SUPP.       +            XXXXXXXXXXX-
 32   BOM-ANAL.BUILD       +            XXXXXXX_____
 33   BOM-FOUND.MAT.1      +            XX----
 34   FOUND.ENGIN.         +            XXXXXXXXXXXX----
 35   BOM-ALLOY P&MAT.     +            X-------------------
 36   ALLOY F/F PIP.E.     +            XXXXXXXXXXXXXXXXXXXXXXXXXXXXXX------
 37   C/S SH.FAB.PIP.E.    +            XX--------------
 38   C/S SH.FAB.PIP.E.    +            XXXXXXXXXXXXXXXXXXXXXXXXXXXX--------
 39   EL.SUB.CON.B/EVAL    +            XXXX-------------------
 40   ELEC1.ENGIN.2        +            XXXXXXXXXXXXXXXXXXXXXXXXXXX--------------------
 41   BOM-ALLOY SH/F P     +            XX--------------
 42   ALLOY SH/F P.EN.     +            XXXXXXXXXXXXXXXXXXXXX------------
 43   BOM-PAINTING         +            XXXXXXXXXXXX-----------------
 44   BOM-INSULATION       +            XXXXXXXXXXXXXXXXXXXXX----------------------
 45   U/G PIP.ENG.2        +            XXXXXXXXXXXXXXXXXX---
 46   BOM-INST&MAT.2       +            XX--------
 47   BOM-FOUND.MAT.2      +            XX----
 48   BOM-ALLOF S/F P.     +                         XX--------
 49   BOM-C/S S/F PIPE2    +                          X--------
 50   BOM-C/S PIPE&MAT.    +                          XX--------
 51   BOM-ALLOY P&MAT      +                          XX-----
 52   PUR.REACT.D501-3     +X-----------------------
----------------------------------+---------+---------+---------+---------+---------+---------+---
```

Figure 3.1   Typical petrochemical project design plan

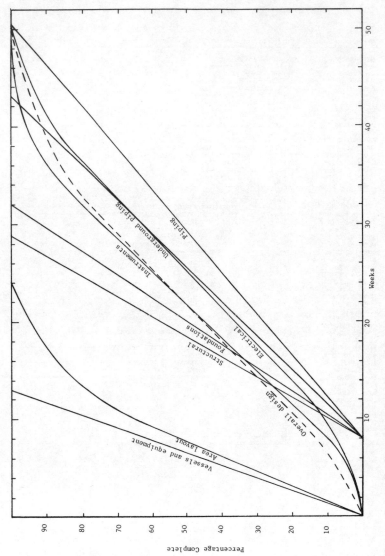

Figure 3.2 S chart for design

– equipment – buildings – structures – routings and evaluations of main pipe runs – vessel orientation – platform locations – evaluation of all equipment – size of structures and buildings – general routing of underground piping and electrical conduits – clearances for maintenance personnel.

These initial activities are not separate from each other, but involve a continuous flow of information backwards and forwards. For example, in order to prepare a layout, drawings of vessels are required so that one of the first jobs started may be to prepare simple line sketches of every vessel. This together with design specifications, are passed to purchasing who obtain vessel drawings from the manufacturers involved. These go to the design section for approval and to the layout group to complete the area layout. A similar process is required for all the major equipment involved.

Once the preliminary area layout is completed work can start in the other functions involved in the project. Most of them have an initial phase which permits the early ordering of the bulk of the material required with the remainder being ordered towards the end of each areas' functional activity, as shown in Figure 3.1. All these activities are interrelated and require a continuous exchange of information. For example, foundation design and layout is effected by vessel and equipment details, underground piping layout and structures; piping design is interrelated to vessel and equipment details of design of structures. Thus though these are shown as several separate activities on the bar chart, there are many micro-interrelationships involved. These can be identified for projects characteristic to any one company and industry. Often it is necessary to ensure progress for information to be made available to interrelated functions before it is accurately defined and different classification of detail are sometimes used. Thus for example, if foundations are located approximately, underground piping runs can be determined and the connections designed a little later when foundations are accurately defined and equipment details available.

The resource requirements for such a plant normally show a peaked manpower curve, with a ratio of approximately 1.67 to 1.0 between peak and average manpower requirements. This poses problems when a design organisation is handling more than one project at the same time. In fact the detail shown in Figures 3.1 and 3.2 were summaries taken from a single project which had five such units in the one project. The contractor's schedule was prepared on a unit basis and only when each functions activities were consolidated was it obvious that they all peaked at the same time and something had to give: usually the schedule. Thus the planning of design and drawing office work has to be done on a multi-project basis and is discussed in a later chapter.

Though the actual work on the development and design engineering phases can be planned and controlled, one vital aspect is very difficult to control, namely, the obtaining of key decisions from a company's senior management, or from a customer. Sometimes it is extremely difficult for the project manager, acting from a subordinate position, to get them to make up their mind and take a key decision which is holding up work. All that he can essentially do is to demonstrate the consequences of delay and clearly outline the alternatives available, but often this is not enough. One project manager stated that in one instance even when told that delay was costing £100,000 per week, one senior manager could not be moved to make up his mind quickly. Not only does this have direct financial consequences for the project, but indirectly it can effect the morale and commitment of all involved from start to finish. This is one area when, if the project manager has the courage, some would say the foolhardiness, a good project reporting system can be a discipline on senior managers. Thankfully, today, the planning and control of design has come to be recognised as critical and most firms give it the necessary emphasis.

Completion and commissioning

The efficient execution of the final completion, that is, inspection, clearing up final odds and ends, and commissioning of a new project can be vital to its success. If not carried out effectively, considerable time and money can be wasted. At this stage almost all the capital has been invested, lying there useless, probably incurring interest charges, not making the profit envisaged, not contributing to the company's cash flow, and missing the market opportunity by allowing competitors to be established. A £10m project could be incurring interest of £40 thousand per week. The contractor would also still be maintaining men and supervision on site and not be able to obtain final payment and holdback. Therefore delay at this stage is very, very expensive for everyone concerned, and these final stages must be planned and controlled as effectively as any other stage, with attention being given to the following points.

Considerable time can be saved if the phased completion of the different areas or modules can be planned. If certain sections can be completed early, inspection, checking and handover can be commenced much earlier than if it is left until the end of the complete project. Often the specialised personnel required are in short supply, and probably the owner's people involved are limited to the operation staff, who are much fewer in numbers than the construction staff available.

Careful planning is particularly critical because there is normally a large organisational interphase. The contractor's staff or owner's construction staff are handing over to the owner's or operations staff and unless the work is dovetailed, that is, jointly planned, cracks will occur and momentum will be lost. Planning for phased completion can be commenced long before a project is nearing completion. The more lead time obtained, the better the phased completion can be obtained. Thus it should not be planned when construction is 90 per cent complete, but much earlier, and in fact, commenced, or taken into consideration during the design and procurement stages.

A major problem at the final stages of a project is the exception, or 'but' lists. During the closing stages of a project the owner and, or contractor will prepare complete detailed lists of unfinished work in each area. These must be checked by all concerned for completeness. The best timing for preparing exception lists must be judged carefully. If done too early, the work becomes burdonsome, because the list is too bulky and the expediting effect is lost. On the other hand, the task of final inspection entails substantial effort and cannot be accomplished in a few hours, or even a few days.

However, allowances must be made to give time for omissions or deficiencies to be rectified.

Another problem near the end of a project is maintaining pace and momentum. Two failures can commonly occur. Work progresses rapidly until handover occurs, and then only slowly. The final checking and commissioning is not started immediately, because the other organisation has not planned and organised effectively. Alternatively a contractor finishes 95 per cent of the work, then withdraws the bulk of his men and the key high-grade personnel involved, and the remaining two to five per cent is left for a minimum number of men, with lower-grade supervision. Pressure must be maintained on this final two to five per cent of the job. It needs to be planned, organised, and controlled with the same pace and attention as the rest of the project, otherwise it can take almost literally forever.

Hierarchy of project plans

Three of the principle problems in planning the planning process are thus:

1. The information necessary for planning the later stages of the project in detail only becomes available as work on earlier stages approaches completion, necessitating a rolling wave concept of planning.
2. Despite this, it is necessary to integrate the planning of the earlier and later stages.
3. Differing levels of detail may be required for different functions and levels of management.

Thus, though on small projects a single level of plan is generally quite sufficient, on larger projects a hierarchy of plans, with varying level of detail, is often used to overcome these problems. Each single activity in the higher levels of plan, being expanded into several activities, or even complete arrow diagrams, or bar charts in the lower level plans. The plans being linked together at key events or milestones as shown in Figures 3.3 and 3.4. In medium sized projects, two levels of plans may be adopted, whereas on larger projects

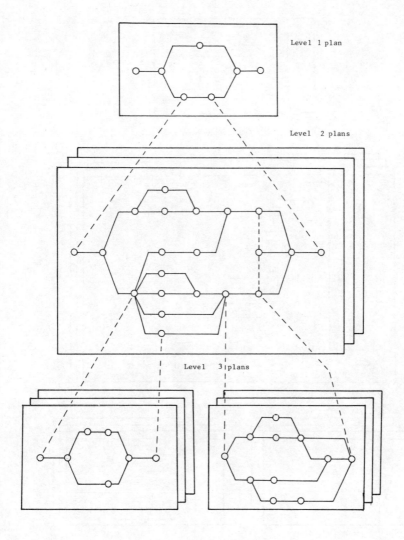

Level 1 plan

Level 2 plans

Level 3 plans

Figure 3.3 A hierarchy of network plans

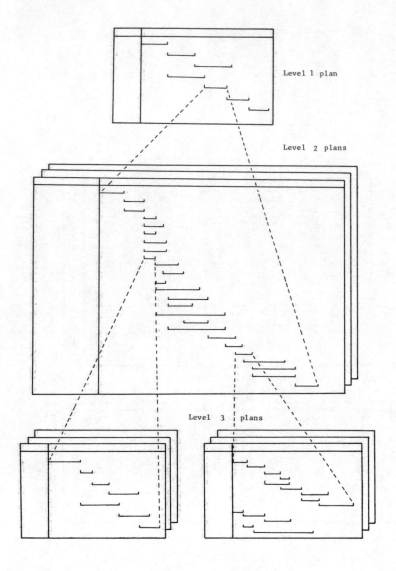

Level 1 plan

Level 2 plans

Level 3 plans

Figure 3.4   Hierarchy of bar charts

three or more levels of plans may become necessary. A three-level plan hierarchy would include the following levels of plan:

1. Level 1. A summary plan.
2. Level 2. An intermediate level plan.
3. Level 3. A detailed plan.

Level 1 plan

A level 1 plan is essentially a summary plan of the project, which outlines the project in skeleton form. It is used throughout the project as a top management reporting and review document, but it is also essentially the only plan possible in the evolution, or project strategy phase, and is thus also the initial plan of the project. At the evolutionary stages of the project, it is normally only possible to build this highly aggregated plan, with the activities being large sizeable increments of work, such as work breakdown structure elements, or cost accounts.

Such a plan shows only the principal activities and the major milestones associated with the project. It is normally a broad scale plan embracing design, procurement, manufacturing and, or construction, and commissioning. It contains the first appropriate estimates of the overall timing of each stage, rough estimates of resources required, and permits certain key points in the schedule and major interrelationships to be approximately estimated. It should show up which critical parts of the total project should be emphasised, and gives the first indications of requirements for materials, and equipment delivery dates. In the initial stages it acts as a strategic planning tool to establish the project objectives and strategies and can be quickly constructed and modified to show different ways of carrying out the project, and yet allows key points to be located and major relationships determined. However it is very coarse scaled and on large projects cannot be used for the complete integration of the various project stages, which leads to the development of a level 2 plan.

Level 2 plan

This plan shows the broad sweep of activities with both major and minor milestones included. It collects together under one description several detailed activities whenever possible. It permits a detailed examination of the project's structure to be made, and allows relationships which exist between the various parts of the project to be seen and studied. It defines the limits, between which individual activities can move, without affecting project completion.

In a level 2 plan the activities in the summary plan are expanded and planned in more detail. It is essentially a middle management decision and control tool, identifying functional responsibilities for items on the work breakdown structure. That is, activities are generally cost accounts, or work packages, and not of a size to permit day-to-day or even week-to-week scheduling and control of work, except perhaps in critical activities. The example network shown in Figure 2.4 is a level 2 plan. This may be a 'skeletonised' plan of the project with strings of activities consolidated into single activities. However, this plan should be in sufficient detail to allow a certain amount of manpower planning to be done, and to show the principal sequencing and interrelationship constraints on work on the project.

Where contracts are put out to tender, the amount of planning possible is based on the amount of design engineering completed, and these factors influence the type of contract used. To enable a contractor to bid for a fixed price contract, the project must be sufficiently defined, that at the very least, a level 2 plan can be constructed for the proposal or pre-tender stages. Otherwise the contractor cannot be in a position to make a fixed price bid, unless he is tendering a 'package' engineering design, procure and construct plant, more or less off the shelf.

Where the contract form is cost plus, normally the design is not at such an advanced stage that a level 2 plan can be constructed, and a summary plan is all that is possible. However, every effort must be made to have at least a level 2 detailed plan at this tendering stage, particularly for the design work, both to enable reasonably accurate prices, resource requirements and completion dates to be estimated, but also so that when approval is given, or contract awarded, the project can be off to a quick start, with the correct priorities.

It is easier to gain time with less resources at the early stages in the project life, than at the end of the manufacturing or construction stages, when literally hundreds, or thousands, of men may be involved. Sufficient planning must be done in the initial plan to ensure that the critical, and near critical paths are determined, before approval of the project is given. The same principles apply whether the client company, or a contractor will develop the level 1 and level 2 plans so that when the contract is awarded, engineering design and purchasing can immediately start work on the critical items.

Level 3 plan

This level shows all the known activities on the project. Level 3 plans are the tool used by lower levels of management to help them manage the day-to-day, week-to-week work on the projects. Level 3 planning can be done in several ways, depending on the size and complexity of the project, information available and experience and preference of the managers involved.

1. A completely integrated plan for the whole project can be made.
2. Each activity in the level 2 plan can be expanded into several activities in sequence.
3. Each activity or groups of activities in a level 2 plan can have its own more or less complete plan at level 3.
4. Detailed planning of the stages of the project can be completed in sequence as separate planning modules, linked together by the intermediate scale level 2 plan.
5. Lower level management and supervisors can be left to construct, or perhaps not to construct, a day-to-day, week-to-week detailed plan, for their area of responsibility, within the framework of the level 2 plan.

The important factor is that someone must plan the

day-to-day, week-to-week work on a project to ensure good management and control. This must take into account resource limitations, interrelationships, time targets and be a basis for budgeting, organisation, and control of progress and cost.

Different techniques of planning may be used with different levels of planning, with commonly, a bar chart or milestone chart being used in a level 1 plan, CPM/PERT and bar charts being used in a level 2 plan, and bar charts and, or milestones charts being used in level 3 plans. However, one, or all of these techniques may be used for all levels of planning.

Rolling wave concept

When three levels of plan are used, a level 1 summary plan must be completed in the evolutionary stage of the project. As information becomes available, the activities on the summary plan can be expanded and planned in more detail following the rolling wave concept. This detailed planning of the later stages of the project must be done with sufficient lead time to ensure that the correct decisions and resource allocations are made in an integrated manner.

Thus, at the evolutionary stage a summary plan would cover all six stages of the project life cycle and information should be available to construct a level 2 or 3 plan for the project development and engineering stage. As this stage approaches completion, sufficient information should be available to construct a level 2 plan for the whole project, and a level 3 detailed plan for the bidding, contract negotiation and engineering design stages. As work proceeds on engineering design information becomes available to complete level 3 plans for the remaining stages of the project. Throughout these stages level 1 and 2 plans are used to integrate the planning and work on the total project.

4 The Science of Project Planning

The science of project planning is concerned with the techniques used, of which the two most common are bar or Gantt Charts, and network analysis methods, which are used under the various names of critical path method (CPM), critical path analysis, PERT, and precedence diagrams. Another much less common basic planning technique which is used occasionally, is the Line of Balance. Its use is normally confined to projects involving small batch production, for example, military hardware or a housing estate. These are basic planning techniques, which are used as tools to outline and determine the timing of the work involved on a project, by means of a visual or mathematical model, that is, what is to be done, when, and then to communicate this information to those involved.

Bar charts and network methods in their simplest form, are satisfactory for the smaller project, but their effective use in larger projects, and in multi-project situations, has problems which necessitate sophisticated methods to overcome them, and the use of supplementary techniques for analysis and control. The most common of these techniques are manpower charts, S curves and milestone charts.

These basic planning systems must be used as project planning and control information systems and

1. Be able to formally schedule all the necessary activities on the project in a manner which will permit the evaluation of actual progress against plan, and which will identify the interdependencies between activities.
2. Permit the project staff to quickly build, change and update the project plan.

3. Be able to be used to control the project.
4. Be able to be integrated at some level, with the financial control system.
5. Permit the project staff to have immediate access to the data to use the system as an information system.
6. Above all they must be able to be used for manpower planning and control.

Before going on to critically review the actual techniques, it is worthwhile to outline the basic requirements of this manpower planning.

Manpower planning

In their simplest form the basic planning techniques are used to determine what is to be done when it is to be done; this is far from sufficient for project planning and control. They must also be used to determine *who* does what and when, as it is farcical to plan the work on a project, without planning and controlling the resources required, primarily manpower. Manpower is a scarce, valuable, expensive and sometimes troublesome resource, which must be actively managed.

This involves forecasting the manpower requirements from the initial plan, comparing these requirements with the manpower available or which can be recruited, and also comparing the pattern of manpower requirements to good practice. These factors often impose restraints on the project plan and require it to be modified to take into account such factors as

1. Resource/manpower limitations.
2. The avoidance of undue fluctuations in manpower levels.
3. The overall resource pattern and its effects on productivity.

There are often limits to the manpower available for work on a project, both skilled tradesmen and professional engineers. In such cases the project is said to be resource limited, and this becomes a major factor in preparing the project plan and may dominate all other factors. It may make nonsense of the critical path and considerably extend the project life. In such cases recognition of the constraint at an early stage can lead to better balancing of work and reduction of peak manpower needs to avoid these constraints.

The naive preparation of a project schedule based on the basic planning techniques may lead to considerable fluctuations in the number of skilled men required. This may have been possible in days gone by, when management could hire and fire at will, but these days are gone. The effect of such a policy today leads to low productivity, poor industrial relations and, when skilled tradesmen are in demand, a reluctance to be employed on such projects. If the manpower is kept constant, when requirements vary, it is not only expensive but also generally leads to low productivity and in turn to poor industrial relations.

The skilled manpower required should be built up and run down in a planned manner, and violent fluctuations in the numbers of each trade or profession required should be avoided. This necessitates scheduling the activities on a project so that the cumulative requirements are less than, or equal to the manpower available and that the numbers required do not fluctuate unduly. Thus manpower planning and work scheduling interact, and both are necessary for effective project planning. This will not guarantee higher productivity and good labour relations, but if not carried out, there will be low productivity and poor industrial relations.

The normal way of portraying this manpower plan is to construct a manning curve, that is, a graph of manpower against time, and this is derived from the bar chart or network plan of the project. It is made up for the individual trades, groups of trades, as shown in Figure 4.1, and for the total manpower for a project as shown in Figure 4.2.

This manning curve can show clearly
1. The estimated number of men required throughout the job.
2. The actual number of men used on the job to date.
3. The manning correction needed to get back on schedule.

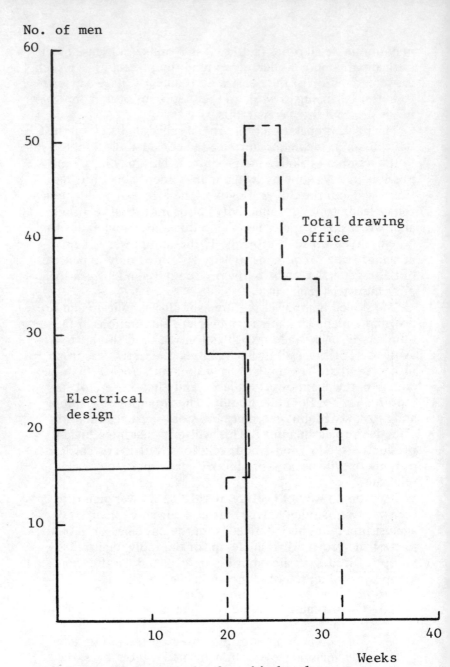

No. of men

Total drawing office

Electrical design

Weeks

Figure 4.1 Manpower plan for critical trades

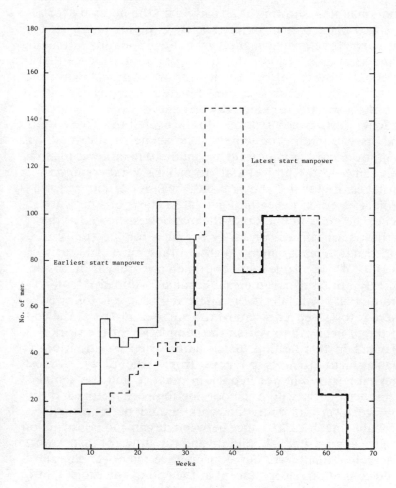

Figure 4.2   Project Manpower

4. Probable schedule delays if it is not practical to make up lost time.
5. The rate of manpower build up and run down.

It has the advantage that it is very sensitive to the effect of undermanning, showing at an early date the necessity for a changed plan to meet objectives. By applying restraints to the curve, for example, manpower limits, it permits estimating a practical completion date. It has the disadvantages that it does not show the effects of changes or additional work, and that it is only as accurate as the estimate of manpower required and the associated productivity estimates.

Attention has also to be paid to the overall resource pattern and its effect on productivity. The shape of the total manpower curve is important as a guide to manpower planning and can help the project staff to avoid several common mistakes. Figure 4.2 shows typical manpower curves for a project based on the earliest and latest starts of a network plan. The rate of build-up of the manpower shown for the earliest start curve is probably too high for the ability of construction management to absorb these men efficiently on the job. Where a large number of men are brought on to site quickly, the supervision can become overloaded and productivity will fall. If the latest start curve is followed there is too steep a descent of the number of men at the end of the project. All too often the completion of the work is planned in this fashion, particularly when construction management attempts to recover from earlier delays. Almost inevitably this will not happen in practice and the actual manpower curve will overshoot due to many factors and the job will over-run. Thus the work should be scheduled, probably involving a balance between design and construction, to give a more gradual build up and run down of manpower. The actual manpower curve in practice may over slip and tend to give this steep descent at the end of the project, but this should not be planned at the beginning.

Sharp peaks on this curve should also be avoided as these will achieve little, considerably increase the supervisor's loads and thus probably reduce productivity. There is a limit to the maximum number of men that can be employed on any size of project without adversely affecting manpower productivity. Too much reliance should also not be placed on costly overtime to make up for the extra manpower required. Working overtime on a regular basis may be required to attract manpower, but it is an expensive way of increasing work output. Actual increases in achieved work may vary from country to country and from time to time but most contractors have sufficient data to give characteristic curves of productivity gains due to working regular overtime, one example of which is shown in Figure 4.3. This productivity loss does not occur when work is machine paced, or is for short periods for specific tasks.

Thus manpower, or as it is generally termed in CPM/PERT methods, resource planning, must be integrated with the work planning, or planning becomes a waste of time.

Bar charts

The oldest formal planning technique in use today is the bar chart, sometimes termed a Gantt or multiple activity chart. This technique was developed during World War 1, by one of the early management consultants, Henry L. Gantt, a contemporary of Frederick Taylor the father of scientific management. Figure 4.4 shows a bar chart for the project outlined in Figures 2.4 and 2.5.

The technique has the advantages that it is

1. Clear: the chart forms a pictorial model of the project.
2. Simple: with very little training almost anyone can learn to construct and use a bar chart, and it is easily understood by all involved in the project.
3. It can be used to show progress.
4. It can be used for manpower planning.

However, it does have disadvantages which limit its applicability, namely

1. The bar chart, by itself, cannot show interrelationships between activities on large, complex projects, and this can lead to problems in co-ordinating the work.

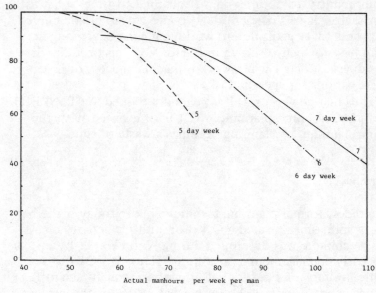

FIGURE 4.3 PRODUCTIVITY WITH OVERTIME

Example:

1. 6 days @ 12 hour   =   72 actual manhours per week
    Productivity   =   0.88
    Effective manhours   =   72 x 0.88 = 63.4

2. 7 days @ 12 hour   =   84 actual manhours per week
    Productivity   =   0.77
    Effective manhours   =   84 x 0.77 = 64.7

N.B. Curves are only illustrative.

Figure 4.3   Productivity with overtime

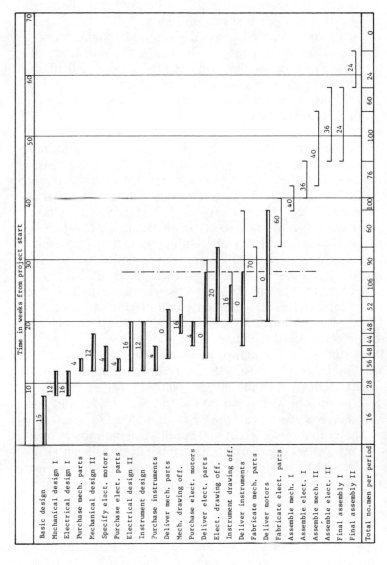

Figure 4.4 Bar chart

75

2. There is a physical limit to the size of a bar chart, which limits the size of project that can be planned using this technique, unless a hierarchical planning system is used, as shown in Figure 3.4.
3. It cannot easily cope with frequent changes or updating. Each change necessitates the redrawing of the chart. In smaller projects this can be handled by having each job represented by a moveable strip, but this soon becomes impractical as the size of the project increases.

When the number of activities is not too great, the bar chart is perfectly satisfactory and thus it is by far the most common technique used to plan and control work on smaller projects. It is a good communication medium, as the chart forms a clear picture of the project. It is clearly understood by all those involved in a project from Managing Director to foreman, and with very little training, almost anyone can learn to build and use a bar chart on the smaller project. It can be used to show progress by drawing a second bar for each activity to represent when the work was actually carried out, or alternatively, the percentage completion of the activity. In Figure 4.4, certain tasks are shown ahead of schedule, on schedule and behind schedule.

It can be used for manpower planning, or resource allocation, by marking on it the numbers of different men of different trades required, in each activity for each time period, as shown. Total manpower for each trade, and for the project as a whole, can then be summed up for each time period and a manpower chart and cumulative manpower chart, that is, an S chart constructed. On smaller jobs the activities can be rescheduled with little difficulty, as progress varies from plan and changes occur. It is also quick to construct and change.

Its one disadvantage on smaller jobs is that it cannot show interrelationships, critical paths and the spare time on an activity, but this can be overcome by using a bar chart in conjunction with an arrow diagram. This enables float, or spare time on activities to be determined and manpower planning carried out by rescheduling activities within their float to achieve a phased build up and run down of labour and avoid severe fluctuations. If resources are still limited, then the finishing date may have to be extended to take this into account as described later.

Unfortunately as the project size increases, the bar chart technique has difficulties in handling the number of activities involved, the mass of data and complex interrelationships between activities. This can be partly overcome by using a hierarchy of bar charts, sometimes termed tiered bar charts as shown on Figure 3.4. This does enable the bar chart method physically to cope with a large number of activities in a systematic manner. It does not enable them to display, or take into account interrelationships and it does tend to give an inflexible plan, as changing and updating requires significant time and labour. In addition integrating manpower planning over the total project becomes very difficult. Thus the bar chart method, when used by itself has limitations in the detailed planning of large projects and this leads to the development of network methods for project planning.

CPM/PERT − network analysis

CPM/PERT or to give these techniques a more generic name, network methods are used in project planning and control under many names and guides. Common names are Critical Path Method (CPM), critical path analysis, Project Evaluation & Review Technique (PERT) and precedence diagrams. The critical path method was developed by E.I. du Pont d'Amours and was first successfully applied in 1958 on a construction project in Kentucky. At the same time the USA Navy's Polaris special projects office, in conjunction with consultants, developed a basically similar PERT system. PERT as originally conceived, used three time estimates for each activity, one optimistic, a most likely and a pessimistic, and used a probability distribution to combine these. This is rarely used today in industrial projects in this form, though the name is now often applied to the basic network methods, and it is interesting to note that there is a growing interest in risk analysis and simulation in project planning using probabilities in a different manner. Figure 2.4 shows a network or arrow diagram for a simple project, and Figure 4.5 shows the normal time analysis output from the calculations involved.

Precedence networks, with an activity on the node or event, as opposed to the activity on the arrow used in the other methods, followed in 1962. It is similar and supposedly slightly simpler in its handling of dummies and ladders, but the activity on arrow, that is, CPM/PERT still tends to be the most common network method used in project planning.

The network method has the following advantages:

1. The method effectively handles the interrelationships between activities on complex projects.
2. It identifies those activities which are critical to finishing the overall project on time and shows the spare time, or float, on the other activities.
3. It can handle very large and complex projects with the present maximum size being between 25,000 and 75,000 activities, depending on the systems used.
4. It can be used with a computer and this permits the integration of the project management information systems.

Thus, because projects were becoming larger and more complex, and their planning more critical to project management efficiency, there was a trend to the widespread adoption of CPM/PERT in the 1960s and early 1970s. Its use became accepted as typifying good practice in project planning, and those who did not use it were considered to be old fashioned, or even immoral!

Bar charts versus CPM/PERT

Despite the fact that it was fashionable to use CPM/PERT, bar charts were still widely used, in these years, in both small and large projects. CPM/PERT never really got established in the planning of the smaller project, because it was not really required, its increased sophistication discouraged its use and bar charts were, and still are, an adequate and effective way of planning and controlling the smaller project. Even with

TIME ANALYSIS

#	ACTIVITY	I	J	T	ES	LS	EF	LF	TF	FF	
1	BASIC DESIGN	5	10	8	0	0	8	8	0	0	CRI.PATH
2	MECHANICAL DESIGN 1	10	15	4	8	18	12	22	10	0	
3	ELECTRICAL DESIGN 1	10	20	4	8	8	12	12	0	0	CRI.PATH
4	PURCHASE MECH.PARTS	15	25	2	12	24	14	26	12	0	
5	MECHANICAL DESIGN 2	15	30	6	12	22	18	28	10	0	
6	SPECIFY ELECT.MOTORS	20	35	4	12	16	16	20	4	0	
7	PURCHASE ELECT.PARTS	20	40	2	12	14	14	16	2	2	
8	ELECTRICAL DESIGN 2	20	45	8	12	12	20	20	0	0	CRI.PATH
9	INSTRUMENT DESIGN	20	50	8	12	24	20	32	12	0	
10	PURCHASE INSTRUMENTS	20	55	4	12	14	16	18	2	0	
11	DELIVER MECH.PARTS	25	60	8	14	26	22	34	12	2	
12	MECH.DRAWING OFF.	30	60	6	18	28	24	34	10	0	
13	PURCHASE EL.MOTORS	35	65	4	16	20	20	24	4	0	
14	DELIVER ELECT.PARTS	40	70	16	16	16	32	32	0	0	CRI.PATH
15	ELEC.DRAWING OFF.	45	70	12	20	20	32	32	0	0	
16	INST.DRAWING OFF.	50	80	8	20	32	28	40	12	12	
17	DELIVER INSTRUMENTS	55	80	22	16	18	38	40	2	2	
18	FABRICATE MECH.PARTS	60	75	8	24	34	32	42	10	6	
19	DELIVER MOTORS	65	75	18	20	24	38	42	4	0	
20	FABRICATE ELCT.PARTS	70	80	8	32	32	40	40	0	0	CRI.PATH
21	ASSEMBLE MECH.1	75	85	4	38	42	42	46	4	0	
22	ASSEMBLE ELEC.1	80	90	6	40	40	46	46	0	0	CRI.PATH
23	DUMMY	85	100	0	42	46	42	46	4	4	
24	DUMMY	90	100	0	46	46	46	46	0	0	CRI.PATH
25	ASSEMBLE MECH.2	85	110	12	42	46	54	58	4	4	
26	ASSEMBLE ELEC.2	90	110	12	46	46	58	58	0	0	CRI.PATH
27	FINAL ASSEMBLY1	100	110	12	46	46	58	58	0	0	CRI.PATH
28	FINAL ASSEMBLY2	110	115	6	58	58	64	64	0	0	CRI.PATH

Figure 4.5   Time analysis

79

larger projects, bar charts were often used as the primary planning technique, principally because they were simple, easy to use, project staff were familiar with them and they were often adequate for the state of the art of planning.

However, even in the late 1970s, contrary to all the publicity and literature produced on CPM/PERT, many companies were actually discarding CPM/PERT and returning to the use of bar charts, even on larger and complex projects. For example:

> One engineering manager from a large US aerospace/ weapons contractor commented in 1979 that CPM/PERT had fallen out of favour in his company, very few of the company projects use this technique and he had not been associated with PERT for five years.
>
> A senior project manager from a large UK chemical company went out to tender on a £20 million project in 1979, and on a preliminary survey of possible contractors found that most of them were not using CPM/PERT. Though in the past the US Department of Defense enforced the use of PERT on their contractors, they now state they 'do not require contractors to use any specific scheduling technique. PERT, Line of Balance, Gantt and Milestone Charts are all good techniques which are effective when properly employed'.

Thus in the late 1970s there was a trend in some companies away from the use of CPM/PERT, even on the larger project, back to using bar or Gantt charts for project planning. Even when CPM/PERT is used, it is often used only as a sales factor, or because the home office or the client insisted upon it. This trend away from CPM/PERT has arisen because many companies had experienced difficulties in using the technique, and the disadvantages and limitations of CPM/PERT came to be more widely appreciated. In addition to the general problems with planning described in the last chapter, the use of CPM/ PERT has the following problems:

1. CPM/PERT is more complicated than bar charting, and this in turn leads to a lack of regard for human factors involved.

2. There are many problems associated with the application of the CPM/PERT techniques on large projects, and these are not widely appreciated
3. There were problems associated with the computing systems used.

Human factors

CPM/PERT is more complicated than bar charting, and requires a greater degree of knowledge and skill with the technique itself, and with the associated computer-based support for it. Many managers and engineers lacked this knowledge and skill, and adequate training was not given to them. As a result many firms employed specialist planners, or set up separate planning departments, and this lead to the problems described in the last chapter.

One of the major advantages of bar charting is that it is a relatively simple technique, requiring little training, and the individual manager or engineer can construct his own with little difficulty and everyone involved can understand them.

Problems with the CPM/PERT technique

Though a simple CPM/PERT application can be carried out with relatively little training, realistic size applications cause many problems in practice, which few, if any, of the textbooks or training courses on the technique attempt to cover. In addition to general problems with the art and science of project planning and difficulties with the computing system, many troubles were experienced due to the following causes

1. Difficulties in communication
2. Difficulties in monitoring and controlling progress
3. The fact that by itself a network and its associated time-analysis is not an operational plan or schedule
4. There was a widespread misinterpretation of the concept of float.

Communication

One of the major difficulties of network analysis at the supervisory level, and often for others, is that an arrow diagram is a very poor means of communication. A large network is difficult to understand even for the specialist, and much more difficult for the general manager or supervisor, who is actually carrying out his part of the project. With some training, the manager can easily understand a simple arrow diagram, or one made up of macro-activities, such as is used for communication purposes with senior management. A large and detailed network looks more like a map of the heavens, than anything else, and is generally unintelligible to those who have no training. Even with training, it can still be very difficult to follow and to use.

The time analysis output of network analysis, as shown in Figure 4.5, is even more confusing, and much worse for communication down the line. Often this is what is handed out to front line management and supervision, and when used for transferring planning into action generally fails. Even if the person concerned can identify the activity to be done, all he has is the earliest and latest start and finish times for the activity. As far as he is concerned, as long as he can get the activity done in these times, everything is on schedule. When he gets the time analysis output for the whole project, the interrelationships of activities are extremely difficult to decipher.

Control

Simple network based methods have no way of showing progress against plan to the manager. Normally the network is time analysed, and possibly resource analysed at periodic intervals to update it and replan, if necessary, the activities on the project. This can be done at very short intervals of a day or a week, in such critical applications as maintenance shutdown scheduling, but more normally on large jobs the network is updated and re-run once a month. This essentially produces a new plan or schedule for the remainder of the work. Unfortunately, there is the problem of relating one network to another. Sometimes no effort is made to check one run of the network with another and the project is continually slipping without people being aware of it. Float is being consumed all the time and managers are completely unaware of the problems building up.

A network is not an operational plan and schedule

All that simple network analysis tells you is:

1. It shows the jobs on the critical path with their start and finish times.
2. It shows the spare time or float on the other jobs with the permissible earliest and latest start and finish times.
3. It shows the interrelationships between activities.

It does not actually tell you who does what, when. It is thus not an operatonal plan and schedule. A critical path schedule is really only a loose planning guide. Except for the critical activities, network analysis produced only a permissive framework, with some limiting dates that can be used to guide the scheduling of the project. The bulk of the results are a long way from being a schedule, that a project manager, functional manager, or construction superintendent can use effectively.

It has two major omissions:

1. It assumes infinite resources are available and no recognition is taken of any limitation in manpower, i.e., no manpower planning.
2. Non-critical jobs are not scheduled.

An operational plan and schedule includes manpower planning, sometimes equipment planning, and someone deciding when the so-called non-critical jobs are to be done. Thus the arrow diagram and time analysis output of a network are not the final plan and schedule for a project, but simply the basis, or first step, in preparing an operational plan.

Problems with the concept of float

There are major problems in the use of network analysis with regard to the misinterpretation and misuse of float. For example, the construction supervision may be planning to delay the start of the first activities in an area, by not assigning resources until some time after its scheduled early start, but before its latest start. If this is done, it will reduce the float available on later activities on that path, and make the float shown in the critical path output for later activities unrealistic with respect to the project schedule.

The concept of float as spare time on a job is a very useful one in planning by network analysis. Unfortunately, three types of float are in general use, namely, total, free and independent float, and very few people completely understand the meaning of any of these. Total float can be taken as the spare time on an activity, the consumption of which will affect the amount of float on both previous and subsequent jobs. Free float can be taken as the spare time on an activity which, provided that the previous activities have been carried out to plan, will not affect any subsequent job. Independent float is the spare time on any activity, the consumption of which will not affect either previous or subsequent activities. The tendency today is only to display total and free float, as independent float tends to be rarely encountered, and activities having independent float also have free float. Total float can be taken as the free time basically on a path through the network; that is not on any particular activity but on a sequence of activities. In other words, the macro-activity or consolidated activity. Unfortunately, very few people, particularly at the supervisory level, understand the meaning of the various types of float. If the word float is shown against the job, it is assumed to be the spare time on that job. Almost inevitably this is then used up in the first half of a project, with the resultant effect that many activities, if not all, become critical in the second half of the project. In practice a project can appear to be progressing to schedule, in that updates of the network show unchanged completion time for the project, but in fact all the non-critical jobs may be slipping badly and float is being consumed.

Problems with the computing system

One of the major reasons for CPM/PERT falling into disfavour is the inadequacy of the computing system used in the past, and the overhead cost of specialist planners and data processing personnel to handle this side of planning. In practice, though there is discussion over the size of the network that justifies the use of a computer, it could be reasonably stated that 'if you don't need to use a computer for CPM/PERT, you don't need to use CPM/PERT'.

In the 1960s, computer-based CPM/PERT planning systems used batch computers implying a complex and powerful sophisticated system, designed to do specific calculations at discrete intervals. Thus the CPM/PERT programmes were also batch-orientated and were not, and could not be effective project management information systems. These systems were able to do the calculations involved in CPM/PERT analysis quite satisfactorily, but suffered from many of the disadvantages of batch computing. Batch computers generally require data processing staff to operate them, who act both as an interface and a barrier to access to the computing system by the project staff. Specialist staff were required because of the complexities involved in using these machines; involving such things as job control language, use of punched cards, file handling and formatting of data. This inevitably meant delay in getting a turnround of the plan, no real quick access to data, and thus no 'feel' or interaction with the planning system. In addition, runs of the project planning computer program had to queue with other jobs waiting to be done by the company's computer, and thus response tended to be slow. The best that could probably be achieved was a 24 hour turnround of the program, though in some cases this could take a week. This was completely inadequate, particularly in the early stages of plan development. Computer cards had to be punched and verified in a fixed format to hold the base data for the plan. Inevitably there would be mistakes, such as data out of place in the formatted card, activities omitted, duplicated activities, activities placed in a loop to give an infinite completion time and activities with no connection, that is, dangling activities. It would probably take several runs before a satisfactory output would be obtained and this could involve a considerable elapsed time.

Thus the speed of development of a plan was slow, just when it was critical that it should be fast to guide the initial work and identify critical activities and problems. It is also at this stage that it should be possible to use a computer-based planning system to simulate alternative ways of carrying out the project and for manpower planning. If this takes several days to get the output from each alternative, then it is unlikely that this strategic use of planning will be carried out. Similarly, when changes and delays occur, there will be delays before management can evaluate their effect and the different courses of action arising from them, and this will not be real time planning. It will also not be possible to query the system to extract information; report formats will also be inflexible and this will discourage its use as a management information system.

Conclusion

Thus for a number of reasons network methods have not been as successful as was once anticipated. Some of the reasons for this were directly attributable to difficulties with the technique, some to the state of computing technology in the 1960s and 70s and some to general problems with the Art & Science of planning large projects. However, management experience, education and general professionalism in the art and science of planning has increased, and many more managers and engineers are using plans as tools to assist them, on a real time basis, in managing their projects. In practice this is probably more critical to the success of planning than the actual planning technique used. The essential factor in project planning is that all the work should be formally scheduled in a manner which will permit the evaluation of actual progress against plan and which will identify the interdependencies of individual activities, and not which technique is used.

In many small and medium sized projects, bar charts will be the favoured primary planning technique, but whenever it is necessary CPM/PERT should be used to support them. In larger projects, although hierarchical bar charts can be used to actually plan and control the project, CPM/PERT should also be used to handle interrelationships. In addition computer-based CPM/PERT is a very efficient way of producing and updating bar charts, and for manpower planning. In fact its use can almost be completely justified for its ease of handling bar charts. Whenever CPM/PERT is the primary planning technique, it should always be complimented by the use of bar charts. In many cases centralised planning should be carried out using both CPM/PERT and bar charts, and then bar charts issued to functional managers and supervisors, who often need not be aware of the use of CPM/PERT. CPM/PERT and bar charts both have advantages and disadvantages, but they are both effective planning techniques which should be used in *conjunction* with each other, and with other techniques such as manpower histograms, S curves and milestone charts. The combined use of these techniques is now much easier with modern computer systems and project planning program packages.

Modern computer-based techniques

Where network methods have a major advantage is that they are amenable to computer manipulation and can be integrated with computer-based project management information systems. In this computer age, it is illogical not to use a computer, if it can be of assistance to management. In the past computer-based project systems have had a bad reputation in project work, primarily because they were based on batch computers, operated by data processing personnel and the packages, which had been devised by data processing or operational research staff, were sometimes not very suitable for practical use.

Today, revised project planning computer program packages and modern computing systems can overcome the problems with project planning outlined in this chapter. From the mid-1970s revised, or new project management, planning and control computer packages, based on practical experience and the identified needs of users, began to be used with interactive computers. These systems are capable of being effective project management planning, control and information systems and are now rapidly coming into use. They allow the project staff direct access to the computer, with more or less immediate response to the requests for information, construction or updating of the plan.

These interactive project management systems were

generally based on research into just what users wanted from such a system, and not what data processing specialists thought should go into it. Thus in general they have the following advantages over the older systems, namely,

1. They are easier to use, both for the novice and experienced user.
2. They are much faster in response.
3. The manager, planner or engineer can use them directly with no data processing interface to go through.
4. They are very flexible in that they can produce bar charts, manpower plans, float charts and S curves if required for any part of the project.
5. They are more powerful than the batch systems, not necessarily in the straightforward calculations, but in the sorting and manipulation of data and output.
6. They are more tailored to the practical needs of the project staff.
7. They can be integrated with data base management information systems.

Computing systems

A major factor in the success of the new systems is the type of computing system used for computer-based project planning, namely, interactive real time computing. There are three types of interactive computing systems used in project work and technological change is leading to emphasis on one of them, namely,

1. The company's main data processing computer.
2. A bureaux-based system.
3. A computer dedicated to the project management function.

Company computer

The nominally cheapest way of providing computer-based project management systems is to use the company's data processing computer. However, it is essential that it be an interactive computing system and it must have ample capacity so that there are no limitations on the use of the system by the project staff. Then with a terminal in the project office they can have access to the project management system for as long as they want, and at any time they want it. Most computer manufacturers have program packages for critical path analysis, though sometimes they are expensive and not up to modern standards of flexibility, which provide a basis for building the project management systems. Though there may be internal charges made for the work, these are normally nominal bookkeeping charges and no 'real' money is involved. However, if the system is not interactive and there is not adequate capacity available, then the company's computer does not provide a basis for effective project management systems and some other alternative should be used.

Computer bureaux systems

Most computer bureaux have critical path analysis program packages, which are adequate for project planning, though their sophistication varies from bureaux to bureaux. They also have high level programming languages such as BASIC, FORTRAN and APL, together with other program packages for such things as financial modelling and data base management, with which an effective project management information system can be built.

These systems can be operated from the bureaux office, but the more normal situation is for the user to hire, or purchase a computer terminal (approximately £1,000) and access the computer bureaux through the normal dial up telephone line. This has the advantage of giving the user access to pre-written program packages mounted on a large powerful computer. They provide a quick and easy way of getting started in using computer systems to back up the project management activity.

Unfortunately, with large scale use the costs mount up, and often people with access to the bureaux system do not use it as much as they should. Every time they access it, there is an identifiable charge to the company and though the cost may normally be well worth the service, it is visible, often management start to quibble about it and the use declines. A more logical approach is to determine how much adequate access to the system would cost, and to see if this would justify an alternative way of supplying this service.

A dedicated project management systems computer

In the last few years there has been a growth of computers dedicated to project management information systems, and with the recent developments in computer technology, these are likely to predominate in the future. A dedicated computer has the advantage that it is completely used in one function, the costs are fixed, it is easily accessible and always available to the project staff. When the company's computer is not suitable and bureaux charges are expensive, a small computer dedicated to this one function is an economic proposition.

At present dedicated computers exist for project management systems in two forms

1. Minicomputer based systems, costing from £10,000 to £60,000.
2. Microcomputer based systems, costing from £3,000 to £7,000.

Firms involved in large scale project work can often justify minicomputer systems such as a DEC or a Hewlett Packard. Such systems are powerful and capable of handling up to 35,000 activities or more on a project, and can be linked to data base management packages, but they are expensive and thus probably only suitable for the larger firm.

A more recent development is the application of 8 bit micro-processor-based microcomputers to project management systems for the small to medium sized project. At present these can only handle up to 4,000 activities, but the newer 16 bit microprocessor based computers will extend the maximum number of activities into the tens of thousands, at little extra cost.

Unlike the larger business computers, which require a specially designed room environment and a data processing staff, microcomputers are designed to be used at an individual level. They are relatively inexpensive, can be as portable as a typewriter, fit on a desk or table, with no special electrical or environmental control requirements, and do not need a data processing professional to operate them. More importantly, microcomputers are easy to use, with no real data processing knowledge required. Nearly any person can purchase, install and operate one. They can be set up in the project office or construction site, to work on a turn-key basis, in that those using them need not know how to operate a microcomputer, but just know how to use the particular application required.

Microcomputer-based project management systems are effective practical tools for project managers and enable even the smaller firm to use modern methods effectively. In the coming years they will be adopted extensively in project work and hopefully lead to better project management, planning and control. Whichever kind of interactive computing system is used, these modern computer-based systems can overcome the previous difficulties experienced in planning and controlling projects.

Modern project planning systems

The modern project planning packages in use today are little different from older packages in the basic calculation routines, but are very different in the framework in which they are used. These packages should have the following characteristics.

Ease of use

The project planning program and the computing system it runs on must appear to the non-data processing orientated project user to be simple and easy to use. It should be interactive, not only for the reasons outlined previously, but also to achieve acceptance of the system by having contact with it and to achieve the man-machine combination, which can be more flexible and powerful than either working on their own. The system should be based on an analysis of user needs and desires, not only from a general project management point of view but also for the managers involved on any individual project. Thus it should be able to be used for simple planning, or for sophisticated planning; it should be able to be used for CPM/PERT and bar charts used jointly; for bar charts as the primary technique or for CPM/PERT as the primary technique. User instruction manuals should be as simple as possible with a kindergarten level introduction to planning the simpler project. The programme should have the facility to be used at beginner level, with a 'help' query system and detailed prompts, and at an expert level without these user aids. It should also give a fast response.

Project planning programme

The program should be just as much orientated to bar charts, manpower planning, S charts and milestones as it is to CPM/PERT. It should be a 'project planning' program package and not just a CPM/PERT program.

Integrated project management information system

Many CPM/PERT programs have PERT/COST facilities where an estimated cost, actual costs and a variance analysis can be used for each activity. A more modern approach is to link the data files for the project planning system to a data base management system, so that not only can this method of analysis be carried out but also so that a more modern performance analysis system can be implemented based on the use of the work breakdown structure, cost accounts and work packages. This provides a basis for an integrated project management information system.

Input facilities

This must be simple, fast and as far as is possible limit the chance of error. Either free format should be used, or formatted screens on visual display units, with prompts for beginners should be available. It must be easy to set-up, use, copy and edit multiple data files to hold the data on alternative plans. The bulk of the data may be input using punched cards, at an interactive terminal or held in a data file, and a flexible interactive data editor must be available to correct and add to the data. Library files must be available to hold standard planning modules, described later, which only need to be edited to add to this project data base. It must be possible to quickly establish and modify alternate calendars to provide the time base for the plan.

There must be comprehensive error checking routines which first of all validate the raw data to see if it is complete and within the bounds of reason, and secondly check the logic of the arrow diagram for errors, such as loops or dangling activities.

Operation

The basic calculation routines are well established for both activity on the arrow and activity on the node, but it should be possible on the same data base to analyse all levels of plan used, by summarisation and skeletonisation. In addition to the straightforward time analysis, the program should be able to do manpower planning on four bases:

1. Time limited.
2. Resource limited.
3. User priority code.
4. Manual interaction.

The program should be able to quickly simulate different logic, activity times and resource availabilities in the plan development stage and when replanning the project, using alternative data files. It should be possible to fix the schedule for any activities described, that is, establish scheduled starts (S.S.) and scheduled finishes (S.F.). On updating runs it should be possible to quickly input actual starts (A.S.) and actual finishes (A.F.) and percent complete estimates for any activity.

Output

The program should have a flexible report generator, which on request should be able to generate the following output for the project as a whole, for the hierarchical planning system, for the work breakdown structure elements, organisations, cost accounts and work packages and sorted for any factor or combination of factors.

1. Traditional time analysis.
2. Bar charts.
3. Manpower histograms and tables.
4. Milestone charts.
5. S charts.
6. Variance analysis from plan, and from update to update.

There should also be a connection to the data base management system for cost and schedule performance analysis.

5 Modern Project Planning Methods

The project manager and planner can overcome many of the problems described in the previous chapter and effectively plan and control their projects, with the use of modern computer-based project planning systems.

These systems are much more effective in achieving good communication than the older batch systems because they are designed for, and can be used as real time project management information systems. The project staff can through a computer terminal extract information more or less immediately on request or on a routine basis. This information can not only include normal time and resources data but also many other items of information. This is done by extending the data records held in file for each activity and, or, interlinking the data network data files on a data base management information system. For example, such a computer system can hold for each activity the information shown in Figure 5.1.

The standard set of reports produced by such a system consists of:

1. A time analysis
2. Bar chart
3. Resource histograms and tables of manpower requirements.

This can be produced for the project as a whole, as is shown in Figures 4.5, 5.2 and 5.3, for the individual department or organisation, for each profession or trade, or any other factor as desired, for example, one area of

	Description
	Whose responsibility
I	Preceding event number
J	Succeeding event number
T	Duration
	Number of resources
	For each resource:
	Name
	Amount per time period
	Total amount estimated
	Total amount actual
ES	Earliest start
LS	Latest start
EF	Earliest finish
LF	Latest finish
SS	Scheduled start
SF	Scheduled finish
TF	Total float
FF	Free float
SF	Scheduled float
AS	Actual start
AF	Actual finish
	% complete
FF	Forecast finish
BCL	Budgeted cost labour
BCM	Budgeted cost material
ACL	Actual cost labour
ACM	Actual cost material
UF	User fields (to add any extra sort codes required, descriptions, or any other information)

Figure 5.1   Data base for an activity

construction site, one unit of a chemical plant. Figure 5.4, shows a standard set of reports for the electrical-instruments system design function in the project used for illustration. In addition S curves and milestone reports can be produced as desired for the analysis and control of progress.

The ability to sort output is a very powerful and extremely useful facility and means that reports can be produced that are sorted by responsibility, by date, by resource, by criticality, by function and by many other factors. For example, reports for the following can be produced in any form desired, and these factors can be combined together for special reports on request

1. All activities due to start next month
2. All activities in a particular area
3. All activities which are the specific responsibility of an individual, department or company
4. All activities using a specific resource
5. All activities with zero float
6. All activities with free float
7. All activities with less than ten units of float
8. Number of fitters required over the next six months
9. The activities these fitters would be working on in order of total float
10. All jobs whose float this month are less than float last month.

Thus, for example, a supervisor or manager could be given a time analysis, bar chart and resource requirements table or histogram for all the activities for which he is responsible in the next three months. Such a system is not only effective for communication but is invaluable as a source of information for management.

Using these systems several methods can be used to monitor, analyse and display progress. The most common are

1. Bar charts
2. Time analysis with progress reports
3. Manpower curves
4. S charts
5. Milestones.

```
                              BAR CHART
                              ---------
29  ACTIVITY                MEN :----+----+----+----+----+----+----+
                                :    10   20   30   40   50   60   70
                                :    +    +    +    +    +    +    +
 1  BASIC DESIGN             16 :XXXXXXXX
 2  MECHANICAL DESIGN 1      12 :        XXXX------------
 3  ELECTRICAL DESIGN 1      16 :        XXXX
 4  PURCHASE MECH.PARTS       4 :            XX-------------
 5  MECHANICAL DESIGN 2      12 :            XXXXX------------
 6  SPECIFY ELECT.MOTORS      4 :            XXXX-----
 7  PURCHASE ELECT.PARTS      4 :            XX---
 8  ELECTRICAL DESIGN 2      16 :            XXXXXXXX
 9  INSTRUMENT DESIGN        12 :            XXXXXXXX------
10  PURCHASE INSTRUMENTS      4 :            XXXX--
11  DELIVER MECH.PARTS        0 :                XXXXXXXX------------
12  MECH.DRAWING OFF.        16 :                XXXXX-------------
13  PURCHASE EL.MOTORS        4 :                XXX-----
14  DELIVER ELECT.PARTS       0 :                XXXXXXXXXXXXXX---
15  ELEC.DRAWING OFF.        20 :                    XXXXXXXXXXXXX
16  INST.DRAWING OFF.        16 :                    XXXXXXX----------
17  DELIVER INSTRUMENTS       0 :                    XXXXXXXXXXXXXXXXXXXX-----
18  FABRICATE MECH.PARTS     70 :                        XXXXXXX----------
19  DELIVER MOTORS            0 :                        XXXXXXXXXXXXXXXXXX-----
20  FABRICATE ELCT.PARTS     60 :                            XXXXXXX
21  ASSEMBLE MECH.1          40 :                                XXXX-----
22  ASSEMBLE ELEC.1          36 :                                XXXXXX
25  ASSEMBLE MECH.2          40 :                                    XXXXXXXXXXXX-----
26  ASSEMBLE ELEC.2          36 :                                    XXXXXXXXXXXXX
27  FINAL ASSEMBLY1          24 :                                        XXXXXXXXXXXX
28  FINAL ASSEMBLY2          24 :                                            XXXXXX
                                +----+----+----+----+----+----+----+
```

Figure 5.2   Computer produced bar chart showing activity time and total float

98

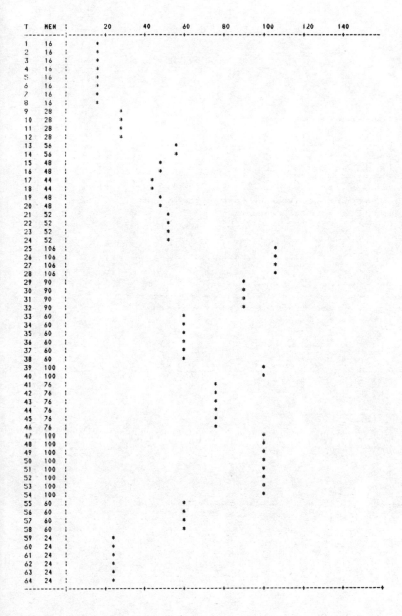

Figure 5.3   Manpower chart

TYPE IN THE CODE NUMBER OF THE RESOURCE REPORT REQUIRED

? 1

TIME ANALYSIS

	ACTIVITY	I	J	T	ES	LS	EF	LF	TF	FF	
1	BASIC DESIGN	5	10	8	0	0	8	8	0	0	CRI.PATH
3	ELECTRICAL DESIGN 1	10	20	4	8	8	12	12	0	0	CRI.PATH
6	SPECIFY ELECT.MOTORS	20	35	4	12	16	16	20	4	0	
8	ELECTRICAL DESIGN 2	20	45	8	12	12	20	20	0	0	CRI.PATH
9	INSTRUMENT DESIGN	20	50	8	12	24	20	32	12	0	

TYPE IN THE CODE NUMBER OF THE OPTION DESIRED(9 FOR THE REDISPLAY OF THE OPTIONS AVAILABLE)
? 4
TYPE IN THE CODE NUMBER OF THE RESOURCE REPORT REQUIRED

? 1

```
                            BAR CHART
                            ---------
29 ACTIVITY               MEN :    10    20    30    40    50    60    70
----------------------------------+---------+---------+---------+---------+---------+---------+
1   BASIC DESIGN           16  :XXXXXXXX
3   ELECTRICAL DESIGN 1    16  :      XXXX
6   SPECIFY ELECT.MOTORS    4  :        XXXX----
8   ELECTRICAL DESIGN 2    16  :        XXXXXXXX
9   INSTRUMENT DESIGN      12  :        XXXXXXXX-------------
----------------------------------:---------+---------+---------+---------+---------+---------+
```

TYPE IN THE CODE NUMBER OF THE OPTION DESIRED(9 FOR THE REDISPLAY OF THE OPTIONS AVAILABLE)
? 6
TYPE IN THE CODE NUMBER OF THE RESOURCE REPORT REQUIRED

? 1

```
                        MANPOWER CHART
                        --------------
T   MEN :     20    40    60    80    100   120   140
--------:---------+---------+---------+---------+---------+---------+---------+
1   16  :    *
2   16  :    *
3   16  :    *
4   16  :    *
5   16  :    *
6   16  :    *
7   16  :    *
8   16  :    *
9   16  :    *
10  16  :    *
11  16  :    *
12  16  :    *
13  32  :        *
14  32  :        *
15  32  :        *
16  32  :        *
17  28  :      *
18  28  :      *
19  28  :      *
20  28  :      *
--------:---------+---------+---------+---------+---------+---------+---------+
```

Figure 5.4   Plan for electrical instrument design

It is relatively simple to produce bar charts showing both planned and actual work on activities by computer for the project as a whole, or sorted by area, responsibility, current jobs, or for activities which are not on schedule.

Time analysis reports can also be produced showing scheduled and actual start and finishes for each activity, plus reports on percentage complete and forecast completion dates, again sorted in any manner desired, as shown in Figure 5.5

Manpower graphs can also be produced by the machine showing planned manpower build up and actual manpower build up as shown in Figure 5.3. They can also be produced for total manpower, and for individual trades.

S Curves

The computer-based system can also produce that very effective control tool, the S curve. An S curve is a graph of the cumulative value of manhours, percentage complete, or cost, against time. The vertical scale can be manhours or cost, or the percentage of planned manhours or budgeted cost, that is, percentage complete. This graph generally takes the form of an S because most projects have a slow start, followed by a longer period of relatively constant activity at a higher rate of activity, and finally a falling off of this rate of activity to give a slow finish.

The S curve is a very sensitive tool for the analysis and control of progress, whether it be based on manhours or cost. In the control of cost, their use has become very sophisticated, and is described in more detail in a later chapter. The big advantage of S curves is that they can be used to identify trends at an early stage, because they can monitor both the rate of progress, and also the acceleration or deceleration of this rate. In manpower analysis the slope of the curve represents the rate of expenditure of manhours, that is the velocity and the rate of change of the curve represents the rate of build up or run down of the momentum of work on the project, that is, the acceleration or deceleration of the pace of work. S curves can be used to represent the project

Activity Description	i	j	SS	SF	AS	AF	% Complete	Forecast Completion
Basic design	5	10	0	8	0	9	–	–
Electrical design I	10	20	8	12	9	14	–	–
Specify electrical motors	20	35	12	16	14	18	–	–
Electrical design II	20	45	12	20	14	22	–	–
Mechanical drawing office	30	60	18	24	13	–	90	25
Instrument design	20	50	20	28	23	–	10	32
Electrical drawing office	45	70	20	32	22	–	15	34
Instrument drawing office	50	80	24	32	–	–	–	33

Figure 5.5 Time analysis report. Electrical design and total drawing office

as a whole, work-breakdown structure items, organisational or functional work packages. Figures 3.2 and 5.6, show the planned percentage manhours S curves for work on the design and construction, respectively, of a petrochemical project.

Three elements of data are required to be graphed on an S curve for effective control of manhours. These are

1. The planned cumulative expenditure of manhours against time.
2. The actual cumulative expenditure of manhours against time.
3. The cumulative manhours equivalent of actual work completed, that is, earned value.

The slope of the curve at the start represents the initial rate of work on the project. If the gradient of the actual manhours curve is less than planned, then it is obvious that there is too slow a start. Thereafter the first critical point is where the curve should turn up at the bottom of the S. If this critical acceleration of work on the project does not occur as planned, that is, the S curve does not turn upwards, the project is going to be delayed, no matter what is done. Once the curve does turn up, the slope of the curve shows the rate of progress. If work is not progressing as fast as planned, the slope of the actual curves very quickly and obviously becomes less than that of the planned work curve. At the top of the curve if the work does not decelerate as planned then there is going to be an overshoot. This is because it is generally not possible to finish off a project without the slowing up of the pace of work, as is represented by the top of the S.

For example, Figure 5.7 shows the S curves for the electrical instrument systems design functions for the functional plan shown in Figure 5.4, at week 17 of the project. The planned manweeks expended curve is simply the cumulative version of the manpower graph shown in Figure 5.4. The actual cumulative manweeks expended is based on the project records. Both these curves are fairly straightforward to obtain data for and to construct, but can be very misleading without the third curve, that is, the earned value of manweeks expended. There is often difficulty in obtaining reliable

103

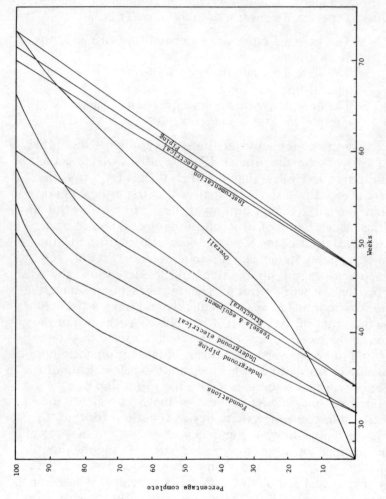

Figure 5.6 S chart for construction

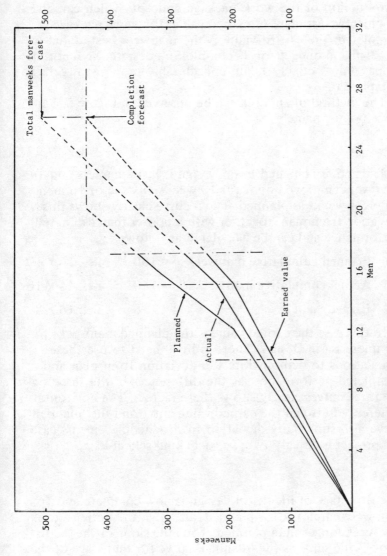

Figure 5.7 S curve for electrical design

105

estimates of this cumulative manweeks equivalent of actual work completed and this is one of the reasons for the introduction of the work package concept, which can give an objective estimate of earned value. If a work package is completed, the earned value is the manweeks estimated in the plan and budget for its completion, despite the fact that it may have actually taken considerably more manweeks to complete it.

The method of analysis can be observed in Figure 5.7 at three points, namely,

Week 10

The activity labelled Basic Design is just complete and 14 men were employed on it for 10 weeks, instead of 16 men for eight weeks as planned. The S curve clearly shows this deviation from plan, together with a poorer than estimated performance and can be calculated as follows

(a) Planned cumulative manweeks = 160   i.e., 16 x 10

(b) Actual cumulative manweeks   = 140   i.e., 14 x 10

(c) Earned value   = 128   i.e., 16 x 8

In this case the earned value is the planned manweeks to complete Basic Design. There is little need to use these calculations to demonstrate the deviation from plan and completed performance, as the differences in the slope of the three curves clearly shows these factors. The horizontal difference between the earned value curve and the 'planned' curve also shows any deviation from schedule; in this case the project is already two weeks behind schedule.

Week 15

The first stage of Electrical Design is now complete and 16 men were employed, as planned, although this activity took one week longer than planned. Thus the slope of the 'actual' curve is the same as the 'planned' curve for that stage of the work, but the 'earned' curve's slope is less than that of the actual. This clearly identifies performance less than planned, and brings it to the attention of the project manager for further investigation.

The project is now three weeks late, as shown by the horizontal difference between curves and performance can be calculated as follows

(a) Planned cumulative manweeks = 290

(b) Actual cumulative manweeks   = 220

(c) Earned value   = 192

(that is, the estimated manweeks to complete Basic Design and Electrical Design I).

It is also obvious at a glance that the pace of work has not accelerated as planned and that the deviation between the curves is increasing.

Week 17

Although the slopes of the actual and earned value curves has increased, they are still less than that of the planned curve. The project is now approximately four weeks behind schedule and an extrapolation of present performance can now be made to forecast the completion date of this segment of the project and the number of manweeks that will be required. If performance is unchanged it can be estimated from the curves that this segment of work will take 26 weeks instead of 20 as planned, and 505 manweeks instead of 432.

The results to date can be calculated as follows

(a) Planned cumulative manweeks = 350

(b) Actual cumulative manweeks   = 275

(c) Earned value   = 235

$$\text{Manpower performance index} = \frac{\text{Earned value}}{\text{Actual value}} = \frac{235}{275}$$

$$= 0.85$$

$$\text{Estimates total manweeks} = \frac{\text{Planned manweeks}}{\text{Manpower performance index}} = \frac{432}{0.85}$$

$$= 505$$

It is obvious that not only are the promised number of men not being committed to the work but that these men are not achieving the expected performance.

Although the points demonstrated on this segment of a project are relatively self-evident from other factors, this is not always the case for large segments of work and the project as a whole. The S curve being a cumulative curve is sensitive to deviations which although small in themselves in any one period, can build up to a significant deviation. When the data for all the activities on a project are consolidated, S curve analysis gives a concise and clear picture of performance on a project. Figure 5.8 shows the complete project, the planned curve being the cumulative version of Figure 5.3, and the same form of analysis can be carried out. For example, at week 32

(a) Planned cumulative manweeks   = 1575

(b) Actual cumulative manweeks   = 1250

(c) Earned value   = 1025

The project is approximately 6 weeks behind schedule because in the 24 weeks, fewer men were committed to the work than planned and they did not achieve the estimated performance. The acceleration of work into the main phase of the project was 4 weeks behind schedule and though the planned number of men are now being committed to the work, they are still not achieving the required performance. The manpower performance index can be calculated on three bases, that is, on the project to date, on the main phase of the project, that is, week 28 to week 32, and for individual segments as desscribed above. For example

Manpower performance index on
project to date $= 1025/1250 = 0.82$

Manpower performance index on
main phase $= \dfrac{1025 - 750}{1250 - 875} = 0.85$

If the earned value curve is extrapolated it forecasts that the project completion will be 13 weeks late. If the manpower is unchanged it forecasts that either 4604 or 4442 manweeks

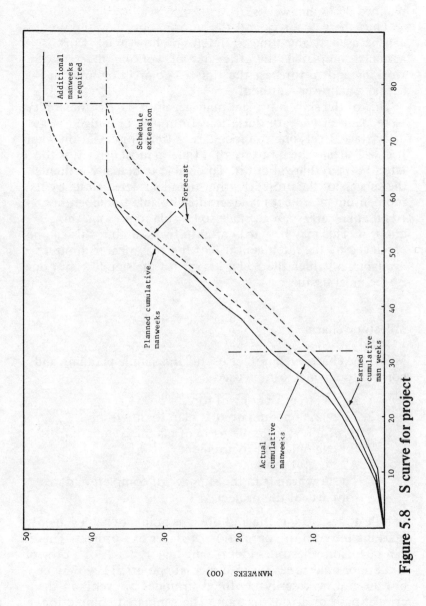

Figure 5.8 S curve for project

MANWEEKS (00)

will be required to complete the project instead of the planned 3776 manweeks.

Thus these S curves and the information they represent can be used at any time to determine how much work is actually completed, the efficiency of working, the rate of working and to forecast the time to completion and the actual manpower required.

One of the skills a project manager must have is the ability to recognise trends, or deviations from plan or budget, at an early stage. Everyone can recognise a trend or deviation when it is well established, but by that time in most cases it is too late to do anything about it. To be able to actually influence the success of the project, rather than be carried along by its momentum, a project manager must be able to recognise a trend at an early enough stage to be able to do something about it. This may be partly an intuitive skill, but this can be enhanced by the intelligent use of the analytical techniques available, of which the S chart is one of the simplest, but one of the most useful.

Milestone charts

Milestone charts are another useful and simple planning and control tool which can be used

1. As an effective control tool,
2. To relate one update of a plan to others,
3. By itself, as a simple form of planning and control, for example, in procurement,
4. As a useful summary plan,
5. To show trends in the slippage of completion dates for parts of the project.

Milestones are specific and obvious points of achievement marking the start or completion of stages of a project. These can be major milestones identifying major phases of a project and minor milestones for intermediate points. They may be, but are not necessarily confined to nodes or events in the critical path or arrow diagram. The estimated completion time of each milestone is determined from the initial version

110

of the plan. Thereafter the re-estimated, or actual completion time, is determined at each update of the plan. This information can be presented in tabular form as shown in Figure 5.9 or a milestone chart can be constructed as shown in Figure 5.10.

In this chart the estimated date of each milestone at the initial construction of the plan is plotted along a horizontal time scale at the top of the chart. Thereafter at each update of the plan, the actual or re-estimated date of each milestone is plotted as shown. As they are plotted, each point is joined up to the preceding one to produce a series of curves, each of which shows the trend in date for that milestone. There may be an optimistic tendency to straighten out these lines at the right hand size, hoping to make up time on these items. Generally, however, delays in the early stages of the plan are likely to be reflected all the way through, as illustrated, and if this seems realistic, it is better to make an early estimate of slippage in project completion date, than be faced with a major revision nearer the end.

This chart can show: the estimated completion date, changes in estimated completion dates between updates, trends towards changes in these dates, causes of these trends, progress, if any, towards returning to schedule, and the actual date of the milestone to give a historical record. It has the advantages that it can permit any significant point to be followed, it can show overlapping items and it is simple and easy to read.

Management of float

Many projects become late because of slippage of the critical path, but many also become late because of slippage of 'so called' non-critical jobs. It is essential that the float, that is, spare time on non-critical jobs be monitored from one update of the network to another, to check for slippages. A general picture can be obtained by the printing out of a graph, or histogram showing the number of jobs with different amounts of float at each update. This, however, only produces a general picture which is not too clear. An alternative method is to print out on a time analysis the previous, or

Event time (Calender week)

	Original Schedule	Review 1 Week 12	Review 2 Week 24	Review 3 Week 36	Present Forecast	Actual
Electrical design I complete	12	12	–	–	–	12
Electrical items orders placed	14	14	–	–	–	15
Electrical design II complete	20	20	–	–	–	21
Mechanical items delivered	24	24	26	–	–	26
Start fabricating electrical	32	32	35	–	–	35
Start assembling mechanical	38	38	42	42	–	43
Start assembling electrical	40	40	44	44	–	46
Start final assembly I	46	46	51	51	54	–
Start final assembly II	58	58	65	65	70	–
Project complete	64	64	71	71	78	–

Figure 5.9 Milestone report week 48

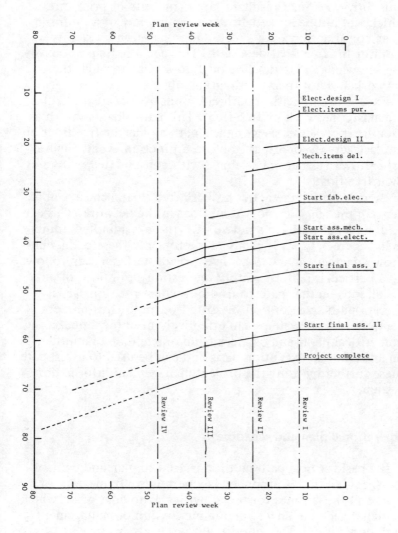

Figure 5.10 Milestone chart

initial float and the present float. Alternatively, the computer can be instructed to print out this information, where present float is less than previous, initial, or a specified level of float. This, however, may result in large amounts of print out, which will not be looked at. An effective way of monitoring float consumption on a shorthand, exception basis is to monitor the free float on a path. This can also help to convey the knowledge that float belongs to a path through the network and not to any individual jobs.

Except on the critical path, all subnetworks are joined to the master network by free float. This path float is shown as total float on activities along the path and as the free float on the last activity on a path before a junction event. Figure 5.11 shows a skeleton bar chart, with consolidated paths and their free float.

By monitoring the activities with free float a check can be kept on the consumption of all float in the network. This can be done for all paths in a network, if there is a limited number as in Figure 5.12, or it can be done for only these paths that show a decrease in free float. The project staff can then follow up a particular path by simply requesting a print out of data for all jobs on that path to find out where the slippage is, using a path trace option or sorted output. Thus modern computer-based systems can effectively monitor slippage on non-critical paths and changes from one update to another, on a total or an exception basis and can be used to investigate these further by using the project management information system.

Operational plan and schedule

If the basic critical path method is used to plan and control a project, all that is produced is a permissive framework of start and finish times for the activities. Who does what, when, is then decided in an *ad hoc* manner by junior management and supervision. This almost always leads to an early consumption of the float available on non-critical activities, resources inbalance and slippages in the completion time of the project. Someone must decide who does what, when, but

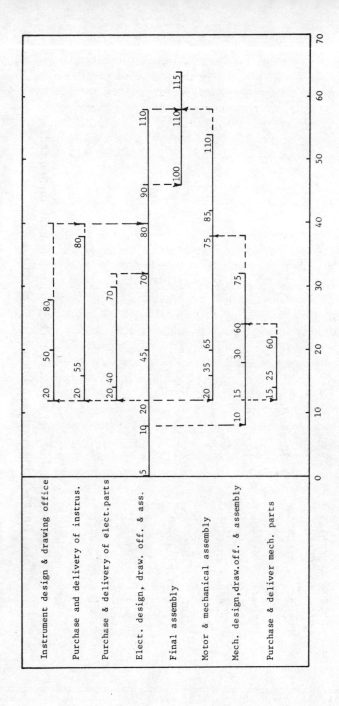

Figure 5.11   Skeleton bar chart showing free float

Description	Path	Initial	Week 12	Week 24
Purchased mechanical items	15-25-60	2	2	0
Instrument design & drawing office	20-50-80	12	8	4
Purchased electrical items	20-40-70	2	2	0
Mechanical design & fabrication	10-15-30-60-75	6	4	2
Purchased instrument items	20-55-80	2	2	0
Motor purchase & mechanical assembly	20-35-65-75-85-95	4	4	2
Scheduled completion week		64	64	64
Total free float		28	22	8

Figure 5.12 Free float monitor. Scheduled completion week remains unchanged, but float is being used up on non-critical activities

it must be done in a planned manner, integrating resource scheduling and time scheduling of activities. It may still be necessary and advisable to leave day to day management, or even week to week management of the work to junior management and supervision, but the amount of latitude delegated to them, must be limited. This day to day, week to week work, must be planned and carried out within the framework of a plan, but this framework must be tighter than the conventional earliest and latest times for an activity. What is required is the *scheduled start* and *finish* of activities and the resources planned. Ideally this detailed planning of the project work should be done in conjunction with junior management and supervision.

Day-to-day management may require changes to the schedule due to a hundred and one factors which cannot be anticipated, but variations must be kept within a tight framework to give management a chance of keeping to schedule. A scheduled start and finish date for activities does not mean the simple suppression of float, but the establishment of an agreed scheduled start and finish for activities by project management, planning staff and junior management and supervision, who then attempt to control the work to this schedule. This has the big advantage of being 'their' schedule and thus they will more likely be committed to it and it is more likely to be achieved.

Thus in planning the project, the preparation of a critical path diagram and its time analysis are merely the start of planning. The next step is to determine the resources required by this plan. This is done by the computer in a similar manner to how it is done manually with bar charts. The data base for network analysis contains the manpower and other resources required (for example, cranes) and the computer can aggregate them in a similar manner to a bar chart for a plan based on both the earliest and latest start times of activities. In addition, non-critical jobs can be easily scheduled to start at some percentage way along the float. This gives the initial graphs and tables of the manpower required, both for individual trades and for the total manpower.

This permits the manager or planner, to examine the manpower profile and compare it to the desired build up and run down of labour, and the labour availability. Where a smooth build up or run down is required, or where resources exceed those available or desired, perhaps to avoid congestion, activities have to be adjusted hopefully within their float, to endeavour to achieve the desired manpower plan, as with bar charts.

There are at least three ways of doing this with computer-based project planning, namely

1. An interactive semi-manual system
2. An automatic resource levelling system
3. A combination of the above

In the interactive method, manpower profiles for the total project and for individual key trades are printed out and examined. When the total project manpower profile is undesirable or where the key trades profile is fluctuating widely or exceeds the numbers available, a time analysis and bar chart are printed out. It is also possible to automatically print these activities contributing to peak demands for any particular trade. Then by inspection, that is, manual planning, activities can be given scheduled starts and/or resource and time requirements varied to achieve an acceptable manpower profile.

To illustrate the flexibility of this combination of human judgement, machine interaction and the quick evaluation of possible alternatives, consider the following example. Figure 4.1 shows the manpower charts for electrical/instrument designers, and for the drawing office. In both cases the manpower assigned to this project varies erratically and probably at the peaks exceeds that available. Good manpower planning would endeavour to avoid these peaks, and have a nearly constant allocation of men to this project. Figure 5.4 shows the full sorted output for the electrical/instrument design activity and shows that two activities have float and thus could be rescheduled without delaying the overall project. By inspection of the bar chart it can be seen that if instrument design can be delayed by eight weeks, this would smooth out the main peak and yet the activity would still have four periods of float. To do this simply involves the following answers to prompts from the program package:

'DO YOU WANT TO RESCHEDULE ANY ACTIVITIES?'
? *YES*
'WHICH ACTIVITY?'
? *INSTR.DES.*
'WHAT IS THE NEW SCHEDULED START WEEK NO?'
? *20*

The program will then recalculate the network data and
produce any reports desired. Figure 5.13 shows the new
manpower chart for the resource in question. This gives a
reasonably satisfactory manpower plan and the next stage is
to see what effect this has on the other critical activity, that
is, the drawing office as shown in Figure 5.14. In fact it has
reduced the peak drawing office manpower requirements
from 52 to 36 but the profile is still too lumpy. By repeating
the process with the instrument drawing office we can get
the manpower chart shown in Figure 5.15. This is still not
too satisfactory and has in fact used up all the float on that
path. A more reasonable plan would be to extend the work
on the Mechanical Drawing Office to take 10 weeks instead
of 6, employing a maximum peak of 28 men on the project
and start work with 8 men on the Instrument Drawing Office
as soon as the mechanical drawings are complete. This would
reduce the peak manpower requirements and still retain two
weeks total float on the instrument path. Thereafter a full
report would be produced to examine the overall effects and
sorted reports for each activity to check the effects on
individual resources.

However, with large jobs, this can get difficult, time
consuming and require many attempts to achieve an acceptable
manpower profile. In addition, as the job progresses and
changes occur, updating the manpower plan can be very
tedious and time consuming. Modern computer-based systems
allow the maximum number of tradesmen per period to be
specified and the computer to automatically endeavour to
carry out this scheduling, using a scheduling algorithm.

There are two types of scheduling carried out on modern
computer-based systems, namely, time limited and resource
limited scheduling. Scheduling starts from the earliest start
schedule. It takes account of the resources required for each

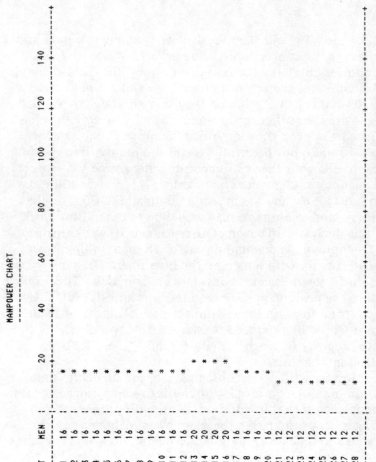

MANPOWER CHART
- - - - - - - - -

T	MEN								
		20	40	60	80	100	120	140	
1	16	*							
2	16	*							
3	16	*							
4	16	*							
5	16	*							
6	16	*							
7	16	*							
8	16	*							
9	16	*							
10	16	*							
11	16	*							
12	16	*							
13	20	*							
14	20	*							
15	20	*							
16	20	*							
17	16	*							
18	16	*							
19	16	*							
20	16	*							
21	12	*							
22	12	*							
23	12	*							
24	12	*							
25	12	*							
26	12	*							
27	12	*							
28	12	*							

Figure 5.13   Electrical designers required after rescheduling

```
                    TIME ANALYSIS
                    -------------
     ACTIVITY             I      J      T      ES     LS     EF     LF     TF     FF
12   MECH.DRAWING OFF.    30     60     6      18     28     24     34     10     0
15   ELEC.DRAWING OFF.    45     70     12     20     20     32     32     0      0      CRI.PATH
16   INST.DRAWING OFF.    50     80     8      28     32     36     40     4      4

TYPE IN THE CODE NUMBER OF THE OPTION DESIRED(9 FOR THE REDISPLAY OF THE OPTIONS AVAILABLE)
? 4
TYPE IN THE CODE NUMBER OF THE RESOURCE REPORT REQUIRED

? 3

                    BAR CHART
                    ---------
29  ACTIVITY          MEN :     10     20     30     40     50     60     70
-----------------------------+------+------+------+------+------+------+------+
12  MECH.DRAWING OFF.  16  :              XXXXXX----------
15  ELEC.DRAWING OFF.  20  :            XXXXXXXXXXXX
16  INST.DRAWING OFF.  16  :                     XXXXXXXX----
-----------------------------:------+------+------+------+------+------+------+

TYPE IN THE CODE NUMBER OF THE OPTION DESIRED(9 FOR THE REDISPLAY OF THE OPTIONS AVAILABLE)
? 6
TYPE IN THE CODE NUMBER OF THE RESOURCE REPORT REQUIRED

? 3

                    MANPOWER CHART
                    --------------

T   MEN :      20     40     60     80     100    120    140
-------:------+------+------+------+------+------+------+------+
19   16 :      *
20   16 :      *
21   36 :          *
22   36 :          *
23   36 :          *
24   36 :          *
25   20 :       *
26   20 :       *
27   20 :       *
28   20 :       *
29   36 :          *
30   36 :          *
31   36 :          *
32   36 :          *
33   16 :      *
34   16 :      *
35   16 :      *
36   16 :      *
-------:------+------+------+------+------+------+------+------+
```

Figure 5.14   Drawing office plan
(after rescheduling of design plan)

121

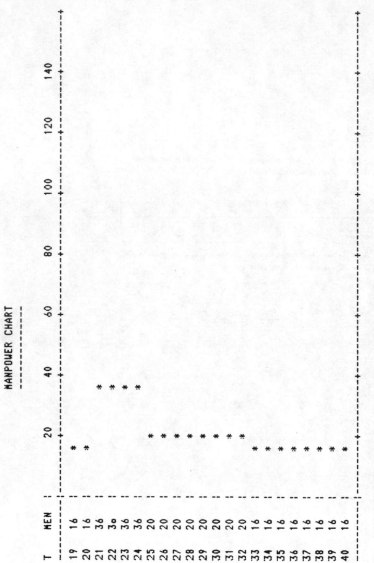

Figure 5.15   Draughtsmen required after rescheduling

activity and their availability, delaying activities where necessary until the required resources are available. Ideally, this can be achieved without missing any target completion dates or delaying the completion of the completion of the project as a whole by rescheduling activities within the float available. It may not be possible, however, to satisfy the constraints of target dates and resource availabilities simultaneously. In this case either the target dates must slip or more resources must be provided. The two types of scheduling, time limited and resource limited, differ only in what happens if both the time limits and resource limits cannot be satisfied simultaneously.

If it is the target dates that are all important, then time limited scheduling will take account of the resource constraints and will attempt to satisfy them, but will provide a schedule that meets the target dates. It will do so even though the requirements for one or more of the resources may exceed the available level for some part of the time. Activities which use resources over the normal availability level set for these resources, will be tagged for future reference and management attention.

If the resource constraints are unchangeable, then resource limited scheduling will provide a schedule which restricts the total resource requirements to the available levels, even though this may result in missed targets or a delay in the project completion date.

Systems using scheduling algorithms generally require a large and faster computer than others and this process can take a considerable amount of time for larger project plans. The human touch tends to be lost and it is difficult for automatic scheduling to take into account complex constraints and intangible factors. However, both methods can be combined to give some human interaction and some automatic resource planning to handle large and complex jobs.

With such systems project and construction managers can use simulation to help them evaluate alternative decisions and changes that occur. For example, the user can enter any changes he requires to activity durations. A rapid analysis would then enable him to discover immediately how the altered durations affect the summary network or how the changes modify a specific area in the network. Resource simulation allows the user to raise or lower resource availability levels and to monitor the effect this has on the completion time and on other resources. Thus such a simulation gives a close approximation to the project resource requirements that can be used later for a fully detailed analysis.

Planning library modules

Many projects are completely new in concept and structure to an individual company, but many others are relatively similar and are characteristic to the industry or the company. They may be widely different in detail, but be similar in general structure; for example, a petrochemical project or an aerospace weapon project. When a company deals with a stream of similar projects in such a situation, considerable time and work can be saved in preparing a plan by the use of standardised logic diagrams, or in other terms, library modules.

These are standard plans, networks or bar charts, or elements of them, which represent the way work is normally carried out on certain activities, or on complete projects. They essentially represent an experienced planner looking at an old plan for a similar project, or parts of such a plan, and using it as a guide or format for the plan of a new project, but taken to a greater degree of sophistication. When project plans are examined for relatively similar projects it becomes obvious that the general structure of their plans is naturally itself similar. In engineering and construction an unreasonable amount of time and manhours are required for the drawing and re-drawing of very similar looking engineering and construction modules in a plan. There may be considerable difference in detail, for example, in a petrochemical plant the number and size of vessels, towers and equipment will be different, but the general logic is the same. In addition when the individual parts of a plan are examined, similar patterns emerge, for example, the design, specification, purchase, delivery and erection of a vessel generates a similar logic for every vessel in a project and in all projects of a similar type.

The interrelationships involved in the design phase and the construction phase also form a standard pattern, and it is possible to have standard logic diagrams showing the design process, the construction process, and the interrelationships between them and for various parts of these processes, for example, in piping or electrical design. In addition, major items of equipment, such as a distillation tower, may have a complete standard plan for the tower itself, its internals, the supporting structure, associated vessels, pumps, instrumentation and piping. There may be similar logic diagrams for up to a dozen or more different types of items in a project, for example, vessels, pumps, heat exchangers, compressors, buildings, etc. In addition, each individual activity in the chain can also be expanded into a standard mini network or bar chart, for example, the design of an individual item or the purchasing and expediting of that item.

Thus, it is possible to have three levels of standard library modules.

1. A micro module for an individual item
2. A midi module for design processes, or an aggregation of items such as a tower and its associated equipment.
3. A macro module for individual stages in a complete project, or the total project itself.

Figure 5.16 shows a macro module for the design of a chemical plant unit and Figures 5.17 and 5.18 show micro modules for individual parts of it.

These library modules can be either handled manually or by computer. In a manual system a drawing or drawings would have the standard arrow diagram or bar chart at a level 1, 2 or 3 for the type of unit or project involved. This would have the key events with event numbers widely spaced. There would also be standard drawings for the micro and midi modules for items goind into this macro module. A planner would then simply take out the number of modules required for the individual project, add the key interrelationship event numbers from the macro modules, perhaps modify it slightly to tailor it for the individual project, then number the events in the various modules and add the names and other details.

With a computer-based system, the planning can be more

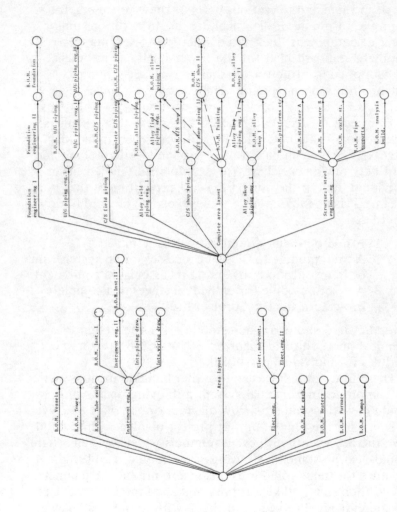

Figure 5.16 Macroplanning module

126

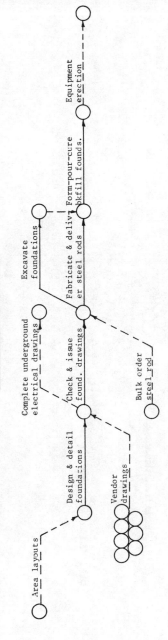

Standard foundation module

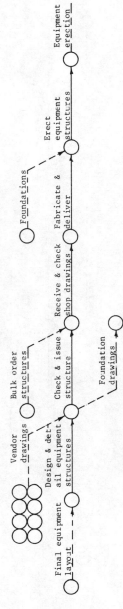

Standard structural module

Figure 5.17 Standard microplanning modules (A)

127

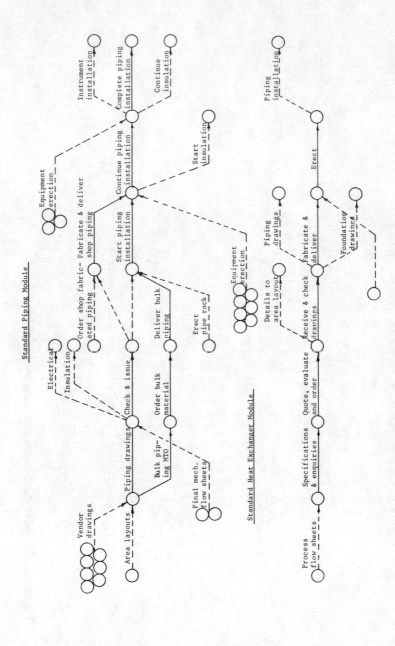

Figure 5.18 Standard microplanning modules (B)

128

automated and instead of drawings, computer files would hold the necessary details. A project plan for a petrochemical plant having, for example, two catalytic crackers, four boilers, twelve towers, fifty vessels, seventy heat exchangers, four large compressors, six buildings, twelve tanks and 150 pumps could be assembled very quickly using this method. The planner would input to the computer the list of these items including names, unit numbers, a code as to the type of item and a code as to its size. The computer would hold the standard logic diagrams for each item, together with the details of the standard duration time and resource required for each activity and for the various sizes of items. The planner would input key event numbers, major interrelation points and the computer would generate a plan and a data base for the total project. This would be reviewed, activities added or deleted and data edited interactively by the planner, before generating a final plan. There is even a move to having computer actually draw the resulting arrow diagram using a graph-plotter. Thus, using this method, either manually or by computer, a plan can be quickly generated at the critical early stages of a project to guide and control the work on it.

Consider a medium to large project, depending on one's point of view, having anything from 500 to 5,000 activities on a plan. Figure 5.19 shows a work breakdown structure for such a petrochemical plant where the overall plan has 1,600 activities at a level somewhere between level 2 and level 3. It had five units, four of which were similar in structure, only one of which is exploded in any detail. The planning for such a project would probably initially be done for each individual unit, in this case using the semi-standard macro planning module for four out of the five units. This macro module will be made up of several medium sized library modules each having several micro modules. Thus, it could be quickly assembled and tailored for the particular unit and give the vertical planning integration for each unit, within this case, approximately 200 activities for each unit.

When each unit level 2 plan is complete, sorting would produce a horizontally integrated plan for each phase or function, and manpower planning could be carried out for each shared resource and the plans adjusted for the resources

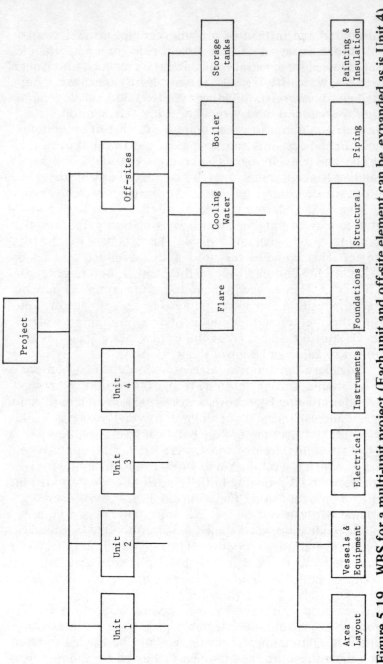

Figure 5.19   WBS for a multi-unit project (Each unit and off-site element can be expanded as is Unit 4)

130

available, any priorities and for phased completion if desired. This would give a satisfactory level 2 plan and adequate integration and manpower planning. It would not perhaps give a plan adequate for control and for efficient functional planning. A further level of planning would probably be necessary, which would explode the 200 activity unit plans into four to six hundred activities to give a level 3 plan for each work breakdown structure element. In addition, or alternatively, the individual functional plans for all the units would be exploded into a level 3 functional plan which would cover such areas as the piping and drawing office work for all the units.

Multi-project planning and control

Where companies are handling several projects at the same time and where the resources must be shared between projects, it is necessary to integrate the planning and control of these multiple projects. Common examples of this situation are:

1. An owner company, for example, a major chemical company, which has several major projects on the go at any one time, each at various stages of its life cycle and each probably with a different contractor.
2. A contractor who has several projects each with a different client company.
3. A factory with a mix of small and medium sized projects, using its own resources and occasionally, when handling large projects, using subcontractors or contractors.
4. A local authority with a large number of minor projects and a few medium sized projects, using a mixture of direct labour and contractors.

The major problem in such situations is the sharing of resources between projects, principally the following:

1. Key management personnel, i.e. project managers, design managers and supervisors, construction managers, and foreman.

2. Design engineers, particularly specialists.
3. Drawing office personnel.
4. Directly employed construction labour, in the last two examples.
5. Floating construction labour availability on a regional basis.

Where resources have to be shared, it is necessary to carry out integrated planning of multiple projects in some form or other. The total availability of these key resources become constraints which must be recognised in the planning of the individual projects. This integrated planning could be carried out in two ways; either the plans for all the projects are integrated into one big multi-project plan, or the subplans for each project for only the resources being shared are integrated in one multi-project functional plan.

When the projects are small, there are few problems in integrating the plans for all the projects into one plan and in carrying out manpower planning. Simply by using artificial activities to impose delays on the starting of each project, or each stage of a project, multi-project planning can be carried out. Another level is added to the top of the work breakdown structure, for control purposes, which represents the multi-project, with the first level of breakdown being the individual projects. Even with larger projects it is physically possible using modern computer systems to integrate these plans together. These systems have multi-project options, which can deal with the individual projects with its own data file, but which can also consolidate these files and plans together into one multi-project plan.

The principal difficulty with integrating large projects together is that the total plan becomes very large and cumbersome, and in practice it is not really necessary. The only integration between projects that is required is where resources are shared. Therefore it is simpler, quicker and more flexible to do this integrated planning for only those functions which are shared. For example, a firm may be handling three projects at the same time, each requiring an average of 40 draughtsmen for five months, that is, a total load of 600 manmonths, with a peak requirement for each project of, say 70 draughtsmen. If it only has 90 draughtsmen available and if it attempts to push all three projects through the drawing office at the same time, there will be total chaos and in-fighting between project managers for priority for their projects. If no other draughtsmen can be obtained, for example, by subcontracting or hiring temporary labour, then there is no way that the drawing office work on these projects can be completed in less than approximately six and a half months.

If it is left to the system to muddle through there will be complete disorganisation and the probability is that it will take considerably longer than this to complete the work. The drawing office plan for all three projects has to be constructed on a logical and a top management imposed priority basis, with a major constraint being the availability of draughtsmen.

Individual project plans would be constructed and the drawing office work for all three projects integrated into one functional plan. This would then be adjusted to level the drawing office resource requirements to that available, by establishing a priority for each project. The rest of the work on each project could then be planned around the drawing office constraint by inputting the necessary scheduled starts and scheduled finishes for drawing office work determined in the integrated drawing office plan. It may then be possible to expedite the highest priority project through the work prior to the drawing office, such that the bulk of its drawing office workload arrives earlier than previously planned. If this can be done the planning and balancing process is repeated so that the completion dates for the drawing office work would be staggered but not significantly delayed.

The same principle can be applied to any function which has its resources shared between projects or parts of a project. When a large number of resources is shared between multiple projects, it will be necessary to carry out fully integrated planning as there will be too many complex interactions between projects and resources. If this was attempted on an individual function basis it would require many iterations and people would become confused. Automatic computer-based resource levelling would have to be carried out with project priorities set by the planner, with limited man-machine interaction. This would produce a final integrated multi-project plan which makes sensible use of priorities to achieve the objectives of all the projects and the company as a whole.

Planning the very large project

The planning of the very large project, sometimes termed a giant or mega-project is more critical than ever to its efficient management and control, but has considerably greater problems than that of planning the medium to large project. There are two extremes in the management, organisation, planning and control of such projects with many variations between them. These are:

1. Complete centralisation, involving the integration of the planning of all areas of the project.
2. Complete decentralisation, with parts of the project being planned separately, and integration occuring only at a macro level, or where resources are shared.

It is physically possible using modern computing systems to use a centralised project plan, but if integrated planning is attempted in any detail it requires anything from 3,000 to 75,000 activities. Such a vast plan would be complex, cumbersome costly, very difficult to create, constantly requiring to be changed and almost impossible to keep up-to-date. The information necessary to build the plan for the later stages would only become available over a very long period of time. The state of the art and science of planning would undoubtedly vary considerably among all the companies involved, and attempting to impose one detailed system would be very difficult and lead to a lot of resistance from many of those involved. In addition, the normal difficulties in achieving good communication and co-ordination are also compounded in these projects, when they are centralised and made more difficult by the many layers of management that are often necessary. Major problems are the time necessary to get decisions made and the sheer superhuman task of handling the mass of data involved. Present day practice is to move some way towards decentralised management of mega projects, and this section of the book outlines only one of the ways that this can be done.

A very large project can be viewed as an aggregation of a number of separate medium to large projects, and is a special case of multi-project management, planning and control. In the following discussion, for the sake of simplicity, a very large project will be termed the 'programme' though in practice programme and project are interchangeable names.

Normally, the owner company, or a principal project management company, would carry out the overall programme management, planning and control, involving the integration of every contributing company's work, and the bulk of the work on the programme will be carried out by a number of construction and manufacturing companies who will have contracts for the various projects making up the programme. Each of these companies will have their own project management staff and will be supervised by either or both of the owners and programme managers staff. These companies will view their contracts as completely separate projects, and the programme managers staff will supervise them, both as separate projects and as part of the interlinking programme.

It is in the planning of these very large projects that the hierarchical and rolling wave principles of project planning are essential. The number of levels of planning used can be considerably greater than the three outlined previously but not all would have to be integrated. The interrelationships required between the individual project plans making up a programme are normally limited to key major decision points or milestones, and the programme plans need only include these to give the necessary overall integration of the programme. The number of levels of plans and their integration will vary from one programme to another, but one example of such a hierarchy is as follows:

Level 1 programme plan This will be a skeleton plan of the programme showing only the key programme decision points or milestones, with most of the activities being individual projects or contracts.

Level 2 programme plan This would be the consolidation of the individual level one project plans into one integrated programme plan, and would identify the major key programme inter-relation points or milestones between projects.

Level 2/3 programme plan It may be necessary in some cases, when there is a large amount of interrelationship between projects, to use another intermediate integrated plan, showing the minor key programme interrelations points or milestones between projects. This would be the consolidation of individual project plans, somewhere between levels one and two.

Individual project plans

Below the above levels, separate project plans can be built for each project using hierarchical principles as described previously, and having the programme's major and minor key milestones shown in them. The individual project level one and level one/two plans will be part of this hierarchy or project plan, and also part of the above project plans.

Progress between milestones can be transferred from the individual project plans to the higher level programme plans to monitor and integrate the total programme. When each project is handled by separate companies each with its own manpower resources, this system can work effectively. Integrating the manpower plans of the individual projects into one programme manpower plan is only required where there are resources shared between projects, for example, in the owner or programme management company, the regional availability of labour, say, in a construction camp, or where space and accommodation are limited as on an oil platform, or where the project is nearing completion. In such cases integrated functional planning must be carried out for the programme as a whole, as discussed in multi-project planning.

The rolling wave concept of the expansion of the programme plans into greater detail and finally into separate detailed project plans is also important in the planning of large projects; earlier projects producing information to permit the expansion of later project plans into greater detail.

The separate project plan could be constructed using any

acceptable technique with which the individual company is familiar, as long as it met the overall effectiveness criteria previously outlined. Where any contributing company's system do not meet these basic criteria, it is often necessary for the programme management staff to impose some level of planning technology on a contributing company. The level of planning technology imposed should be the minimum acceptable level as attempting to move a company's personnel from working by the seat of their pants to interactive computer-based detailed planning in one step is normally impossible. Simple bar or milestone charts are quite acceptable, normally easily implemented, and can identify the key milestones in the programme plan in these individual project plans and permit their integration into the overall programme. Uniformity of planning would only be necessary at the levels of the integrated programme plans, which would be constructed by the programme staff.

If the work breakdown structure concepts are used to explode the programme into its component projects and also to explode the individual projects into their component elements, control and reporting can be implemented as described in the following chapters. This would permit the consolidation of performance analysis and the tracing of deviations from plan and budget down to the individual project and to the individual detailed activity.

This method of management planning and control would force much of the necessary decision-making, communication and co-ordinating down the line to the level where work is being carried out and lead to a simple management structure with fewer levels of management. The organisation structure, or structures, involved in large projects is normally a mixture of functional matrix and divisional organisations. In practice the forms of organisation structure used will be dynamic and change over the life of the project. For example, a very large project may start with a functional organisation, move to a divisional organisation, then to a matrix and, finally, may contain all three types, both in the global organisation and in the component parts of it.

A very important factor in the management of programmes, involving hundreds or even thousands of millions of pounds of expenditure, is the forecasting and management of the cash flow. The forecast cash flow of all the individual projects has to be consolidated into the overall programme cash flows. Then as progress and performance vary, the cash flows have to be planned and controlled, that is, managed. With the present day rate of inflation, this can involve many detailed calculations as described in the next chapter, and computer programmes or financial models have to be used to handle this. These forecasts and models have also to be integrated with the various levels of programme plan.

The line of balance technique

In addition to the techniques previously described, one other basic planning technique is sometimes used in some projects, that is, the line of balance. The line of balance technique is a graphical method of scheduling that was originally developed to improve the planning and reporting of an ongoing production process. This technique was developed by the US Navy in the early 1950s and it is especially suitable for low volume new product situations in integrating research and design with small scale production. In these types of projects, some of the effectiveness of planning and control of the entire project is often lost during the transition phase from development to prototype production and full production. This technique can handle this critical transition stage. Its principal applications in project work are:

1. Where the project is made up of a number of identical units manufactured or constructed in sequence, such as houses.
2. In a similar situation where the project consists of first the design and then the production of a limited number of units based on that design, for example, a pre-production run.
3. As one reporting tool in one-off projects to give a concise presentation of progress against plan.

The line of balance technique is concerned with parts, sub-assemblies, or various stages of construction which make up the finished flow of units. The most important single result of the line of balance technique (LOB) is the development of a schedule for the completion of the component parts or stages of construction, which make up the final product or project. Line of balance can be used to set up the initial schedule for a series of units and it can be used to monitor the progress during the production or construction cycle. In a multi-unit situation such as a housing estate, it is difficult to establish how work is progressing against plan, because the various units will be at various stages of completion at any one time. Some will be being completed, some will be at various stages of partial completion and others will just be starting. Similarly with limited production runs at the end of a design and manufacturing project, the transfer of such a project from design to production is always subject to poor communication and loss of momentum. The line of balance technique can provide a simple and easily understood method of establishing a plan and controlling such situations.

All that is required in the line of balance technique is that an objective made up of the number of units to be completed in each time period is established and a simple plan made for the production, or construction, of one unit. This first requirement is normally termed the 'Objective' for the production or construction process, where a quantity of the end items is being made under contract, the objective is the required delivery or completion schedule. The delivery information used is of two kinds; the planned schedule representing the contractual requirements and the actual schedule showing the calendar date of delivery. The second requirement is termed the 'Programme'. Once the objective is determined, the next task is to define the programme, which is simply the production or construction plan with normally a bar or Gantt chart plotted against the lead-time required before shipment. The monitoring of progress is done against key operations or assembly points in the manufacturing or construction cycle known as control points. These are essentially events in a network analysis system or the end of bars in the bar chart, or milestones in a milestone chart.

Figure 5.20 shows a programme for a simple example, and Figure 5.21 shows an S chart from the cumulative delivery

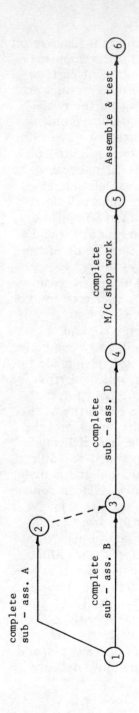

Events in L.O.B.

1. Start work on A and B

2. Sub–assembly A complete

3. Sub–assembly B complete

4. Sub–assembly D complete

5. Machine shop work complete

Figure 5.20 Programme for a single unit in LOB example

140

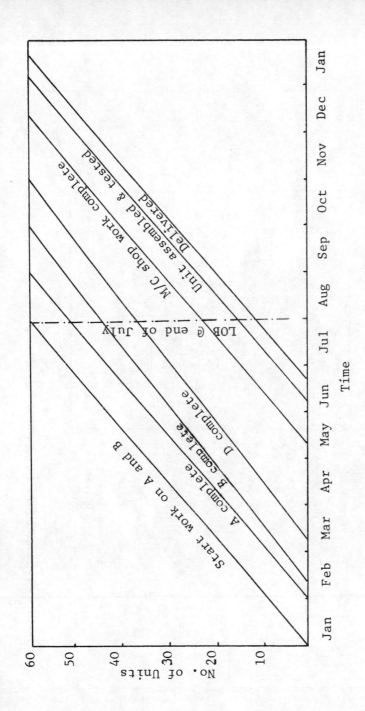

Figure 5.21   S chart for programme

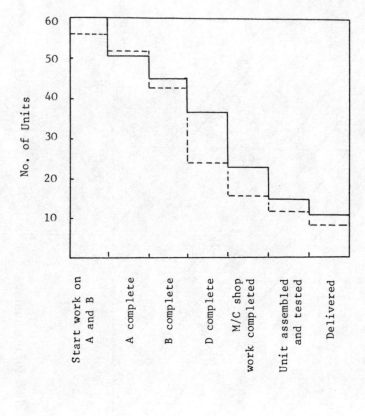

No. of Units

Start work on
A and B

A complete

B complete

D complete

M/C shop
work completed

Unit assembled
and tested

Delivered

Figure 5.22 Line of balance

142

schedule required and also the cumulative completion schedule for these intermediate key events or milestones. This represents the planned completion of the final units and the various intermediate parts or stages. Then by drawing a vertical line through this chart, it is possible to determine how many units should have passed through all the stages at that time. This is the line of balance and it depicts the cumulative number of parts or units which must have been completed by that date if the schedule is to be maintained. Then by determining how many units have passed through the key stages by that date it is possible to measure progress against plan. This can be presented in a compact form as in Figure 5.22 which shows the planned completion at every stage, the actual completions at these stages, and can also highlight any bottlenecks. For example, the figures show that the first three stages are ahead of schedule, whereas the remainder are behind schedule, with the bottleneck being at stage 4.

Although the line of balance technique is more suitable for small scale production or construction of similar units as described, it is also used in engineering design and construction work as an ancillary analytical method of measuring progress against plan and to give a concise picture of this. Using the S charts shown in Figure 3.2 and 5.6, a line of balance can be drawn at week 40 to give a concise pictorial presentation of progress against plan shown in Figure 5.23. This illustrates how clearly the line of balance method demonstrates progress or the lack of progress against plan.

The line of balance technique therefore broadens the other techniques available to allow the inclusion of repetitive activities and is also a useful concise reporting tool. It aids management analysis in that it highlights critical activities that may delay the completion of the project and points to problem areas, as well as to the present status of repetitive activities.

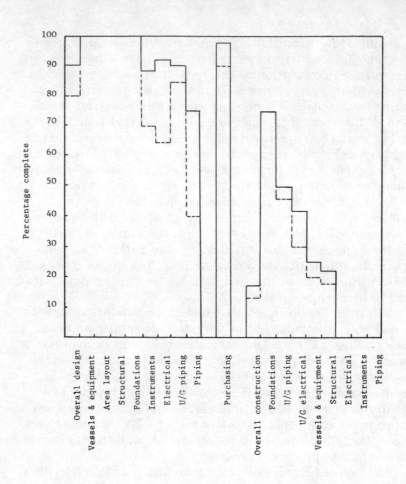

Figure 5.23 LOB at week 40
For Typical Petrochemical Project

6 Estimating the Project Cost

Money, whether it is called, cost, profit or loss, is of extreme importance in project management as it is the ultimate criteria of performance. All good project managers become part accountant and are involved in the estimating, budgeting, forecasting and control of cost for their projects, that is, their financial management.

The difference between an estimate and a budget is that an estimate is the more or less simple tabulation of estimated costs for the work involved on the project. It normally only has a general relationship to how the work on the project is to be carried out, for example, it can be based on a Level 1 or initial project plan. The budget, on the other hand, is a time-phased, detailed financial plan, integrated with a Level 2 or Level 3 plan. Whereas an estimate will normally only show a lump sum allocated to each activity or cost centre, a time-phased budget will show the expenditure for each time period for the activity or cost centre. The estimate and the detailed project plan are thus the basis for the establishment of a time-phased budget. Once constructed, the budget and the plan are tools for the on-going management of the project and the baselines for the project control system.

Importance of cost estimating

Efficient cost estimating of the cost of a project is vital, both to the client and the contractor. Reasonably accurate estimates are essential to the initial decision on whether to proceed with a project or not, that is, the 'go/no-go' decision. If project costs are widely underestimated at this stage, companies can be 'locked in' to uneconomic investments, with low or negative profitability, undertake the wrong project, or run out of funds. They are also required by the client company for the knowledgeable comparison of bids, where contractors are involved, with very low bids being as much a cause for concern as very high bids. A very low bid may imply a contractor anxious to gain the contract and accepting no profit on his bid; it may also imply that some factor has been missed out on a bid, or that corners are going to be cut; or it may simply be errors in the contractor's estimate. If the contractor underestimates the cost to him of carrying out a project at the bidding stage on fixed price contracts, the consequences can be catastrophic for him. At the very least he can be landed with a loss-making contract, and at the extreme he can go bankrupt, which in turn can cause the client considerable trouble and expense. Decisions on tendering policy, that is, whether to bid a low price or the estimated cost plus a reasonable profit margin, should be taken on as accurate an estimate as is possible. Thus the initial cost estimates, both for client and contractor, must be as accurate as the information available permits, and must include allowances for any particular areas of uncertainty.

Accurate estimating is also important throughout the life of a project to evaluate proposed changes, alternative ways of carrying out the work and as a basis for effective cost control. Without a good estimate with which to construct a budget, there is no reliable baseline for evaluation of performance. Project management cannot decide whether work is being carried out effectively, or whether the final cost is going to exceed the originally allocated funds. Accurate estimates of project cost are the basis for decision making and control of work in progress for both client and contractor. If these estimates do not bear some relation to the reality of actual costs, motivation is affected, control is lost and the project will unavoidably cost more than is necessary.

Escalation of costs

The project that is completed to its first estimate of cost is the exception rather than the rule. In reality, it is almost impossible to complete a project to its initial estimate, because of many factors, not the least of which is the lack of information at the early stages of the project life cycle on which to base an accurate estimate. Because of this the project manager is concerned with the escalation of project cost estimates from the day he is appointed to a project, until long after it is finished. This cost escalation has been defined as:

> 'The difference between the final cost, or latest estimate of final cost, and the original definitive estimate.'

It can also be defined, more simply as:

> 'The change in estimated cost over time.'

Cost escalation on smaller projects of 10—20 per cent is relatively common, whereas on larger, longer projects, particularly those with a high development content or considerable uncertainty at the earlier stages, the sky is the limit. For example, cost escalations have been reported of 50 per cent on petrochemical projects, 140 per cent in North Sea oil projects, 210 per cent on nuclear power stations and 545 per cent on Concorde! With high cost escalation many companies can be trapped by the 'sunk costs' principle. That is, some way through a project, cost escalation that makes the whole project uneconomic, becomes obvious, and yet the logical decision is to proceed to completion. The money already spent must be considered as sunk, or written off, and the decision to proceed must be based on the project's rate of return on the remaining forecast costs to completion. One such project was initially estimated to have a 40 per cent rate of return; half way through, escalation had reduced this to 12 per cent for the overall project, but there was still a 30 per cent rate of return on the remaining costs to completion and the logical decision was to proceed to completion.

Some of this cost escalation is avoidable and it is the

project manager's function to prevent it by effective control. However, in almost all projects, some of this cost escalation is unavoidable and allowances for it should be included in the initial cost estimate. Whether this cost escalation is avoidable or unavoidable, the project manager must be aware of the factors which contribute to project cost escalation.

These factors are:

1. Inefficiency.
2. Inflation.
3. The characteristic flow of information on which to base an estimate.
4. Changes to the contract.
5. Form of contract.

Inefficiency of management, supervision, suppliers or labour will naturally lead to cost escalation, but this is one of the factors the project control system sets out to monitor and control. The other factors are not so amenable to straightforward control, but as they are as critical to cost escalation, if not more critical than inefficiency, they must be subject to managerial attention and control.

Inflation of project costs

The cost of materials, equipment, services and labour in project work has considerably increased in the 1970s, and it is no longer practical to simply add a nominal allowance for this inflation to the bottom of a cost estimate. Neither is it something that can be ignored in the evaluation of projects, in the belief that the increase in the cost of the project due to inflation can always be recouped with the inflation in the price of the product. Government imposed restrictions or intense competition have tended to limit price rises. Thus inflation can often have a catastrophic effect on the viability of capital expenditure projects and must always be discreetly evaluated and allowed for in the project estimate.

The consequences of this inflation can be different for a client and a contractor, although it can adversely affect the cash flow of both. However, no contractor will accept a contract over several years without escalation clauses linked to the appropriate indices. One example of such a price adjustment formula is shown at the end of this chapter. Therefore a contractor can be protected against most of the worst effects of inflation. Unfortunately this is not a complete protection as index-linked payments may not apply to all the payments involved in a contract, such as profit margin, administrative costs, and retentions and the effects of inflation in individual projects may be different from that shown in official indices. Material, equipment and labour costs, and thus inflation, may vary geographically within a country, and from country to country, and contracts with subcontractors and suppliers may involve different inflation protection terms than that agreed with a client. These factors may work to the advantage or disadvantage of the contractor, but he must be aware of them and make contingency allowances where necessary.

Payments for the effects of inflation generally lag behind payments for work done, because of the form of the contract and delays in the publication of indices, and this increases the gap between funds in and out and increases the amount of working capital required. Also as inflation goes up, interest rates normally also go up and this increases the cost of financing this working capital. Retentions are also a problem, as by the time they are paid, often long after a contract is nominally completed, inflation may have considerably reduced their value.

The client, on the other hand, has not got any protection against the ravages of inflation and must forecast inflation and take it into account in the 'go/no-go' decision. Therefore, using his time-phased budget and forecasts of inflation over the projected project life, he must prepare a separate inflation estimate and budget.

For control purposes, those involved in managing the project cannot be held responsible for cost escalation due to inflation, and thus cost control data must be deflated or inflated to allow comparisons with estimates on a meaningful basis. Prices or rates used in compiling the control estimate should be those ruling at a particular date, generally referred to as the 'project base date'. The objective in using a common base date for the project is to establish base date estimates against which the anticipated final cost and base date prices and rates can be compared; any variance can then be identified and analysed as to cause and effect and corrective action taken as necessary. Using indices forward from this date permits the control estimate to be corrected for inflation and to be compared with the current costs of materials and labour. To achieve this objective it will be necessary for estimates, tenders, orders, contracts, invoices and changes to be valued at prices and rates ruling at the base date, with actual and forecast escalation shown separately. Since inflation is not under the control of the project manager, the change in costs due to this cause can be taken out, leaving the changes in costs which are under the control of the project manager.

Estimating the effects of this inflation and analysing progress can often involve time consuming and relatively complex calculations, and sometimes small computer program or programable calculators are used. The effects of this inflation can often come as a surprise in long projects because of the characteristic curve of expenditure rate on a project. Figure 6.1 shows a typical curve for the time-phased expenditure on a five million pound project over five years, with the bulk of the expenditure being characteristically in the second half of the project life cycle, and thus it can be markedly affected by the cumulative effect of inflation. It shows the cumulative cost curves for this project with varying rates of inflation: for example, a 15 per cent inflation rate over the life of a project would lead to a 47 per cent cost escalation due to inflation alone. The effects of this would not really be obvious until the end of the third year of work on the project because of the time phasing of expenditure. Simple models on a computer or programable calculator allow project managers to simulate various inflation rates and their effect on the project budget and its viability.

Delays in completion can also have a significant effect on this cost escalation due to inflation. Even without any extra work involved, delays in project completion lead to significant

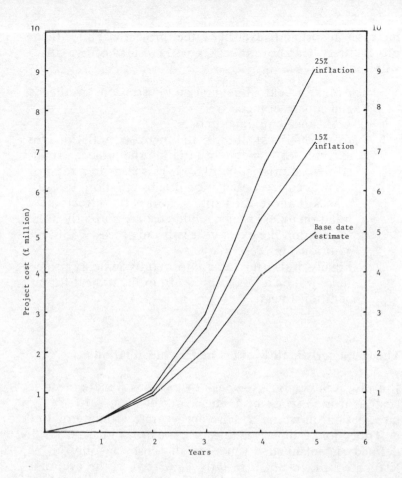

Figure 6.1 Effect of inflation on project expenditure

increases in cost and adversely affect project viability. If the project described above takes six years instead of five, this will lead to:

1. An extra year of general administration, overheads and supervision costs.
2. Additional equipment costs.
3. Additional costs due to the increased inflation, for example, at 15 per cent inflation the project would cost an additional £660,000. This leads to a total of 60 per cent cost escalation due to inflation. It also makes it more difficult to notice the effects of inflation unless progress and cost are correctly linked.
4. In addition the extra year will add at least £550,000 additional interest charge.
5. Finally, but often most importantly in many projects, there will be a loss of profit from the project for an additional year.

The characteristic flow of estimating information

It is just as impractical to speak of a single estimate of project cost, as it is to speak of a single project plan. All the information on which to base an accurate estimate of the cost does not become available until the project has been fully defined and planned. Even then the cost can only be 'estimated' or, to put it bluntly, 'guessed', as the eventual cost is subject to considerable change due to many factors. Until a design has been fully specified, firm quotations obtained from suppliers and the manufacturing or construction work involved fully defined in detail, only imprecise estimates of project costs can be made. Yet decisions have to be made, based on these cost estimates, before all the information is available and a budget based on these estimates established to permit management control. In practice this is handled by developing several estimates through the life of a project, each of which is subject to a level of uncertainty which hopefully declines as the project progresses and more information becomes available. Each of these estimates must be linked together by a system which identifies and controls changes to scope, specifications and estimated costs, so that it should be possible to trace the reasons for differences between each estimate.

In addition, an allowance normally termed contingency or management reserve, must be added to each estimate to cover the following factors:

1. Errors in estimating.
2. Minor changes to the design as it progresses.
3. Minor omissions from the estimates.
4. Minor field extras, or changes, to compensate for field conditions, or 'bits that don't fit together' when it comes to actual manufacture or construction.
5. A management reserve to be used at the discretion of the project manager for changes required to expedite the work, unforeseen minor contingencies, or other minor areas of uncertainty.
6. 'Normal' variations about the averages which are used in estimating data.

Traditionally a nominal 10 per cent of the estimated cost of the project is added for these factors, but this is an oversimplification. The amount of contingency should vary with the degree of uncertainty of the estimate and thus differing amounts of contingency should be allowed for each estimating stage. In addition some parts of the project may have greater amounts of uncertainty than others and may merit additional contingency allowances.

By far the best method of estimating the amount of contingency to allow, is to use experience of similar projects, modified for the particular project, together with the best forecast possible of future conditions. This involves accurate record keeping and analysis to differentiate all the elements that went into cost escalation on previous projects. This is often difficult to do; because the records normally available are insufficiently detailed or reliable to perform such an analysis.

These contingency funds should be treated as the project

manager's own money held in a safety deposit vault in a bank, and only reluctantly released on the basis of formally documented requirements. Contingency funds for particular areas of uncertainty should be documented and controlled in the same manner. If not required, they should be eliminated from the project estimate and not looked on as 'fat' available for use elsewhere on the project.

It must be emphasised that these contingency funds are to compensate for minor changes, errors, omissions and variations in estimates and are not used to cover major changes of scope or specifications. These more significant factors require a change in the estimate and these changes, which occur naturally during the development stage of a project, should also change the amount of contingency funds, that is, if a change adds £100,000 to the estimated cost of the project, an additional £10,000 should be added to the contingency.

Evolution of a project cost estimate

The various estimates of project cost that are made should be made at those characteristic points in the project life cycle where information becomes available to make increasingly accurate estimates, and these points will vary with the type of project. The project life cycle can normally be split up into several phases, for which estimates can logically be made. In a petrochemical project these phases would be at the:

1. Proposal and evolutionary phase.
2. Preliminary design phase.
3. Design and purchasing.
4. Manufacturing or construction.

Figure 6.2 shows the elvel of uncertainty associated with all four phases whereas Figure 6.3 shows an S chart for the design phase which portrays the normal development of a design in this type of project.

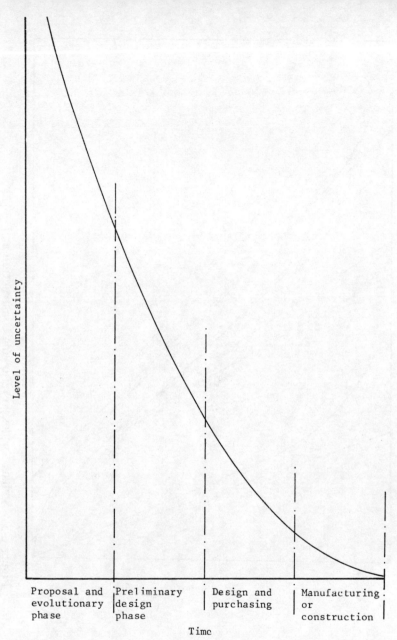

Figure 6.2   Level of uncertainty of project estimate versus time

155

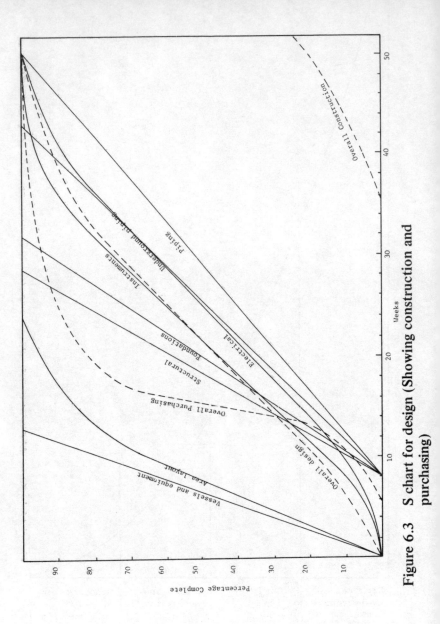

Figure 6.3   S chart for design (Showing construction and purchasing)

156

Proposal and evolutionary phase

Estimates at this phase are 'rule of thumb', 'order of cost' estimates, subject to wide variations in outcome. They are based on experience of similar projects, factored to take into account increases in cost of labour, material and equipment. Thus the early cost estimate for a project, particularly one with a large development content or areas of uncertainty, is often more an expression of hope than a realistic guideline. Unless scope and specifications can be changed to 'design to a price', no one can accurately estimate the cost of such a project at this early stage. It is not until a specific design has been firmed up, that a cost estimate can be made with any degree of reliability. Even then, it can still be widely out if the design has major changes, flaws or omissions. Large development projects fall into a class of their own and no real estimate of final cost can be made until a considerable amount of work has been carried out. It is difficult to estimate the level of contingency funds required at this stage. At the very least, a 20 per cent contingency allowance should be made, but this may bear little relation to the outcome of a development project, or where undue optimism has been used in estimating.

Preliminary design phase

The first real estimates of the cost of the project can be made at the completion of this stage. This estimate is based on a preliminary or outline design of the complete project, tenders for major items and bulk material, and preliminary estimates for manufacturing or construction. The end of this phase is immediately prior to the start of the S curve in Figure 6.3. At this point the first realistic decision on 'go/no-go' can be made. There is still a large amount of uncertainty, but the areas involved will have been identified and adequate special contingency allowances made for them. A 15 per cent contingency allowance is prudent for this estimate; however, significant changes of scope and specification can still occur and this allowance does not cover these changes.

This is the earliest a client company can approach a contractor, and even then the only form of contract which can normally be negotiated at the end of this preliminary design phase is a cost plus contract. The exception from this is when the contractor bids for a complete turn-key design to meet specified performance requirements. Any estimate of cost at this stage still involves considerable uncertainty as shown in Figure 6.2 and a considerable amount of work has to be done to reduce this uncertainty before a reliable estimate for a fixed price bid can be made.

Design and purchasing phase

In this phase, refinement of the project estimate is almost a continual process with the level of uncertainty declining as more information becomes available. The earlier in the design phase a contractor is approached and a contract awarded, the more likely there is to be a greater number of changes to scope and specification, which will change the estimate and be additions to the contract price. The stage at which contractors are involved varies with the industry. In some, such as the civil engineering and building industries, contracts are awarded with tenders based on more or less complete design specifications; this limits the number of changes but does not eliminate them completely. In many other industries contracts are negotiated at some stage through the design process, involving greater uncertainties and the probability of more changes to the design and thus greater escalation of the contract price. This particularly applies to high technology industries, where development, design, purchasing and manufacturing are often overlapped to shorten the project life cycle, at the risk of greater cost escalation. If a fixed price contract is awarded for the design engineering, as well as the manufacturing and, or construction, the contractor must either quote a price which includes allowances for the increased costs that may occur, or he must carry out a large amount of the detailed design before quoting a price. Either way it can cost the contractor and client more.

It is possible to identify various stages in most design processes at which greater refinement of the estimate can be made. These depend on the characteristics of the project life cycle for any particular industry. For example, in the design phase of a petrochemical project, as outlined by the S curve shown in Figure 6.3 these could be as follows.

1. At approximately 15 per cent through the life of the main project work, as shown in the S curve, design is 20 per cent complete, vessels and equipment are 80 per cent specified, area layouts are 70 per cent complete and most important equipment is ordered. Sufficient engineering studies would have been carried out to establish that no significant problems incurring delays or extra costs would be encountered. With this estimate a further project evaluation could be carried out and the 'go' decision reaffirmed, cancelled or the project sent back for a re-specification of its scope. This is the first real point that fixed price contracts can be reasonably negotiated, but the project can still be subject to variations due to changes arising out of the remaining design work. If a contractor is involved, he is partially protected against the effect of changes in design, as these would be considered as extras to any contract, and a 10 per cent contingency would be sufficient for him. However, the client is not protected from the effect of changes and must make provision for them; possibly a 15 per cent contingency at this stage. In tight bidding circumstances the contractor has often to forego any form of contingency.

2. At approximately 25 per cent through the project design is 40 per cent complete and orders are placed for 70 per cent of materials and equipment. Vessels and equipment are completely specified, area layouts are complete and other areas of design are 25 per cent to 50 per cent complete. A definite estimate can be prepared at this stage, with a normal 10 per cent contingency. This estimate gives a good 'fix' on the design and procurement aspects of the cost of the project, with all vital design decisions taken. Thereafter the principal uncertainties are concerned with the remaining detailed design

of less important work and the construction stage, such as site conditions, delays in delivery, management performance and labour productivity. Design changes after this stage are particularly expensive, as they involve considerable disruption of design and construction work and rush ordering of material and equipment. However, design is sufficiently far advanced to establish the first reasonable estimate of construction costs and a construction cost control budget, at least for the initial stages on a rolling wave basis.

3. At approximately 45 per cent of the way through the project, design is 75 per cent complete, construction has started and another estimate can be prepared to finalise the construction budget. At this stage it is hard to differentiate between an estimate prepared as a basis for decision making and the development of a control budget, from a forecast of the final cost of the project. One of the reasons for refining the estimate at this stage is to ensure that the construction budget is realistic.

Contingency versus job schedule

The amount of contingency allowance can be reduced as the project progresses, commitments made and the funds expended. The project manager can use either a graphical method or a formula to reduce this contingency. One such formula is

$$
\begin{aligned}
\text{Contingency} = \ & (0\% \text{ x expenditure}) \\
+ \ & 5\% \text{ x (Commitments } - \text{ Expenditure)} \\
+ \ & 9\% \text{ x (Funds not yet committed)} \\
+ \ & (1\% \text{ x Total cost)}
\end{aligned}
$$

A simpler graphical method, based on experience, is shown in Figure 6.4. Whichever method is used, some funds must be retained to cover corrective work after the project is completed.

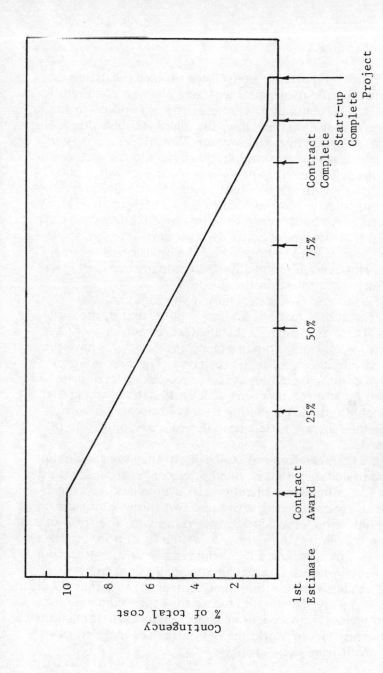

Figure 6.4 Contingency versus schedule

161

Form of contract

The relative importance and effect of cost escalation is different for the owner or client, and for any contractor involved. The contractor is somewhat less exposed to the ravages of cost escalation than the client, though this is influenced by the form of contract. Nevertheless, it may be more immediately catastrophic and obvious to the performance of a contractor than that of a client. A project which costs more than is justified by its return, may be debilitating, rather than immediately obvious to the client's performance. Many a company has been locked in to low profitability with such a project, through poor control, or the sunk costs principle. Other projects have been saved by the inflation of product prices. However, inflation adjusted company accounting will highlight such projects in the future.

The contractor is not generally involved in the stages of a project with the greatest cost uncertainty, that is, the early stages. These are primarily the greatest responsibility of the client company and estimates made at these stages have the greatest probability of high escalation. The first point at which a contractor can be expected to make a fixed price bid is when the project has been sufficiently defined to permit reasonably reliable estimating. If a contractor is involved before this, there is little alternative to a cost plus form of contract.

There are many forms of contract but they are all variations of two basic types, that is, fixed price, and cost plus, with the other forms being modifications to overcome the various disadvantages associated with these two forms. Emphasis on cost control between participants varies with the form of contract, as shown in Figure 6.5. With a fixed price contract, a contractor must have a high emphasis on cost control, and the client's project manager is principally concerned with time, standards and limiting changes arising from other people in his company. The contractor on the other hand may have mixed feelings about client instigated changes as, though they disrupt his flow of work, many contractors make most of their profit from these changes.

Client	High	Low
Contractor	Low	High
	Cost plus	Lump sum

Type of contract

Figure 6.5   Emphasis on cost control

With a cost plus contract the client is very concerned with cost control, whereas the contractor gives it less emphasis; the more the project costs, the more profit he makes. Though contractors may not consciously follow this line, subconsciously the people involved cannot give cost control the same emphasis. For example, are they going to risk conflict with the client's management in order to limit costs, or simply say the client is always right? Thus the cost plus form of contract will normally lead to greater cost escalation, because of the inherent fact that the cost estimate was constructed earlier in the project life cycle and thus was more uncertain, and because of the motivational effects of this form of contract. Thus the forms of contract decided upon can influence the degree of cost escalation on a contract.

It is thus essential that the project manager is aware of the different forms of contract used in project work and their advantages and disadvantages.

Lump sum form of contract

In a lump sum contract a contractor agrees to supply for a fixed price a well-defined and fixed requirement, based on definitive specifications and drawings. The contractor has the opportunity of making a profit by carrying out the work more efficiently than his competitors, but at the risk of making a loss if he under-estimates, or has trouble with the project. The owner is able to obtain a minimum price by putting out the contract to tender for competitive bids.

It can be used when the project design has advanced to a stage where it can be fully specified, where there is no or limited new technology or innovations involved. There is little likelihood of significant changes to design and cost inputs are relatively stable. When project execution extends to a year or more this form of contract is almost always used with a cost escalation clause similar to that described at the end of this chapter.

If these prerequisites can be fulfilled the lump sum form of contract is often preferred by both owners and contractors. It has the advantages for the owner that he is likely to obtain a minimum price through competitive tendering, and even if this is not certain, he at least knows the major part of the final cost of the contract at an early stage; early enough in fact to cancel it if need be. It simplifies the administration and supervision of the project for the owner in that he is not concerned with monitoring the contract's cost. He is only concerned with ensuring that the work is progressing in an orderly manner to meet the desired completion date and with monitoring the quality of the work, that is, is it meeting the contractual specifications and drawings? The rigidity of the contract acts as a restraint on the owner's personnel as any changes or additions to the contract will involve extra payment to the contractor. However, if there are many changes to the contract, it will involve considerable additional charges over and above the fixed price as the contractor has a tied customer, and many contractors make the bulk of their profit from changes to fixed price contracts.

From the contractor's point of view the lump sum form of

contract has the advantage that it is sometimes possible to make a larger profit than with other forms of contract. He also does not have to disclose his costs and efficiency of working to the owner, and is subject to a minimum of interference from the owner's personnel.

The disadvantage of this form of contract is that it theoretically entails a longer project life cycle. The owner cannot get a contractor working until the project has been fully defined, which also means that the various stages cannot be overlapped to reduce the overall project time. The preparation of lump sum bids also takes the contractor longer to prepare, and thus is expensive to the contractor, and in the long run to the customer too. There is also a risk factor involved for the contractor and some contractors in certain industries where development projects are common are reluctant to tender for lump sum contracts, at least for the design and development stages of a project. The owner also has the risk that where a major project gets into trouble and the contractor goes bankrupt, he is left with a partially completed project which may also be entangled with litigation problems.

The motivation and objectives of the contractor may also not be what the owner would like. The contractor will have as his prime objective the minimisation of cost and the maximisation of profit. This may involve trimming the equipment sizes to the smallest possible and using the cheapest quality of materials. The owner has to counteract this by adequate specifications and supervision to ensure they are being met. In the simple lump sum contract the contractor does not have any motivation to complete the project in the shortest possible time. Normally he does not want to extend the project time as this will usually increase his overheads and his costs. Nonetheless if work is short and he wants to spin the project out, or if extending the project will lead to more profit, then it is in his best interest to do so. Sometimes the completion time is agreed with a bonus for early completion and a penalty for late completion, but this does not really solve the problem. The contractor will always try to build in some contingency in time and money to cater for this, and such clauses are very difficult to enforce. Where they exist, every time the owner requests a change the contractor can quite legitimately extend the contract completion time due to the extra work involved, and few contracts have no changes.

Cost plus form of contract

In this form of contract the contractor is reimbursed on the basis of all direct costs incurred plus a percentage of these costs to cover the contractor's overheads and profit. The contractor is limited to a small margin of profit, but he has no risk of making a loss.

This form of contract has several advantages which in certain circumstances outweigh its disadvantages. It enables a contractor to start work before the project has been fully specified and where project phases can overlap, this can theoretically reduce the time to completion. It not only saves time in this way but it also considerably reduces the time required for contract tendering and negotiation, both for the owner and the contractor. The cost plus form of contract is also appropriate to those projects which involve new technology, a great deal of research and development, or are innovative. It is only in the later stages of such projects that it is possible to make a reasonably accurate estimate of how much they are going to cost, and there is little alternative to the cost plus formula for this type of project. Thus in projects where the content is uncertain or where there is the likelihood of many changes to scope and specification, the cost plus form of contract provides a flexible way of employing a contractor.

The main disadvantage of the cost plus form of contract is that the contractor has little motivation to control costs as the more the project costs the more profit he makes; neither does he have any motivation to meet target dates. In practice most contractors are concerned to maintain a good reputation, most people want to do a good job and the contractor must keep in mind the possibility of being barred from future contracts by the owner if he abuses this form of contract. However, in a lump sum contract the contractor normally acts as a constraint on the owner's personnel in so far as changes and requests for additional work are concerned. In the cost plus form of contract this restraint is removed and the very flexibility of this form of contract is a two-edged weapon which can lead to increased cost escalation.

In addition to this the owner does not know until near the end of the project what the project is going to cost, and thus he may be trapped into an uneconomic project. He also has more expense in that he must employ more staff to administer and supervise the contractor. The owner's company project management staff must ensure that the contractor is carrying out the work efficiently, watch out for over-design, give considerable attention to cost control and supervise the contractor to see that he is working efficiently and that his objectives are a fair cost, a minimum time and satisfactory technical standards. This can be a major source of annoyance to the contractor's project staff as they have the owner's staff constantly looking over their shoulders, interfering and questioning their decisions and performance.

Other forms of contract

The other forms of contract used are mostly variations and enhancements of the cost plus form of contract and endeavour to modify its disadvantages. The simplest modification to the straightforward cost plus formula is the 'cost plus fixed fee'. In this the contractor is reimbursed for all his direct costs and, instead of a percentage fee on top of them, a fixed fee is negotiated to cover his central overheads and profit. In order to use this form of contract the scope and specification of the project have to be reasonably firmed up so that the fee can bear some relation to the amount of work involved.

Another variation is the convertible form of contract where the contractor starts work on a cost plus formula on an ill-defined project and when it has been defined, a fixed price for the remaining work is negotiated. This gives a quick start to the project and lets the owner know at an earlier stage what the total cost is going to be. It does, however, limit the possibilities of competitive tendering, as, though it is theoretically possible to use competitive tendering for the second stage of the work, it rarely works in practice.

Where the design work is reasonably well completed, but where exact quantities of construction work may be subject to wide variations, a bill of quantities form of contract may often be used in some types of projects. In order to use this, the order of magnitude of the quantities involved such as excavation or concrete, have to be known as costs vary quite considerably with the scale of work.

There are also many forms of cost plus contract where some form of bonus penalty enhancement is made in order to give the contractor some motivation to meet time and cost targets, one such form is the Target Cost Contract outlined below. Under this form of contract, as used by a one owner, the total net cost of the work is paid by the owner as it is actually incurred and the contractor's profit is paid separately as a fee subject to upper and lower limits. The amount of fee is determined by comparing the actual cost of the works with the target cost submitted with the tender, which is subsequently updated at regular intervals. Although the principle function of the target cost is to provide an incentive to the contractor it also provides a viable basis for budgetary control of the project.

The bill of quantities submitted with the tender is priced by the contractor at rates which will cover all cost which would normally be allowed for in pricing a measure and value contract, but which excludes all profit. Profit is dealt with separately by means of a variable fee. The total amount of the bill of quantities before the addition of the fee represents the initial target cost. The final target cost is established by measurement of the work as executed in precisely the same way as would be the contract price in a normal measure and value contract.

If the actual cost of the work is equal to the final target cost the fee to be paid to the contractor would be 4.5 per cent of the final target cost. If the actual cost is less than the target

cost, the basic fee to be paid to the contractor would b
increased by one third of the difference between the actu
and final target cost, provided that the total fee payable t
the contractor including the basic fee does not exceed 7 pe
cent of the final target cost of the project. If the actual cost
exceeds the final target cost the basic fee payable to the
contractor would be reduced by the amount corresponding
to one third of the difference, and the actual and the final
target cost, provided that the total fee payable to the
contractor would be not less than 2 per cent of the final
target cost of the works. This can be expressed by a simple
formula

Contractor's fee $= 0.045 \text{ FTC} + 1/3 \text{ (FTC} - \text{AC)}$

where   FTC   = Final target cost

          AC   = Actual cost

This form of contract can be further modified to give a time
incentive by incorporating a time bonus penalty as shown by
a second form of the formula

Contractor's fee $= \overline{0.034 \text{ FTC}} + 1/3 \text{ (FTC} - \text{AC)}$

$$\frac{1 + 2 \text{ (TCT} - \text{ACT)}}{\text{ACT}}$$

where   TCT   = Target completion time

          ACT   = Actual completion time

This enhancement of the cost plus form of contract
endeavours to give an in-built performance incentive for the
contractor to achieve an actual cost at the end of the job less
than the target cost as presented at the tender stage. This
necessitates running the job in a normal measured contract
form to establish this and target cost. One of the advantages
of this type of enhancement is that it endeavours to establish
a contractor/client management relationship such that most
major decisions are taken jointly and the risks are agreed and
accepted. The owner is then aware of the basic cost and the
deviations and has most of the information to participate in
budgetary control. One basic failure of any such formula is

that in the event of the contractor falling down on both cost and time, he can immediately revert to his minimum fee, which is in this case 2 per cent. This gives an adverse incentive to make the overall cost as high as possible to achieve a desired return at 2 per cent. Although not by any means an attractive rate of return, in periods of economic depression or lack of work, contractors may still find this acceptable.

Thus the form of contract used has important implications for both owner and contractor alike and influences their motivation, their costs and is the basis of their relationship. In addition it is important, whatever form of contract is used, that it is well constructed with no 'grey' areas. If a contract is poorly worded and is capable of being misinterpreted, there will inevitably be misunderstandings and disagreements leading to owner/contractor conflict. If a project is to be successfully completed it is essential that both the owner and contractor's staff work together in a reasonably harmonious relationship. Either party can easily make life difficult for the other, but only at the cost of disrupting the project with the consequences of increased cost for both and delays to completion. Any form of contract cannot cover all points and eventualities, and the owner and contractor's staff must give and take in an atmosphere of mutual trust and respect for the good of the project. The owner's staff recognising that the contractor should make a reasonable profit, and the contractor's staff accepting that they should give a reasonable performance for this profit.

If any individual owner gets a reputation of being tight and unreasonable, the inevitable consequences will be that the contractors who tender will add a contingency for this in their bids. Thus, though the owner's staff may congratulate themselves on not permitting any changes and scoring over the contractor, the initial bids they receive will be higher than necessary to allow for this.

If a contractor proves unsatisfactory in performance once a contract is awarded, there is very little an owner's project manager can do within the scope of that particular project. The project manager has as the basis for his authority only the terms of the contract, the contractor's desire for the maintenance of goodwill and hope for future work. If this is insufficient then the owner's project manager is trapped into a project which will cost more and take longer than necessary, affect his reputation and which will give him a very troublesome and unpleasant personal life for the life of the project.

Thus the selection of a contractor for a project is a two-stage process, namely, the preparation of the bid list and the evaluation of tenders, with the first stage being the most important. The starting point to obtaining good project performance from a contractor is to choose reliable, competent contractors to ask to tender.

The preparation of the bid list, namely, the list of contractors who will be asked to bid on a project, is thus one of the most important stages of a project. This is a real decision-making phase as thereafter one step inevitably follows another without any real option. On many occasions arguments will be made against awarding firm A a contract, even though firm A is the lowest bidder. These are very difficult decisions to justify on any grounds, as these very same grounds should have been used to keep firm A off the bid list.

In order to prepare the bid list it is necessary to prescreen the contractors to be considered in the following areas

1. The owner's previous experience with the contractor.
2. The contractor's planning and control system.
3. The contractor's technical ability to handle the type of work involved.
4. The contractor's ability to handle the size of the project, both from a managerial and financial point of view.
5. The contractor's present workload.
6. The contractor's key personnel available for the project.
7. The contractor's policy with regard to cost plus and lump sum projects.

Example of a cost escalation clause

BEAMA contract price adjustment formula

The contract price shall be subject to variations in accordance with the BEAMA Contract Price Adjustment Formula (January 1979). If the cost to the contractor of performing his obligations under the contract shall be increased or reduced by reasons of any rise or fall in the rates of wages payable to labour or the cost of material or transport above or below such rates and costs ruling at the date of tender, or by reasons of the making or amendment after the date of tender of any law or any order, regulation or byelaw having the force in the United Kingdom that shall affect the contractor in the performance of his obligations under the contract, the amount of such increase or reduction shall be added to or deducted from the contract price as the case may be, provided that no account shall be taken of any amount by which any cost incurred by the contractor has been increased by the default or negligence of the contractor.

Variations in the cost of materials and labour shall be calculated in accordance with the following formula

(i)   Definitions: for the purpose of this formula:

'Contract price' means: the total sum certified in each Interim Certificate less the total sum certified in all previous certificates in respect of the Plant Works.

'Contract period' means: the period between the date of acceptance of the Contractor's tender or the date of any earlier written instruction to the Contractor to proceed with the work and the date of the Contractor's application for the individual Interim Certificate concerned.

(ii)   Labour element

45% of the Contract Price will be regarded as the Labour Element and will be varied proportionately to the difference between the Basic Labour Cost Index and the Mean Labour Cost Index expressed as a percentage of the Basic Labour Cost Index. The Labour Cost Index will be the BEAMA Labour Cost Index for the Mechanical or Electrical Engineering Industry as appropriate to each section of the works. The Basic Labour Cost Index will be the Labour Cost Index at the base date; the Mean Labour Cost Index will be the average of the Labour Cost Indices published during the second half of the Contract Period.

(iii)   Materials element

45% of the Contract Price will be regarded as the Materials Element and will be varied proportionately to the difference between the Basic Materials Index and the Mean Materials Index expressed as a percentage of the Basic Materials Index. The Materials Index will be the Department of Trade and Industry Price Index Order VII (excluding MLH 342) — Table 1 — Mechanical Engineering Industries: Materials Purchased or the equivalent Index for Electrical Machinery as appropriate to each section of the works (1970 = 100) published monthly in *Trade and Industry*. The Basic Materials Index will be the Materials Index *last published* before the base date: the Mean Materials Index will be the average of the Materials Indices so published during the middle three-fifths of the Contract Period.

7 Budgeting, Analysis and Control

Effective control of a project is vital to its successful completion, but unfortunately in many projects, control is too weak and too late. It is important to understand why there is so much emphasis on control, rather than just getting on with the project and collecting the cost of it for the record, which is unfortunately the final result of what many people do. One answer is that without effective control, an organisation and the people in it will tend to grow slack, and cost and time to completion will inevitably increase.

It is true that one function of a control system is to monitor efficiency, and cost and progress are criteria of efficiency in management, design engineering, procurement, manufacturing and construction. Nevertheless, there is a more positive side to control. A project is a large complex dynamic organism which is difficult to co-ordinate and which is subject to many changes. In a project, work rarely ever goes as planned or budgeted and management must have some means of determining how the project is progressing, where the problem areas are and what changes are occurring, in order that it can take action to minimise delays and cost over-expenditures, before they get out of hand. An effective control system that quickly brings to the attention of the manager deviations from the plan and budget as soon as they occur, to enable him to take action, that is, to manage his project, provides this means. Effective control is essentially the ongoing management of a project.

Thus the project control system has basically two functions

1. To monitor efficiency, progress and cost.

2. To permit the manager to maintain a grasp of the project, so that he can manage it.

Execution is the normal function of the managers involved in a project, both project and functional and is considered to be their normal duty, and what they are trained for and experienced in. Control of technical factors is thus relatively straightforward, and something engineers and technical personnel are normally fully competent in. Control of work in progress, money, changes to design specification, procurement of bought-in items and a host of other factors is much more difficult than the control of technical factors. This difficulty is magnified in project work, not only because of the dynamic characteristics of this type of work, but also because of the fact that the project manager is welding together several companies and, or organisations within one company, into a single organisation, without the normal permanent relationships between managers and without an established information system. Technical personnel involved in a project are thus often not experienced, interested in, or trained in this area of control, and control of the project is thus one of the prime responsibilities of the project manager.

Responsibility for the ultimate cost and time to completion of the project is one area of the project for which the project manager has little competition from functional line managers. This in fact makes a great deal of sense, as he is the only manager in the organisation at the centre of the project information system who is able to put together cost and progress for all the stages of the project, in order that managerial analysis can be carried out and control action taken. This is particularly so for large projects, where it may be over a year between the major part of engineering design work being completed, and the main manufacturing or construction costs coming in. He is the one manager who can evaluate the future costs of decisions taken early in the project, and make trade-offs between time, money and quality. Thus the normal project manager spends a large part of his time on the control of his project, which in reality is merely the ongoing management of a project.

Cost accounting and cost control

Often in project work, the only formal control function or system is in the hands of the project accountant, and to some people project control and cost control are thought to be synonymous with one another. Sometimes, the situation is even worse, and the only control and information system on a project is a cost accounting system. In reality, cost control is only one sub-system of the overall project control system, and cannot be separated from control of other factors without it becoming ineffective. Cost accounting, in turn, is only one sub-system of the cost control process, and is not really concerned with the management function. Thus before continuing, it is worthwhile to clearly define what is meant by cost accounting and cost control in project work.

Cost accounting systems are traditionally concerned with: 'accumulating actual cost, ensuring these costs are properly allocated against the operations that have to support them, verifying that the work is actually being carried out, is billed correctly, the legal requirements of accounting and establishing the capital account for depreciation purposes'. Standard accounting procedures and systems of checks are employed to ensure the validity of such costs. This form of cost accounting is of course essential, but totally inadequate by itself as a control system for project management.

Cost control on the other hand can be defined as 'the maintenance of cost within budget by taking corrective action where necessary, as indicated by the analysis of predicted cost relative to budget'. This involves cost analysis, prediction and reporting, together with management action to correct deviations, in addition to cost accounting.

However, even this traditional definition of cost control is not adequate for a project and a different definition of cost control has to be used. Cost control in a more modern idiom appropriate to project work can be defined as follows. 'Cost control is the correct application of the technical sciences in our industry to produce the least costly product within given guidelines'. Thus in reality the project manager is concerned with the financial management, planning and control of his project, with the objective of 'minimising the overall costs, subject to satisfactory time and performance constraints'.

Unfortunately, even this approach to cost control has proved unsatisfactory in practice, partially due to the inadequacy of the historical accounting methods to forecast expenditure and to control cost effectively, but also due to the incompleteness of any project cost control system. Cost control systems are not sufficient in themselves to control project work, as there must be a combination of technical, accountancy, and managerial factors, together with the integration of progress and cost in the control of projects.

It must be remembered that the objectives of the project manager, with regard to control of his project, are involved with more than costs. On some occasions he may be more concerned with minimising time, subject to cost and performance constraints, or in fact, as in the early North Sea work, project managers may on occasions be concerned with only minimising time, subject to performance constraints. In these early North Sea oil projects, time was the prime objective, and cost was secondary and this was a contributing factor to the 130 per cent or more cost escalation experienced. One of the problems of multiple objectives is that normally all of them cannot be maximised, or minimised at the same time. Some compromise has normally to be made and one objective chosen, such as the time or cost objective, with the others looked on as constraints. The mix of objectives, or balance, may vary from project to project, but in general the project manager is concerned with somehow minimising both time and cost, or some balance of these two factors, subject to a satisfactory technical performance or standard. He then attempts to control cost and progress, because by doing so he believes he can reduce the overall cost and time to completion of the project.

One of the essentials for this effective control of a project is the integration of all the subsystems for control. It has been found that it is essential that the subsystems for planning, budgeting, information and control of both progress and cost must be integrated with the work to be done, who is to do it,

177

organisation structure, and that this integration is the basis of an effective project management system. It establishes personal responsibility for progress and cost right down the line to the place where the work is actually being carried out. All these systems must go together, as the control of progress and cost are inseparable, and interact with plan and budget, with the budget being based on the plan of how the work will actually be carried out. Unless project managers are backed up by such effective systems, there will not be an effective project management, and projects will inevitably cost more and take longer than necessary. Thus the project management requirements for control are often completely different to that of a traditional proprietorship accounting system, and this generally requires a separate management information system to the normal accounting system of a firm. This system must integrate progress and cost, be faster and thus be more up to date, and cover many more areas.

Therefore the project manager has to have an information system that integrates all these factors. In addition, just as critical to the success of projects are a number of factors which, though part of the overall project control system, justify treatment on their own and are covered in later chapters, namely

1. The importance of cost consciousness, particularly in the early stages of a project.
2. Change control systems.
3. A system to control procurement of bought-in items.
4. The influence of project management on labour productivity in construction projects.

Budgeting

The baselines for any project control system are the project plan and a time-phased budget based on it. The project estimate of costs, and perhaps manhours is not sufficient on its own to permit effective control of costs on a project. Once an estimate of project cost, which will probably be roughly

178

based on how the work is going to be carried out, is completed, it must be expanded into a time-phased budget of expenditures based on the project plan. The cost estimate and the project plan must therefore be integrated into a time-phased budget, with cost centres based on planned activities, each having budgeted expenditure for every time period involved. This involved considerably more work, than simply preparing an estimate, but except on small projects, if it is not done, financial control and thus overall management control is lost, and the project manager cannot manage his project.

Figure 7.1 shows a project plan for a very simple example, and Figure 7.2 shows the time-phased budget for this project. This budget can be constructed manually from a bar chart and estimate in the same way a manpower chart is constructed. However, the amount of work involved in budget preparation can be considerably reduced by simple computer systems, which can take the project plan and estimate, and automatically produce a project budget for an even rate of working on each activity. This can then be modified inter-actively for activities where the rate of work, or expenditure is not even.

Unfortunately it is not possible to maintain either of the two critical performance measurement baselines, that is, the plan and time-phase budget, as static baselines. As mentioned previously, nothing ever seems to go to plan and budget in project work, and at times there are debates on whether the original plan and budget should be the baseline or whether these should be revised to take into account changes that have occurred. One argument put forward against changing them is that if the plan and budget are frequently changing, they are merely being adjusted for inefficiency and they do not provide valid baselines. The counter argument is that many changes do occur in project work, and if the plan and budget are not changed to take some of these into account, they soon lose all credibility as control baselines.

It must be remembered that the plan as well as being a control baseline, is a management tool to assist the project manager to make decisions and to allocate resources to achieve his objectives. It must be used in an adaptive way to remain a real time aid to project management. It is also true

179

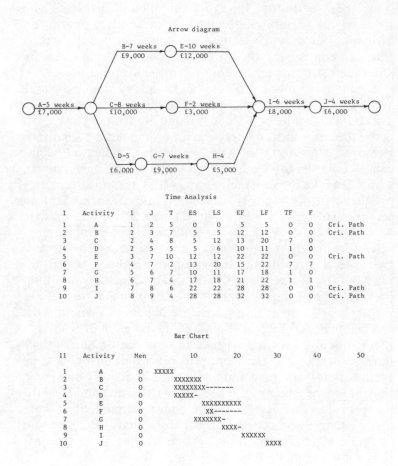

Figure 7.1   Project plan for simple example

Activity	I	J	£ Estimate	Monthly Budget (£)							
				1	2	3	4	5	6	7	8
A	1	2	7000	5600	1400						
B	2	3	9000		3857	5143					
C	2	4	10000		3750	5000	1250				
D	2	5	6000		3600	2400					
E	3	7	12000				4800	4800	2400		
F	4	7	3000				3000				
G	5	6	9000			2571	5143	1286			
H	6	7	5000					3750	1250		
I	7	8	8000						2667	5333	
J	8	9	6000								6000
			75000	5600	12607	15114	14192	9836	6317	5333	6000

Figure 7.2   Project budget

that budgets should not just be changed because costs to date are higher than budgeted, and progress is less than planned. They should not be changed merely to compensate for variances already experienced. The budget is a performance baseline, built up from estimates of how much the work should cost and how long it should take, if carried out in a particular way.

If a budget is hopelessly inaccurate, it is useless as a control tool and it is counterproductive not to change it, as otherwise no one will pay any attention to it. The budget after all is a basis for comparing actual costs and when they occurred, with estimated costs and when they were supposed to occur. It is thus one way of measuring efficiency and progress, but primarily it is a means of attracting management's attention to any deviations from planned progress and estimated cost. Thus it is wrong to be dogmatic about changing a budget and it should be changed whenever it serves some managerial or control purpose to do so. There is no real reason not to do so, as analysis can easily be carried out with more than one budget baseline when using computer-based systems, by simply using different data files.

However, in addition to changes in performance affecting the budget, there are a number of factors which quite legitimately require the budget to be changed. During the life of a project, any budget is subject to an almost continuous series of minor alterations to cope with changes to schedule, changes to the scope of work and adjustments to compensate for inflation. These do not alter the essential structure or base-estimates of the budget, and are not really 'changing' the budget. Whatever changes occur to the budget, it must be maintained as an up-to-date, valid baseline, against which to measure performance, and it must be tight, but not unrealistic.

Thus there are a number of factors which must be formally incorporated into a dynamic approach to project budgeting and control, if the budget is to remain such a valid baseline. The principal factors are

1. The characteristic flow of information in the development phase of a project.

2. Changes to the project.
3. Variations in the plan.
4. Inflation.

During the development and engineering design phases of a project, the project estimate will be refined as more information of increasing reliability becomes available, as discussed in the last chapter. Thus when the project estimate is changed, the project budget will require to be changed to take this into account. No matter how indefinite the estimate is in the early stages of a project, a budget should be constructed early in the project life cycle to show the proposed time-phased expenditure, otherwise there is no control baseline. It is probable that the estimate for the early work on the project will be more defined than that of the later work, similar to the development of different levels of a plan, and the budget will be a reasonably accurate control tool for these early stages.

However, even when a definitive project budget is established, it is still not normally possible to keep it static. There will probably still be design changes to the project, and as these are made, appropriate changes must also be made to the budget for this work. Occasionally this involves adding to the budgets for existing cost centres, at other times it may be necessary to add new cost centres for which performance data must be collected.

When work on a project actually starts, changes to the time phasing of work are almost inevitable, and whenever the planned schedule of work changes, so must the time-phased budget. If an activity is replanned to start later than originally scheduled, and, or to take longer, then the period to period time-phased budget should also be changed. This is a relatively simple change, with the baseline estimate remaining the same, and merely the time phasing of the expenditure changed to correspond to the new plan. The only changes to the total expenditure would be for associated overheads, allocated on a time-phased basis, and any adjustment for inflation due to the extended timescale to the project.

In many projects, inflation makes nonsense of the original

figures used in a project budget, therefore it must be incorporated in the budgeting process. Performance measurements can be made on an inflated or deflated basis, with more or less the same results. Actual costs can be compared to inflated budget estimates, or deflated actual costs can be compared to the original budget estimate. It should make little difference whether the analysis is carried out on an inflated, or deflated basis, provided like is always compared to like. Often both methods have to be used for differing purposes, and for, or by, the different parties involved in a project. The estimated costs at the base date prices can be compared with the actual costs deflated to the base date prices, or the base date estimate can be inflated to current prices and compared with actual costs. The actual budget for control purposes would be varying dynamically, but would still provide a valid baseline for control purposes. The project budget is thus normally subject to a number of minor revisions due to these factors throughout the life of the project. In addition to this on many projects, there often comes a time, despite these minor revisions, when a major revision of plan and, or estimate, and thus the budget becomes necessary. The original plan and estimate may have been widely optimistic, or even pessimistic, unexpected cost, schedule or technical problems may have occurred, or there may be changes to the project strategy in how the project is to be carried out. Whatever the reason, the existing budget is now totally unrealistic, or has been subject to so many changes that it is extremely complex and difficult to follow, does not provide a valid performance baseline, and thus serves no purpose.

In such cases it is necessary to re-plan, re-estimate and re-budget the project, so that the best decisions and resource allocations can be made in the light of the changed circumstances, and yet control of the project is maintained. This kind of revision is not undertaken lightly, and certainly should not be carried out more frequently than once per year. Even then, the revision of the budget should not happen more than once or twice in the life of an important project, and there should be substantial remaining work on the project after the last budget revision.

An exception to this is where there is a change of project management. When project managers are changed during long life cycle projects it is prudent for the new project manager to do a full analysis of his project when taking over. This is necessary to familiarise himself with his project, but also to clearly establish 'his' performance baseline so that he cannot be held responsible for delays and over-expenditures of the previous management.

Cash flow forecasting

As well as being a performance baseline, budgeting and control systems perform another function, namely, cash flow forecasting. With the high cost of capital today and the problems many companies have, both client and contractor, in maintaining a positive cash flow, cash flow forecasting and its management are important activities for many firms. In the contractor's case, care must be taken to maintain a balance between funds obtained from the client, and payments made to direct labour, equipment and material suppliers and to subcontractors. The situation which must be avoided at all costs is the 'hysteresis. form of cash flow in and out, as shown in Figure 7.3. The vertical difference between cash in and cash out must be maintained as small as possible, preferably zero or positive, if the contractor is extremely lucky. This is especially important in foreign contracts as contractors must also manage their foreign currency dealings. In many such cases, the profits from this can exceed the profits from the project; in others, if this is not managed effectively, the losses from foreign currency commitments can bring about large losses on a project and can lead to bankruptcy.

The budget is the tool that is used in the initial stages of a project to forecast cash flow, but as soon as work starts the budget forecasts of cash flow must be modified by the analysis of performance. These forecasts are not revised budgets, and the budget should not be revised simply to provide a better forecast of cash flow. Thus as work progresses, cash flow

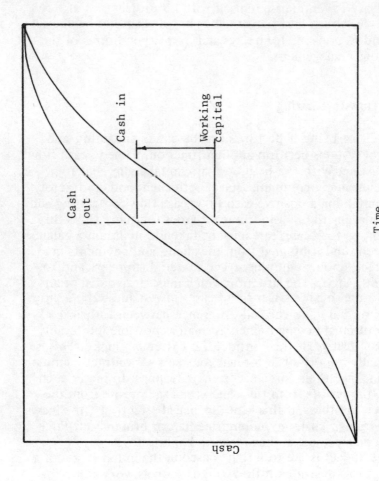

Figure 7.3 Hysteresis cash flow

Activity	Budgeted Costs in Period	Cumulative Budget to Date	Actual Cost in Period	Cumulative Actual Cost to Date	Variance for Period	Cumulative Variance to Date
A	£20,000	£45,000	£22,000	£50,000	£2,000 (Unfavourable)	£5,000
B	£15,000	£30,000	£13,000	£33,000	-£2,000 (Favourable)	£3,000

Figure 7.4   Variance analysis

forecasting should be based on an analysis of the existing budget modified in the light of performance and progress to date.

Variance analysis for project control

The traditional form of budgetry control is variance analysis, that is, the comparison of actual costs with budget costs. For example, the analysis for two activities on a project is shown in Figure 7.4.

This form of accounting-orientated analysis is inadequate for the control of project work. It merely tells you whether you have, in the time periods concerned, spent more or less than you budgeted for. It does not tell you whether you are getting the work expected for the money spent, that it is the 'earned value'. Without additional information you cannot tell whether the activities are going to cost more or less than budgeted for. For example, if this were excavation work, £20,000 might be the expected cost of 500 cubic yards, and £22,000 might be the cost of actually 400, 500 or 600 cubic yards? There is also a tendency to collect and summarise costs by function or type of equipment on a project, for example, all excavation, all pumps, all piping. This may be useful as a form of summary for overall control and feedback to estimating but should be a secondary form of analysis.

Variance analysis of cost must be integrated with variance analysis of progress, through some measurement of progress, for example: milestones, percentage complete on an activity, or a bill of quantities, on individual activities or linked groups of activities. Even a bill of quantities may be insufficient as a criterion of progress or performance, as, for example, though 500 cubic yards of excavation may be estimated to be required for a particular foundation, because of ground conditions, 700 cubic yards may be required. Therefore the unit cost may be satisfactory, but the cost of excavation for this foundation will be well over the budgeted figure.

Early attempts at integrating time, physical progress and cost for variance analysis, involved allocating cost to individual activities on a bar chart or network, for example, PERT/COST. This permitted variance analysis to be carried out on each activity for the following factors, for each time period and cumulatively, as appropriate.

1. Scheduled start versus actual start.
2. Scheduled finish versus actual finish.
3. Scheduled time for activity versus actual time for activity.
4. Budgeted cost versus actual cost.
5. Budgeted manhours versus actual manhours.
6. Scheduled quantity versus actual quantity.
7. Budgeted unit cost versus actual unit cost.

Unfortunately, though this has worked on small projects, experience on larger projects has not been very satisfactory. This form of control permits only the comparison of scheduled time and budgeted cost with achieved time and cost for an individual activity. This is satisfactory for individual activities, and for the smaller project, but it does not give adequate control on larger projects. The only consolidation of activities, reporting and analysis is at the level of the project itself, and a large amount of subjectivity has to be used to estimate overall progress. Individual small activities can be monitored, but large activities, segments of the project and the project itself, could not be subject to satisfactory control analysis. This traditional variance analysis also only looks backward in time to analyse historical performance on completed activities, whereas a project manager requires to have a forward looking control system to help him manage his project. In addition there tends to be rationalisation about historical performance and many reasons are often given to explain why what has happened in the past will not happen in the future; unfortunately this tends not to be the case.

The other problems are concerned with the difficulty of achieving a match between the break-down of the project into activities, necessary for physical and time-planning, and those convenient and suitable for budgeting, action and control, with the level of detail required. It is almost impossible to construct a network such that cost distribution is identical to the mode of cost collection and reporting in at the level where work is carried out. This led initially to the concept of 'cost hammocks', in which several activities were aggregated together by a hammock activity spanning them. This was an improvement, but only the start of the development of an effective system. Hammocks give a disordered, rather random set of cost centres, and do not necessarily provide a match between physical and financial planning and control.

Of equal or even more importance is the level of detail required to give effective management and control. There is no point in developing a finely detailed planning, budgeting and control system which serves no managerial purpose and will not be operated. The principal purpose of preparing a time-phased budget is to assist project management to minimise the cost of executing the project by effective control. To achieve effective control, a project management information system is required which works and works quickly. Having approximately accurate information at the end of the month is much more helpful to the project manager, than having accurate information two or three months after the event.

In conditions most projects work under, you cannot expect to get the project, design engineering, manufacturing or construction staff to operate a management information system which returns very detailed information, and thus often massive amounts of it, accurately and quickly. Nor, often, is very detailed information of much use. There are always variations in cost and schedule on individual small activities. Time and cost estimates of activities are based on average performance, and there must be many variations about these averages. It is the performance of the organisation with these variations averaged out, which is the concern of the manager.

Thus some compromise on the size of control centres for planning, budgeting and control analysis must be made. They must be large enough so as not to overload the management and supervision with too much detail, but small enough to provide effective control, in that deviations from plan and budget are identified, before they are the size to adversely affect the overall project. It must be possible for costs to be estimated and budgeted for these control centres, and the actual costs and progress to be identified, and collected without difficulty. Ideally it should be possible to not only integrate the plan, budget and information system, but also to establish individual responsibility for these control centres. Also it must be possible to consolidate the information gained at the lower levels to perform an analysis for the overall project, segments of the project and the organisations involved in the project. This can be done by using the modern methods of project control.

8 Modern Methods of Project Control

Modern methods of organising project control systems, sometimes termed 'Performance Analysis' are based on the use of

1. Three different types of control centres to control progress and cost, with differing modes of analysis,
2. The work breakdown structure to provide a framework to integrate the subsystems and to consolidate reporting,
3. The earned value concept for work done.

The most sophisticated application of these concepts is seen in the US Department of Defence, Cost Schedule Control System Criteria (C/SCSC) and Cost Performance Reporting systems (CPR). These are primarily for the US defence projects, but the concepts and techniques used are just as applicable to manufacturing and construction projects in industry.

Control centres

There are three types of control centre required for effective project control, each involving different methods of analysis, namely

1. Work packages: Essentially discrete tasks, or activities as on a bar chart or arrow diagram, on which analysis is by relatively straightforward budget versus actual variance measurements, as in PERT/COST.

2. Overheads: On which analysis is based on an expenditure rate over time.
3. Cost Accounts: Essentially the aggregation of work packages into separate sections of the project, the largest of which is the project itself, on which a full performance analysis, forecasting of final cost and completion dates are required.

Work packages

The basic building block of the modern planning, budgeting and control system is termed a 'work package'. A work package is simply a discrete task, activity or job, which has an observable start and finish, and an end product of some form. It is normally related directly to one level of the project plans, be they bar charts or networks. In the simple example shown in Figures 7.1 and 7.2, each activity could be considered as a work package. A work package can be a single activity, a cost hammock covering several activities in series, or several activities progressing in parallel. For example, a work package can be the excavation, setting of shuttering and reinforcing, pouring of concrete and placing of a single vessel, or piece of equipment. Alternatively, it could be those activities for all the equipment on one area of a project, or it could simply be the excavation, or any other individual activity in the sequence, for all the equipment on the project, or in one area of the project.

Each work package is thus a significant amount of work, which is large enough to simplify the estimating, budgeting or collection of costs and other information, but which is also small enough to pick up deviations before they become dangerous. This concept attempts to achieve the objectives and the compromise outlined at the end of the last chapter.

Analysis of progress on work packages is by simple variance analysis, as carried out in PERT/COST, and this is quite adequate for these short timespan activities. However, work packages are different in concept from the activities used in PERT/COST, and are only the base element of the project control system. They are not simply cost centres, but are

193

more information or control centres. They are in effect small pseudo-subcontracts between the project manager and the individuals contributing to the project. They describe the work to be done, are the assigned responsibility of one individual, have an estimated cost and a time schedule, and their completion gives an objective means of monitoring progress and cost.

The size of the work package used is not tied to the size of the activity necessary for physical planning purposes, but can vary between functions. The key factor of the work package concept, from the point of view of monitoring progress and cost is that they should be relatively short. Work package durations should be measured in terms of weeks rather than days or months. With short term work packages, overall progress and cost analysis can be based mainly on completed work packages. Subjective estimates of progress are limited to 'open' work packages, that is, work packages that are started but not yet completed. Ideally, as control analysis is normally based on monthly reporting, most work packages should be from one to two months duration. No attempt should be made to artificially achieve this and work packages should be natural subdivisions of the work. When work packages are longer they should be subdivided by objective milestones, or 'inchstones' with separate estimates and schedules for each segment. On these short work packages, there is little need to carry out an analysis of cost and progress until they are completed. As they normally span two, or at most three reporting periods, an optimistic subjective assessment of progress in the first reporting period is quickly corrected in the second. This short timespan of a work package is essential to reduce the amount of subjectivity and error in performance reporting.

Thus project performance analysis at work package level is based on variance analysis of completed work packages, and analysis of performance on larger segments of the project and for the total project can be based on this foundation. However, one cannot wait until a project or substantial segments of it, are completed, before carrying out an analysis of performance. A project can be made up of anything from 30 to many thousands of work packages and variance analysis of completed work packages is inadequate to give a clear picture of what is the overall project performance, or to forecast the final cost and completion date. This is where simple PERT/COST fall down and where the more sophisticated 'performance analysis' based on 'cost accounts' and work packages, can give more effective control of projects.

Overheads

Direct costs, such as labour, materials and subcontracts can normally be easily allocated to work packages. However, many other activities can exist on a project which are more general or supportive in nature, and cannot be identified as belonging to specific work packages. They cannot be easily and logically allocated, and are termed indirect, or overhead costs. The allocation of these overhead costs are a problem area in project management, just as they are in production management, and if wrongly handled they can distort the management decision process and make control of a project difficult. It is here that accounting for management control often differs from standard accounting practice.

The traditional accounting practice is to endeavour to allocate, or apportion these costs to work packages based on some criteria of the presumed benefit the work packages receive from these indirect activities. Unfortunately, there is often no direct link between work packages and these overhead costs, and the criteria used can be artificial or arbitrary. An overhead rate for the overall organisation is sometimes derived on an annual basis, and applied to work packages, or cost accounts, on the basis of the proportion of total manpower used, or as a percentage of total expenditure. To do this, estimates are made of total annual company activity and the total overhead cost, and a simple division used to establish an application rate for overheads.

This can result in an arbitrary allocation, and may be necessary and satisfactory for historical or proprietorship cost accounting, but is generally useless and counterproductive for management control purposes. Many of the sources of these costs are not activities for which good or bad performance on work packages can influence, or vice versa, nor can the project management influence them, as they have little responsibility or authority over them. To achieve effective management control in project work, overheads must be treated in a different manner than in traditional cost accounting.

Overheads in project work can be divided into two classifications, and each must be handled differently, that is

1. More or less direct overheads, which can be allocated or apportioned in a logical manner.
2. Indirect overheads.

Some overheads are more or less direct overheads and can be directly traced as supportive effort to particular work packages, or cost accounts, and are dependent on, or related in direct proportion to the performance on them. These can be logically allocated on a meaningful basis to particular work packages, or may even form separate work packages within cost accounts, each with its own budget which may be based on a percentage of the related work package cost. For example, a design department may be working on three projects, and the departmental overheads can be split among these projects and have some meaning.

Other overheads cannot be directly traced to individual work packages, or cost accounts, for example, central company overheads, project management or general administrative costs. It is wrong, from a management point of view, to allocate these arbitrarily to work packages or cost accounts. These costs must be separated from that which is measurable, to avoid distorting performance analysis.

Separate budgets can be made for these indirect overheads, and allocated to the project as a whole, or to discrete segments of it. For example, the budget for the project management costs can be allocated to the overall project and the budget for construction management allocated to the total construction phase. Generally these overheads are time based, and are simply budgeted as a cost per period, though in fact the level of expenditure may vary from period to period. Measurement is on the basis of an expenditure rate over the passage of time, and if the project is extended, these costs are unavoidably increased.

Cost accounts

Carrying out a control analysis of a relatively long on-going activity, such as the project itself, or a major part of it, is entirely different from the simple budget versus actual variance analysis for short span activities, that is, work packages. One difference is that for effective control analysis, there must be a reliable measurement of progress that is percentage complete, or to give it another name, the 'earned value' of work done.

In practice this tends to be a highly subjective estimate, made with 'rose coloured spectacles', unless some systematic method is used. Many projects, and segments of projects, have had optimistic estimates of progress made until these estimates are obviously shown to be widely inaccurate, and by then it is too late to do anything about it. These projects tend to be reported 'on schedule and budget' up to 80–90 per cent complete, at which stage they stay that way until the actual work catches up with these estimates, the project completion date is extended, and the budget over-run. Modern methods of analysis endeavour to limit the amount of subjectivity, that is, opinion, used in the measurement of progress and thus make control action possible at an earlier stage.

The type of information the project manager needs to have for effective progress analysis and control are objective answers to the following questions, which can be called 'performance analysis'.

1. Are we on schedule, ahead of schedule, behind schedule, on the project as a whole and the individual parts of it? If we have a variation from schedule, where did it occur, why did it occur and who is responsible for it? What effect will it have on the other parts of the project, and what can we do about it?
2. Is the work being completed to the budget estimate,

197

or less than the budget estimate, or is the work costing more for the project as a whole and the individual parts of it? If we have a variation from budget, where did it occur, why did it occur, or what caused it, who is responsible for it, and what can we do about it?

3. Are we *going to be* on schedule, on budget, or over schedule and over budget? That is, what is the trend of progress and cost? It is vital to become aware of trends at an early stage or there is little possibility of influencing them. When work progress or cost is obviously varying, it is normally too late to do anything about it. The secrets of real control are to pick up trends as soon as they start to occur and to be able to do something about them.

4. Thus project management needs to be able to forecast the final cost, and the completion date for the project and for the individual parts of it.

5. We are also concerned with monitoring against plan and budget the rate of build-up of cost and progress. This is analogous to the acceleration of the project, just as cost versus time is essentially the velocity of the project. (It is in this that S charts are an effective tool.)

On small projects, the project manager will only want this full 'performance analysis' for the project as a whole, with the simpler budget versus actual variance analysis for work packages. However, as projects get larger, this limited analysis becomes too aggregated and does not give sufficient control over the project. The project must then be broken down into segments, for which a full performance analysis is also carried out in order to answer the above questions for each segment. Performance analysis for only the complete project is too insensitive and slow to react to wayward variances on any part of it. These segments can be called 'cost accounts.' In a small project there may be only one cost account, the project itself, on slightly larger projects there may be only a handful of cost accounts. In very large projects, hundreds of cost accounts may be required to provide effective control.

These cost accounts are key points for the management's

planning, analysis and control of work on a project. All parts of the project information system must be integrated at these points, including budgets, schedules, work assignments, organisational responsibilities, cost collection, progress assessment, performance analysis, problem identification and corrective actions.

The lowest level of cost accounts is located immediately above the work package level and is normally made up of several work packages. Figure 8.1 shows the work breakdown structure, cost accounts and work packages for the example shown in Figure 7.1. Costs are accumulated, progress measured and performance analysis carried out at this 'basic' level. The measurement of progress is based on completed work packages and work packages being worked on in the period in question. Subjectivity is limited to estimating progress on work packages started, but not yet finished, and this considerably reduces errors in estimating progress and quickly corrects any optimistic estimates. These lower level cost accounts should not be exorbitantly long, or there is a danger that there would be the use of funds for later work for earlier work in the cost account and the information system might have difficulty in differentiating this. At this basic level nine to twelve months is a reasonable maximum length.

Each cost account is a natural subdivision of the work on a project and should have formally assigned to it

    1. A description of the scope of work to be performed.
    2. Who is responsible for this work.
    3. A time-phased budget for the work.
    4. The resources required.
    5. A plan, with scheduled starts and finishes.
    6. The work packages making up the cost account.

In addition to these lower level cost accounts, there should also be a hierarchy of higher level cost accounts, as shown in Figures 2.7 and 8.1, built up from these basic cost accounts, each with the above information assigned to it, the higher level cost accounts being work breakdown structure elements. It should thus be possible to carry out a performance analysis on a summarised basis for segments of the project, the project as a whole and for the organisations working on the project.

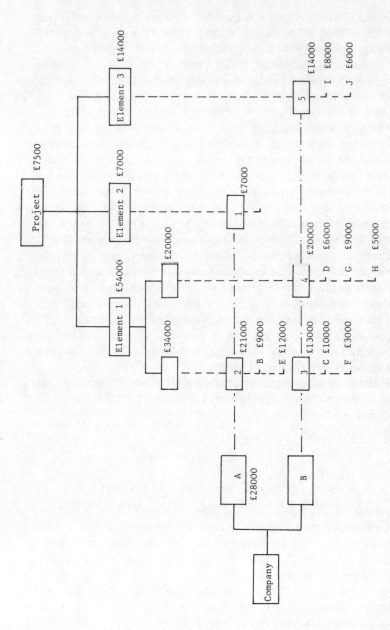

Figure 8.1 WBS and estimates for simple project

The structure of this matrix hierarchy of cost accounts, and the size and level of the basic cost accounts are important decisions to be made at the outset of a project in designing the project management information system. These factors should be carefully considered at the outset of a project to ensure that the work will be properly defined into manageable units and that functional responsibilities are clearly and reasonably established. This is where the work breakdown structure is an invaluable tool in structuring the hierarchy of cost accounts.

The interaction of the work breakdown structure and the organisation structure, at the lowest level of the work breakdown structure as shown in Figures 2.7 and 8.1 is a logical point to integrate all the project subsystems and establish the lower level cost accounts. The assignment of lower level work breakdown structure elements to responsible lower level functional managers, provides a key automatic integration point for all these subsystems and for management analysis, planning and control.

The work represented by this intersection is the basic cost account. This more or less self contained entity can be considered as a separate contract with a particular organisation and identifiable person responsible for it, a planned start and finish time, resource requirements and a time-phased budget. Just as these factors are defined for the overall project contract, so they must be defined for those key intersection points, which are essentially external subcontracts or internal pseudo-subcontracts.

Not only must the project systems be based on these key intersection points, but so must the people involved view them as binding subcontracts. This attitude of mind contributes much to the effectiveness of project management. For example consider the simple example shown in Figure 8.1 which shows the basic level cost accounts, made up of one or more packages, the higher level cost accounts and work breakdown structure elements consolidating these for segments of the project, and two organisational cost accounts. The budget for each of these cost accounts can be constructed as shown in Figure 8.2 and performance analysis carried out for each of them.

201

These cost accounts and the concept of representing them as individual contracts are extended up the work breakdown structure and to the organisation structure to form a matrix hierarchy of costs accounts or pseudo or real subcontracts. These basic cost accounts can be consolidated up the work breakdown structure for analysis and reporting on higher level work breakdown structure items. This forms a natural hierarchy of the work breakdown structure cost accounts, each with its planned start and finish, time-phased budget and analysis and reporting systems. They form a structure of the planning and control system for the overall project, with all subsystems integrated at each level in the hierarchy. Each work breakdown structure cost account can be considered as a separate contract and controlled as such, with the ability to trace variation, changes and trends right down to the lowest level cost account.

The basic level cost accounts can also be consolidated horizontally, and all the cost accounts for each organisation can be considered as a functional cost account, or pseudo-contract for that organisation. Again the organisation's total work on the project will have a plan, budget, information feedback, and be subject to analysis and performance reporting.

The highest level cost accounts are the project itself on one axis, and the performing company or companies on the other axis. A full performance analysis can be carried out on schedule and cost performance for all levels of cost account. Any variance in the project can be traced down the work breakdown structure to the basic level of cost account, the work package involved and to the organisation responsible for it. Performance of the companies, sub-organisations or departments involved can also be analysed in a similar manner. Reporting can be kept to the minimum and yet be expanded to identify a cause and who is responsible for any variance.

Performance analysis

The methods of analysis that should be used at cost account and higher levels of the work breakdown structure and the

202

project as a whole, are based upon earned value concepts and S chart analysis. The earned value concept is based on the measurement of the budgeted value of work actually carried out, and its comparison with the budgeted value of the work that should have been carried out and what it actually cost. The concept has been crystallised and defined in the Cost/ Schedule Control Systems Criteria. Previously a project manager could measure progress against a pre-determined schedule and measure actual cost for work performed against the budget. The problem was that the project manager could not determine, for the money spent, whether or not he was getting the progress he should have obtained; how much should he have spent for the progress achieved, and how did this actually compare with what he actually spent? Often he tried to evaluate value by making a subjective estimate, usually subconsciously based on the percentage of funds expended. The success of the modern methods of project control is based upon removing this subjectivity.

This method of analysis uses three basic terms with which the project manager should become familiar. These are partially new concepts, and partially the formalisation and 'jargonisation' of previous methods. The terms used are

1. BCWS — the Budgeted Cost of Work Scheduled.
2. BCWP — the Budgeted Cost for Work Performed.
3. ACWP — the Actual Cost of Work Performed.

Using these three data elements, it is possible to quickly evaluate for each lower level cost account and for the hierarchy of cost accounts

1. Its cost variance   = BCWP-ACWP
2. Schedule variance in cost terms   = BCWP-BCWS
3. Cost performance index (CPI)   = BCWP/ACWP
4. Schedule performance index in monetary terms (SPI)   = BCWP/BCWS
5. Estimate to complete the project (ETC) (where BAC = Budget at completion)   = (BAC-BCWP)/CPI
6. Estimate at completion, that is, the forecast cost (EAC)   = ACWP + ETC

Control Centre	Estimate	Monthly Budget (£) in Period							
		1	2	3	4	5	6	7	8
Cost Account No. 1									
Work package A	7,000	5,600	1,400						
Total	7,000	5,600	1,400						
Cost Account No. 2									
Work package B	9,000		3,857	5,143					
Work package E	12,000				4,800	4,800	2,400		
Total	21,000		3,857	5,143	4,800	4,800	2,400		
Cost Account No. 3									
Work package C	10,000		3,750	5,000	1,250				
Work package F	3,000				3,000				
Total	13,000		3,750	5,000	4,250				
Cost Account No. 4									
Work package D	6,000		3,600	2,400					
Work package G	9,000			2,571	5,143	1,286			
Work package H	5,000					3,750	1,250		
Total	20,000		3,600	4,971	5,143	5,036	1,250		
Cost Account No. 5									
Work package I	8,000						2,667	5,333	
Work package J	6,000								6,000
Total	14,000						2,667	5,333	6,000
Department A									
Cost Account No. 1	7,000	5,600	1,400						
Cost Account No. 2	21,000		3,857	5,143	4,800	4,800	2,400		
Total	28,000	5,600	5,257	5,143	4,800	4,800	2,400		
Department B									
Cost Account No. 3	13,000		3,750	5,000	4,250				
Cost Account No. 4	20,000		3,600	4,471	5,143	5,036	1,250		
Cost Account No. 5	14,000						2,667	5,333	6,000
Total	47,000		7,350	9,971	9,393	5,036	3,917	5,333	6,000
Total Project	75,000	5,600	12,607	15,114	14,192	9,836	6,317	5,333	6,000

Figure 8.2   Manual calculation of project budget for cost accounts

204

Budgeted cost for work scheduled (BCWS)

BCWS is simply another name for the time-phased budget against which performance is measured for the project and for the individual cost account. It is normally determined for each individual cost period and on a cumulative basis, though in small projects it may only be determined on cumulative basis. For any given time period, budgeted cost for work scheduled is determined at the cost account level by totalling the budgets for all work packages scheduled to be completed, plus the budget for the portion of in-process work (open work packages) scheduled to be accomplished, plus the budgets for the overheads for that period. Figure 8.2 shows the BCWS for each period for the simple example.

Budgeted cost for work performed (BCWP)

The budgeted cost for work performed consists of the budgeted cost of all the work actually accomplished during any given time period. This can be determined by individual time period, and on a cumulative basis. At the cost account level BCWP is determined by totalling the budgets for work packages actually completed, plus the budget applicable to the completed in-process work with open work packages, plus the overhead budget.

The major difficulty encountered in the determination of BCWP is the evaluation of work in progress (work packages which have been started but have not been completed at the time of cut-off for the report). As discussed previously, the use of short span work packages, or the establishment of value milestones within work packages will significantly reduce the work in progress evaluation problems, and the procedures used will vary depending on work package length. For example some contractors prefer to take 50 per cent of the BCWP credit for a work package budget when it starts and the remaining 50 per cent at its completion. Other contractors use formulae which approximate the time phasing of the effort, while others prefer to make physical assessments of work completed to determine the applicable budget earned. For longer work packages many contractors use discrete milestones, with pre-established budget, or progress values to measure work performance. The method used largely depends on work package content, size and duration. However, the use of arbitrary formulae should be limited to very short work packages. Figure 8.3 shows the manual calculation of BCWP for period 3 in the simple example.

Actual cost of work performed (ACWP)

This is simply the costs actually incurred and recorded in accomplishing the work performed within a particular time period. These may be collected at cost account level, though more commonly they are collected at work package level, or individual activity level, depending on the size of the activity.

Cost/performance analysis

Using these three elements of data, it is possible to carry out an analysis of performance which integrates schedule and cost. Combining this with the work breakdown structure permits this analysis to be carried out at will, for any part of the project, for any contributing organisation and for the project as a whole. On larger projects, these comparisons are carried out for the latest time period, and on performance to date, that is, on cumulative basis, whereas on smaller projects they are sometimes only carried out on a cumulative basis.

Cost variance shows whether the work done costs more or less than was estimated, and schedule variance will give a cost measure of how far behind, or ahead of schedule the cost account, work breakdown structure item or the project is. Estimates to complete (ETC) and estimate at completion (EAC) produced by this method are mechanistic methods of forecasting final costs, but do tend to show the outcome if no improvement is made or action is taken. In essence they challenge 'Show why we should not take these as the likely outcome'.

This form of analysis can also be shown graphically using S charts, both for the total project and for individual cost accounts. Figure 8.4 shows an S chart for a typical project. The cumulative data elements are plotted as shown, and both the cost and schedule variances are clearly shown. In addition it can graphically show the estimate to complete (ETC) and

	Estimate	% Complete	Cumulative BCWP	Previous BCWP	BCP for Period
Cost Account No. 1					
Work package A	7,000	100	7,000	7,000	0
Total	7,000	100	7,000	7,000	0
Cost Account No. 2					
Work package B	9,000	85	7,650	3,240	4,410
Work package E	12,000	0	0	0	0
Total	21,000	36	7,650	3,240	4,410
Cost Account No. 3					
Work package C	10,000	85	8,500	3,800	4,700
Work package F	3,000	0	0	0	0
Total	13,000	65	8,500	3,800	4,700
Cost Account No. 4					
Work package D	6,000	100	6,000	3,600	2,400
Work package G	9,000	0	0	0	0
Work package H	5,000	0	0	0	0
Total	20,000	30	6,000	3,600	2,400
Cost Account No. 5					
Work package I	8,000	0	0	0	0
Work package J	6,000	0	0	0	0
Total	14,000	0	0	0	0
Department A					
Cost Account No. 1	7,000	100	7,000	7,000	0
Cost Account No. 2	21,000	36	7,650	3,240	4,410
Total	28,000	52	14,650	10,240	4,410
Department B					
Cost Account No. 3	13,000	65	8,500	3,800	4,700
Cost Account No. 4	20,000	30	6,000	3,600	2,400
Cost Account No. 5	14,000	0	0	0	0
Total	47,000	31	14,500	7,400	7,100
Total Project	75,000	39	29,150	18,340	11,510

Figure 8.3 **Calculation of budgeted cost of work performance (BCWP) for period 3**

207

estimate at completion (EAC). Figure 8.5 shows a similar analysis for a Cost Account in the simple example.

Cost variance and schedule variance when considered together, given an integrated picture of the position of the project, or individual cost account, as shown below.

BCWS	BCWP	ACWP	Cost variance	Scheduled variance	Analysis
4	4	4	0	0	On schedule, on cost
4	4	3	1	0	On schedule, under cost
4	4	5	−1	0	On schedule, over cost
3	4	4	0	1	Ahead of schedule, on cost
3	4	3	1	1	Ahead of schedule, under cost
3	4	5	−1	1	Ahead of schedule, over cost
5	4	4	0	−1	Behind schedule, on cost
5	4	3	1	−1	Behind schedule, under cost
5	4	−5	−1	−1	Behind schedule, over cost

Figures 8.6 and 8.7 show the performance analysis reports for periods 2 and 3 for the simple project shown in Figure 7.1. To illustrate the terms used, consider the cumulative performance analysis for Cost Account 2 in period 3 as shown in Figure 8.7.

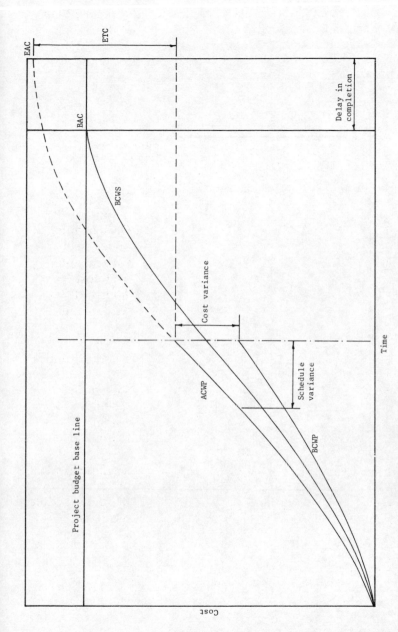

Figure 8.4 Typical project S curve

209

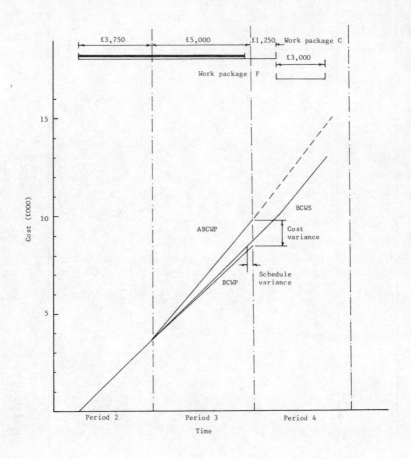

Figure 8.5   S curve for cost account 3

PERFORMANCE ANALYSIS FOR PERIOD 2

COST AC. NUMBER	BUDGETED COST WORK SCH.	BUDGETED COST WORK PE.	ACT.COST WORK PE.	VARIANCE SCHEDULE	VARIANCE COST	PERF.INDEX SCHEDULE	PERF.INDEX COST	BUDGET	EAC	VARIANCE
1	1400	1450	2150	50	-700	1.03571	0.674418	7000	7700	-700
2	3857.13	3240	3270	-617.13	-30	0.840002	0.990825	21000	21194.4	-194.4
3	3750	3800	3825	50	-25	1.01333	0.993464	13000	13085.5	-85.5
4	3600	3600	3672	0	-72	1	0.980392	20000	20400	-400
5	0	0	0	0	0	0	0	14000	14000	0
PROJECT	12607.1	12090	12917	-517.1	-827	0.958983	0.935975			

CUMULATIVE PERFORMANCE ANALYSIS FOR PERIOD 2

COST AC. NUMBER	BUDGETED COST WORK SCH.	BUDGETED COST WORK PE.	ACT.COST WORK PE.	VARIANCE SCHEDULE	VARIANCE COST	PERF.INDEX SCHEDULE	PERF.INDEX COST	BUDGET	EAC	VARIANCE
1	7000	7000	7700	0	-700	1	0.90909	7000	7700	-700
2	3857.13	3240	3270	-617.13	-30	0.840002	0.990825	21000	21194.4	-194.4
3	3750	3800	3825	50	-25	1.01333	0.993464	13000	13085.5	-85.5
4	3600	3600	3672	0	-72	1	0.980392	20000	20400	-400
5	0	0	0	0	0	1	0	14000	14000	0
PROJECT	18207.1	17640	18467	-567.1	-827	0.968852	0.955217	75000	78516.2	-3516.2
DEPT.A	10857	10240	10970	-617	-730	0.943	0.933	28000	30010	-2010
DEPT.B	7350	7400	7497	50	-97	1.001	0.987	47000	47619	-619
PROJECT (BY DEPT.)								75000	77679	-2629

WORK PACKAGE ANALYSIS

WP	BUDGET	ACTUAL	VARIANCE
1	7000	7700	-700

Figure 8.6 Performance report for period 2

211

PERFORMANCE ANALYSIS FOR PERIOD 3

COST AC. NUMBER	BUDGETED COST WORK SCH.	BUDGETED COST WORK PE.	ACT.COST WORK PE.	VARIANCE SCHEDULE	VARIANCE COST	PERF-INDEX SCHEDULE	PERF-INDEX COST
1	0	0	0	0	0	0	0
2	5142.84	4410	5100	-732.84	-690	0.857502	0.864705
3	5000	4700	6000	-300	-1300	0.94	0.783333
4	4971.42	2400	3540	-2571.42	-1140	0.482759	0.677966
5	0	0	0	0	0	0	0
PROJECT	15114.2	11510	14640	-3604.2	-3130	0.761535	0.786202

CUMULATIVE PERFORMANCE ANALYSIS FOR PERIOD 3

COST AC. NUMBER	BUDGETED COST WORK SCH.	BUDGETED COST WORK PE.	ACT.COST WORK PE.	VARIANCE SCHEDULE	VARIANCE COST	PERF-INDEX SCHEDULE	PERF-INDEX COST	BUDGET	EAC	VARIANCE
1	7000	7000	7700	0	-700	1	0.90909	7000	7700	-700
2	8999.97	7650	8370	-1349.97	-720	0.850002	0.913978	21000	22976.4	-1976.4
3	8750	8500	9825	-250	-1325	0.971428	0.865139	13000	15026.5	-2026.5
4	8571.42	6000	7212	-2571.42	-1212	0.7	0.831946	20000	24040	-4040
5	0	0	0	0	0	0	0	14000	14000	0
PROJECT	33321.4	29150	33107	-4171.4	-3957	0.874813	0.880478	75000	85181	-10181
DEPT.A	16000	14450	16070	-1350	-1420	0.916	0.912	28000	30702	-2702
DEPT.D	17321	14500	17037	-2821	-2537	0.837	0.851	47000	55229	-8229
PROJECT (BY DEPT.)								75000	85931	-10931

WORK PACKAGE ANALYSIS

WP	BUDGET	ACTUAL	VARIANCE
1	7000	7700	-700
4	6000	7212	-1212

Figure 8.7   Performance report for period 3

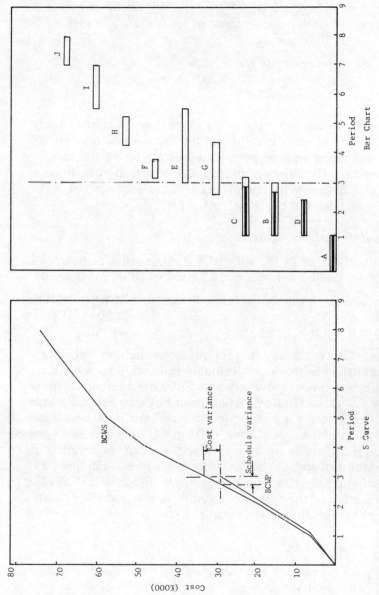

Figure 8.8 Integration of cost and schedule

Cost variance analysis

The comparison of BCWP and ACWP shows whether completed work has cost more or less than was budgeted for that work, for example

Cost variance $= $ BCWP $-$ ACWP
$= 7650 - 8370$
$= -720$

Thus the cost account is costing more than budgeted. Analysis of the differences should reveal the factors contributing to the variances, such as poor initial estimate for the task, technical difficulties requiring additional resources, the cost of labour and materials different from planned, or a combination of these or other factors.

Schedule variance analysis

Comparisons of BCWS with BCWP relate work completed to work scheduled during a given period of time, for example

Scheduled variance (in terms of cost) $= $ BCWP $-$ BCWS
$= 7650 - 9000$
$= -1350$

Thus this cost account is significantly behind schedule. Although this provides a valuable indication of schedule status in terms of monetary value of work accomplished, it may not clearly indicate whether or not schedule milestones are being met, since some work may have been performed out of its planned sequence. A formal time scheduling system must therefore be used to provide the means of determining the status of specific activities or milestones, as described in the chapter on planning. For example, Figure 8.8 shows the integration of the cost and schedule analysis at the end of the third month in this example.

Performance indices

On quickly scanning such a report, varying figures for cost and scheduled variance may at first glance not show up significant deviations clearly enough because of differences in magnitude of the figures involved. For example, a cost variance of £20,000 on one cost account with a BCWP of £200,000 is not as important as the cost variance of £20,000 on a cost account with a BCWP of £100,000. The use of cost scheduled performance indices overcomes this problem and provides at a glance a reliable indication of danger spots.

Cost performance index (CPI)   = BCWP ÷ ACWP
Schedule performance index (SPI) = BCWP ÷ BCWS

A performance index of 1 then represents 'par' performance. An index performance of less than 1 represents performance poorer than planned; an index greater than 1 represents a better performance than planned. Thus in the above examples, the first cost account would have a cost performance index of 0·91 and the second cost account would have a cost performance index of 0·83, clearly a greater problem. In the case of Cost Account 2 in Figure 8.7

$$\text{CPI} = 7650/8270$$
$$= 0·914$$
$$\text{SPI} = 7650/9000$$
$$= 0·85$$

These variances and performance indices are required at the cost account level and at higher levels. Performance analysis of higher level cost accounts consists of direct summaries of the results of such comparisons at the basic level and there is less need for further calculations at higher levels to determine project status and organisational performance at all levels of into both the work breakdown structure and organisational structure from the basic cost account level to provide both project status and original performance at all levels of management. Cost favourable variances in some areas may be offset by unfavourable variances in other areas, and higher level managers will normally see only the most significant variances at their own level. However, the accumulation of many small variances which may be adding up to a large overall cost problem, not attributable to any single major difficulty, will also be evident.

In this simple example, the project is the only higher level cost account, on the vertical consolidation axis, for which performance analysis is carried out. On the horizontal axis, performance analysis is carried out for the two departments involved. Figure 8.7 shows this analysis carried out for these three higher level cost accounts.

Forecasting the final cost

Forecasting the final cost of the project and parts of it, that is, cost accounts and work breakdown structure level items, are pieces of information often requested of project managers by anxious senior management and are vital to the project cash flow, the viability of the project and sometimes whether to cancel the project after it has started. No matter what the reason, as soon as work has started, this information is frequently and urgently requested.

A great deal of management judgement should go into these estimates, but this system does provide a mechanistic way of estimating these final costs, as there is a danger of relying too much on subjective estimates. This analysis provides a starting point for more judgemental estimates and a benchmark to compare them with. The method used is a simple extrapolation of performance to date. The forecasts are calculated for each cost account and higher level accounts, including the project, for which a full performance analysis is carried out. They are calculated by dividing the budget for the remaining work to be carried out by the CPI and adding it to the actual cost of work performed, for example

Performance to date (CPI) $= BCWP/ACWP$
Budgeted cost for the remaining work $= BAC-BCWP$
Estimate to complete (ETC) $= (BAC-BCWP)/CPI$
Forecast cost at completion (EAC) $= ACWP+ETC$

Using this method forecasts of the final cost for segments of the project can be made for

1. Individual cost accounts that have been started.
2. Work breakdown structure items that have been started.
3. Organisational cost accounts, that have been started.

Thus, forecasts of the final cost of all activities and cost accounts that have been started can be made, based on performance to date. In addition, using average performance to date, forecasts for the expected total cost of the project can also be made.

In the example

Performance to date (CPI) = 0·88
Budgeted cost for the remaining work = £75,000-£29,150
= £45,850
Estimate to complete (ETC) = £45,850/0·88
= £52,073
Forecast cost at completion (EAC) = £52,073+£33,107
= £85,180

One drawback is that at first sight no forecast can be made for those segments not started, except to take into account the average overall performance. This is where the hierarchical cost account structure permits a logical extrapolative forecast for many cost accounts not yet started. For example, where an organisation is responsible for several cost accounts, performance on their initial cost account can be used to forecast performance in later cost accounts. Admittedly there are many factors to take into account, but the extrapolative forecast is a good starting point and any change in it must be justified. Similarly forecasts of final cost on higher level breakdown structure items, can be based on performance on the early work.

In this example Cost Account 5 is not started but the CPI for the department involved is 0·85. Using this as a measure of future performance the EAC for Cost Account 5 can be forecast as £16,451.

There are thus three methods of forecasting the final project cost, namely

1. The average overall performance to date.
2. Organisational performance.
3. Work breakdown structure performance to date.

In this example, only two methods are used, namely average performance to date on the overall project, and performance by the individual organisation. This gives an EAC of £85,181 and £85,931, respectively, compared to a budgeted figure of £75,000.

This form of performance analysis can be carried out simply and quickly using the computer, with no more data required than that which is normally available. Figure 8.9 shows the layout of a typical computing system, which requires only three raw data files to hold the data involved, and Figure 8.10 shows the contents of these files.

File 1 — contains the simple network data.

File 2 — contains the estimate for each work package, the cost account to which it belongs, and the hierarchical structure of cost accounts.

File 3 — contains the data required to produce a performance report for each period.

The network programme module takes as input File 1 containing activity data as shown, and calculates the time analysis and bar chart. It produces the scheduling data as a report to management, and creates a data file to hold this information for the remaining programming modules. In more realistic cases, manpower data would be used to produce manpower loading details and some rescheduling carried out, before producing the final schedule. The budget programme takes the schedule data held in the file, the estimated cost for each work package, or activity, and the cost account code from File 2 and produces a time-phased budget as shown in Figure 8.2. This can be produced for each work package, cost account, work breakdown structure item and organisational cost account for each time period and on a cumulative basis, that is, BCWS and cumulative BCWS.

Thereafter as actual costs and progress on work packages are reported, the analysis programme calculates the ACWP, BCWP, cost and schedule variances and performance indices, and forecasts of final costs for all cost accounts and the project as a whole as shown in Figures 8.6 and 8.7. This is done simply and automatically involving no more work, or probably less, than is done in manual systems.

This is a simplistic example, but no more data files are required for each activity for a project with several thousand

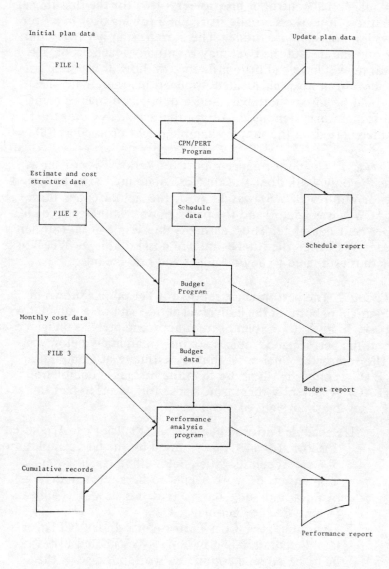

Initial plan data

FILE 1

Update plan data

CPM/PERT Program

Estimate and cost structure data

FILE 2

Schedule data

Schedule report

Budget Program

Monthly cost data

FILE 3

Budget data

Budget report

Performance analysis program

Cumulative records

Performance report

Figure 8.9   Flow chart for computer programs

activities, to produce the same type of performance analysis with the same ease. This type of analysis can give a project manager real control of his project, often for the first time. Without it he is essentially sitting in a rowing boat in a river, with no oars and no rudder. The current simply carries him along and he and the boat may eventually reach his objective, but he will have had little influence on how or when he got there. In more sophisticated applications these data files would be in one data base and a data-based management information system used. A hypothetical analysis for the first three periods in the simple example might proceed as follows.

Period 1. The performance report for Period 1 is not shown, as the only work done was on Cost Account 1. The budgeted expenditure (BCWS) was £5,600; the actual expenditure (ACWP) was £5,550 and the package was estimated to be 80 per cent complete. Thus, earned value was £5,600 (80 per cent of £7,000, the total estimated cost) that is, BCWP. Work is thus estimated to be on budget and on schedule.

Period 2. The performance report for Period 2 is shown in Figure 8.6, both for the individual period and on a cumulative basis. In both, the expenditure is approximately as budgeted and the performance indices are only marginally below par. The forecasted final cost, that is, Estimate at Completion (EAC) is only slightly more than the budget at completion (BAC). Apparently there is no cause for alarm. In fact these are several small signs of problems

1. Schedule Performance Index (SPI) for Cost Account 2 is low at 0·84. This is caused by the late completion of Cost Accounts which delay its start. However, the momentum of work seems to be approximately as planned and budgeted, so that this slow start appears to have been overcome.
2. The cumulative Cost Performance Index (CPI) for Cost Account 1 is now reliably estimated at 0·91, being based on a completed work package. If this is used for Department A's performance, it raises the EAC for its work to £30,010; if used for the project

as a whole it forecasts an EAC on £82,417 which is rather more worrying.

3. The CPI in Period 2 is 0·67 and this abnormally low value is caused by the system correcting for the previous period's optimistic estimate of percent complete of 80 per cent, as against a more realistic value of 72 per cent as can now be estimated with 20-20 hindsight. This demonstrates how the system rapidly corrects and highlights previous optimistic subjective estimates of progress. It also calls into question the reliability of the percent complete estimates of the three work packages that are open in this period. If they are similarly overestimated, then the project is heading for a major over-run. However, it is early days yet, the signs are not conclusive, and the project manager would have difficulty in persuading other people, but at least he would be alerted.

Period 3. The performance report for Period 3 is shown in Figure 8.7 and the problems are now more obvious. Though the rate of expenditure is only slightly below budget, the work achieved for this expenditure is much less than expected. The significant pointers are

1. Both the SPI and CPI for the work done during the period are very low, indicating both that the work on the project is not going well and that the previous period's estimates of completion were highly optimistic.
2. The forecast final cost of the project (EAC) is now £85,131 based on overall performance, or £85,931 based on departmental performance.
3. Both departments' performance are well below par, with Department B's being especially iow at 0·837 for schedule and 0·851 for cost.
4. Work on Cost Account 4 is well behind schedule and well over budget, that is an SPI of 0·7 and a CPI of 0·83.

Thus performance analysis using the earned value concept on cost centres, termed work packages, each looked on as a discrete subcontract, and structured into cost accounts using the work breakdown structure, can provide effective control of projects. The size of the work package can be varied, according to the size of the project and the sophistication of the information system used. The schedule and cost variances, coupled with schedule and cost performance indices give sensitive and reliable indicators of progress achieved against plan and budget. The system also automatically produces forecasts of final cost for parts of the project and the project as a whole. The performance of contributing organisations is automatically monitored and gives an effective feedback to those involved. Hopefully the use of performance analysis will lead to more effective control of projects in the future than in the past.

Project management systems

At first sight the methods of planning, budgeting, analysis and control outlined in these chapters may look too sophisticated and require too much work to be of any practical use in project work. Many project managers may comment that they do not have the time, or the people to carry out these methods, or that they are not appropriate to their size of project, cannot get the kind of information required, or that future events are too uncertain to justify the effort involved.

These comments are basically unjustified in that these methods require no more data than is available for any project, and the effort required of the project manager, or his staff, can be less than that required for the more traditional and less effective methods of planning and control. However, the management of projects is a highly skilled professional branch of management, and the methods used have to be sophisticated to a certain extent, if projects are to be managed efficiently.

One of the secrets of efficient management, planning and control of projects is an effective integrated project management information system based on; the use of the work breakdown structure to structure the project and its systems; the use of the work package concept to ensure objectivity in reporting; the use of forward looking performance analysis, as well as variance analysis where appropriate; and the systematic processing of the data available, whether done manually or by computer.

All project managers must be backed up by effective project systems, as it is impossible to manage a complex entity, such as a project, without planning, budgeting, analysis and control systems to assist the manager in his function. If he does not have this back up, his planning and budgeting will be too slow, and they will not be used to help him organise and control his work. Without a good information system, he cannot really control his project, as he will not know until too late what is happening, must spend a lot of his most valuable and scarcest resource, his time, on simple supervision and the collection of information, and any information he does get will inevitably be out of date.

All project managers do have back-up systems of one kind or another, ranging from the most elementary manual systems to extremely sophisticated computer-based systems. Some of these systems of both types are excellent but others are not worth the effort put into them and sometimes hinder or confuse, instead of helping the project manager. Often the simplest systems are too slow, do not carry out an adequate analysis, even though the raw data is there, and are not organised as an integrated project management information system. In other cases, sophisticated computer-based systems produce piles and piles of data print-out and very little information in a digestible form for the project manager. The computer is used as a high speed typewriter simply to reproduce large amounts of data, or to give a veneer of respectability to unreliable data. This distinction between raw data and the information extracted from it, is critical in project work. There may be from hundreds to tens of thousands of activities involved in a large project, and there can be a tremendous amount of data produced. Unless this data is analysed and filtered in a systematic manner to produce meaningful information for the project manager in a summarised and exception basis, it will snow him under and land up in the wastepaper basket.

There should be at least four subsystems to an integrated project management information system, namely

1. Planning and budgeting.
2. Analysis, reporting and control.
3. Change control.
4. Procurement and expediting.

Although the discussion up to this point has been confined to the first two subsystems, the change control and procurement subsystems are just as essential to successful project management as the others and will be covered in later chapters.

It is essential that the speed of the project manager's planning and budgeting systems must be fast enough to manage the pace of project work, both in the initial stages of the project and in the periodic updating required. In the initial stages, plans and budgets must be established quickly, otherwise decisions will be made and resources allocated without the logical guidance provided by planning and budgeting, and there will be no effective baselines on which to evaluate progress and cost. They must also be able to be used quickly, when changes or deviations occur, to evaluate alternative ways of carrying out the work and keep the control baselines current and up to date.

It must be possible for variance and performance analysis, as described, to be carried out quickly as timeliness is important to allow management to act in time to correct deviations. It is more important to have approximate information quickly, than accurate information when it is too late to do anything about it. The project manager must have information in a summarised form and on an exception basis, on slippages to schedule, variances from budget, delays in procurement and escalation of costs, etc. or he will not be able to manage and control his project. Important points should be highlighted automatically in a digestible form. Once a deviation is identified he must be able to trace it down to its source and produce further information right down to the relevant raw data.

The systems used will vary with the size, complexity and value of the project, but they must always provide these basic essentials. It is not uncommon for project managers to become involved in a 'systems audit' of their own firm's, the clients' or contractors' systems. This is carried to an extreme in the US Department of Defense, Cost /Schedule Control Systems Criteria standards where contractors' systems are evaluated according to 35 criteria.

These systems can be manual or computer based. Manual systems can work effectively with the smaller project, if the system is structured as described in the previous example. Although this information can be produced manually for the small project, as the size of the project increases, manually-based systems become ineffective. The manually-based collection and processing of data, and its analysis to extract information and planning, budgeting and control is tedious, involves considerable manual work, is time consuming, slow and rarely up to date, very inflexible and often inaccurate. It is necessary to use what seems like sophisticated methods to plan and control the larger project and there is a great deal of analysis of data required if the manager is to maintain control. If this has to be done manually, on all but the smaller project, it will simply not be done and effective control of the project work will be lost.

In this computer age it is illogical not to use a computer if it can be of benefit. We use a computer because it allows us to do things that were perhaps not possible before, but much more likely to do things faster and more accurately, particularly if they have to be repeated several times, with far less effort than is required with manual systems. Normally it carries out functions which can be carried out manually but which take considerable time and labour and thus are not done or are not done adequately. With a computer, integrated project management information systems become reality for even the smaller firm. Even a simple PET personal microcomputer costing £700 can carry out computer-based budgeting and analysis effectively for smaller projects. If a firm is handling projects involving more than one or two hundred activities, it must really use a computer for planning and control analysis. At the very least the modern microprocessor-based microcomputers can handle one to two thousand activities, and if larger networks are involved, project planning and hence effective project management is impossible without using a computer. The cheapest system is based on the PET personal computer which costs approximately £2,500 for a complete system consisting of the microcomputer, a pair of floppy disks and a printer. This is less than the annual cost of a labourer and extends the availability of computer-based systems to even the smallest of firms. A larger system can be based on more powerful microcomputers such as the Cromemco System 3 which costs about £5,000 for a complete system, but is more flexible and has a greater capacity.

Figure 8.9 shows an integrated project management information system, as mounted on a Cromemco System 3 microcomputer set up to handle a network of up to 2,000 activities. There are three programmes in this system

1. A network, or critical path analysis programme.
2. A budget programme (a) labour manhours and money, (b) materials and equipment.
3. A performance analysis programme.

Initially the network data is processed by the planning programme to produce

1. A time analysis.
2. A bar chart, including total float.
3. Manpower table and histogram.

These can be produced for the project as a whole, for any specific trade and responsibility code. Then either automatic or interactive resource levelling can be carried out to match the plan to the manpower and equipment restraints. This can then be modified interactively as desired to establish schedule starts and finishes to those activities which are not restrained by other factors to give a definitive plan or schedule for the project, both as the printed report and as a data file for further processing.

For each plan update, information as to the actual starts and finishes of activities can be input, and if required the above process repeated to produce an updated plan. Options are available to produce a free float consumption report, a milestone report and manpower S charts.

The schedule data file and a file containing the estimate data and cost account structure can then be input to the budget programme to produce a cash budget and a manpower budget for activities, work packages, basic cost accounts and the hierarchical cost accounts as desired. This gives printed reports and a budget data file for further processing in the performance analysis programme.

At each reporting period data and cost to date together with the budget and schedule files are used to produce variance and performance analysis reports as described previously. Very little effort and no more data are required than with traditional methods to use this integrated project management information system, which can effectively enhance real time planning and control of projects at a cost most firms can afford.

Project reports

The principal time that this analytical effort is applied to the control process is for the periodic project report. The reporting period for projects can vary with the stage of the work, but the normal period used for reporting is one month. This is not to say that the process of analysis and reporting should be confined to the monthly report time. When there is an important development on a project such as the discovery of a significant design problem, or a failure of an important piece of equipment, which would set the project back by several months; or an industrial strike, this should be reported immediately. One firm uses a red-bordered reporting form for this initial problem report, sometimes termed a 'Red Bandit' to provide early visibility of potential problems and expeditious management response.

Many people complain about the labour involved in preparing these monthly reports and consider them a waste of valuable time. In fact these reports are not only an extremely important link in the control cycle of a project, but lead to the more effective management of a project in several ways. The discipline of formal reporting compels all the managers involved to sit back, take stock and measure progress, assemble and analyse facts and figures and crystallise opinions. Project reports should be built up in a fast hierarchical process with

227

all the significant managers responsible for segments of projects making reports for their particular area of responsibility in such a manner that they are built into the project manager's report. This then forces everyone involved to use their brains and imagination to achieve insights on the progress and problems involved in their project, to lift their eyes from day to day problems and to look ahead. It may be that the only time they perform the real function of a manager rather than just acting as glorified firefighters is during the few hours they take once a month to analyse and report progress. This discipline of formal reporting is essential to good project management.

The principal purpose of the project monthly report is to ensure control analysis and actions are carried out and to communicate information on the progress and problems of the project to senior management and to all those involved in the project. It highlights and gives a brief description of the status of the project, reports the results of variance and performance analysis in terms of time, money and manpower, shows the present status of the project plan, reports significant events and any changes to estimate and budget. It should in particular identify problems and the steps taken to overcome them.

These reports also perform secondary, but important functions. They are a means of maintaining the involvement of all those concerned in a project by keeping them informed of progress. By circulating these reports to everyone concerned on the project they can be kept in the picture, see how what they are doing fits into the overall work and thus help to motivate them, achieve better co-ordination of work and maintain a good team spirit.

Reports are also one of the ways a project manager can achieve and maintain his authority and influence over the people from organisations contributing to his project. The fact that he automatically has the 'ear' of senior management through this report and that deviations from an agreed plan, manpower commitment and budget are picked up and reported, greatly increases his control authority in a matrix organisation. This need not necessarily be an explicit expression of power, but is implicit in the running of 'tight' systems.

This monthly report also forms a historical record of the project, its management, plan and cost, and it makes it possible to analyse and determine what happened in the project. This contributes to the better management, planning, estimating, budgeting and control of future projects as without this record, all too often important experience is lost.

Format of the report

Reports should be uniform in style and format, to simplify comparison with previous reports and with reports on other projects. The US Department of Defense has extremely formalised reporting formats termed Cost Performance Reporting (CPR). These reports should contain the following three sections

1. Summary.
2. Written progress report.
3. Back up data, charts, tables and photographs.

The summary action of the report will be the most widely read part and the most important section for communication purposes. It should be short, one or two pages long, and cover the main points of the overall report. This not only enables senior management to quickly review progress and performance, but also gives the project manager a place to express the more intangible opinions he has about his project, for example, hunches, or the first small signs of an adverse trend.

The main body of the report covers a written description, the general state of the project as a whole and the principal sections of it. It highlights the exception performance reports, forecasts of final cost and completion dates, significant developments, important decisions taken, problems encountered and corrective action taken.

The data section of the report includes details of the variance and performance reports, as outlined previously, S charts, updated summary plans and milestone schedules, manpower charts and details of changes to the project. In construction projects it should also contain one or more coloured photographs of the construction site, taken from the same viewpoint each month to show visible evidence of progress.

In addition to these monthly reports, it is essential that a final report is made at the end of a project. This report should not just be a summary of the final results, but should be based on a full 'post mortem' (perhaps post-audit is a less emotive term) analysis of performance on the project. It is important that a full and frank analysis is made of what happened on the project, the effectiveness of planning, estimating, analysis and control methods, what went wrong, what went right, the mistakes made and the achievements. All too often valuable experience is lost, or not communicated, and the personnel involved rationalise their experience, make the same mistakes on the next project and do not improve their systems. This should not be a witch hunt or an attempt to find scapegoats, or an attempt to put as good a light as possible on project performance, but an effort to learn from what happened so that a better job can be done on the next project. Normally by the time a large project is completed, most of those involved have been reassigned to other projects, but it is well worthwhile to gather them together for a day to carry out this post audit analysis.

File 1. - Plan Data

Tail No.	Head No.	Duration	Description
1	2	5	A
2	3	7	B
2	4	8	C
2	5	5	D
3	7	10	E
4	7	2	F
5	6	7	G
6	7	4	H
7	8	6	I
8	9	4	J

N.B. This data file can be extended to include all the items in Fig. 5.1

File 2 - Cost & Coding Data

			Cost Code	
Tail No.	Head No.	Estimate £	Field 1	Field 2
1	2	7000	1	1
2	3	9000	2	1
2	4	10000	3	2
2	5	6000	4	2
3	7	12000	2	1
4	7	3000	3	2
5	6	9000	4	2
6	7	5000	4	2
7	8	8000	5	2
8	9	6000	5	2

Field 1 identifies Cost Account that the work package belongs to.
Field 2 identifies Department that the work package belongs to.
This simplistic cost code can be expanded with additional fields
to include more structural information.

Field 3 - Progress Data for Period 3

Tail No.	Head No.	ACWP	% Complete
1	2	0	100
2	3	5100	85
2	4	6000	85
2	5	3540	1000
3	7	0	0
4	7	0	0
5	6	0	0
6	7	0	0
7	8	0	0
8	9	0	0

Actual cost of work performed (ACWP) is the cost incurred in
Period 3.

Figure 8.10   Data files for simple example

9 Additional Factors in the Control of Projects

Introduction

There are a number of aspects of project control which are not covered by the conventional planning, analysis and control cycle concept, and are often not carried out by many firms. The traditional emphasis on control, as described in the last chapter, is to 'control to plan and budget'. In practice this is inadequate on its own, and may be essentially likened to 'closing the stable door after the horse has bolted'. Conventional control systems must be supplemented by attention to other practices and systems, and thus this chapter discusses the following additional factors influencing efficiency and control of projects.

Cost consciousness in design. One of the factors with considerable influence over the eventual cost of the project is the basic project scope and design, as this 'sets' the eventual cost of the project, and all that conventional control practices can do is to ensure good performance.

Change control system. Another important factor leading to late completion of the project, low productivity and cost escalation is design changes.

Labour productivity. One factor influencing the cost and time to completion of projects, particularly construction projects, is labour productivity. Although the main treatment of labour productivity in construction work falls more into the realm of construction management or industrial relations, the efficiency of project management can significantly influence it.

Cost consciousness in design

Traditionally the emphasis of cost control has been on the construction, or manufacturing phases of a project, with emphasis on labour productivity and fundamental management efficiency. This is illogical in the extreme, and attention to cost control must commence much earlier in the project life cycle.

The actual distribution of cost between phases of the project will vary from project to project and industry to industry, but the general shape of the cost distribution curve is often similar to that shown in Figure 9.1. The principal phases of a project and the approximate percentage of project cost incurred in each of them are:

1. Project evolution and preliminary design — 2 per cent (1 per cent — 5 per cent)
2. Design engineering — 13 per cent (8 per cent — 20 per cent)
3. Purchased materials and equipment — 55 per cent (40 per cent — 70 per cent)
4. Construction or manufacturing — 35 per cent (15 per cent — 45 per cent)

This rough distribution of cost between phases has the same general pattern for the construction and manufacturing industries, except that for long manufacturing runs, the proportion given to evolution and design engineering is reduced. In some projects, operation and maintenance costs must also be taken into consideration by one or more of the parties involved, that is, Life Cycle Costing (LCC), and these may dwarf the actual cost of the project, for example, chemical plants, military aircraft systems.

If we consider that a combination of management efficiency of functional management and labour productivity can vary the costs of each phase by a plus or minus 10 per cent, theoretically the difference between good and bad performance in the construction or manufacturing phase is only 7 per cent of the total project cost. However, if the same concept is applied to purchasing, the difference between good and bad performance is 11 per cent, half as much again;

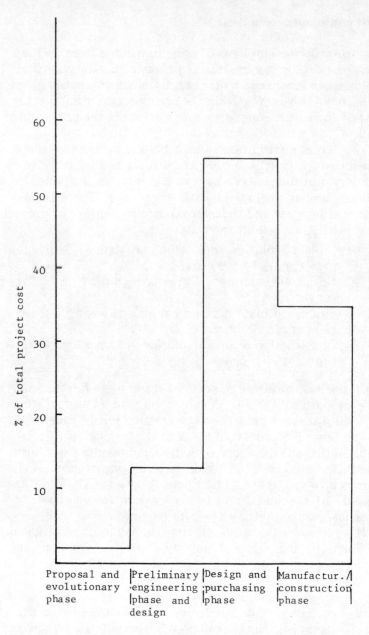

Figure 9.1   Distribution of project cost between phases

therefore, efficiency in purchasing is as important, if not more important, than efficiency in manufacturing or construction. (Unfortunately, in construction work the minus 10 per cent figure is often exceeded.)

Thus management efficiency and labour productivity undoubtedly can influence the cost of each phase, but the main influences on what could be called the basic cost of a project are the decisions made and work done in the early stages, that is, the project evolution and preliminary design, and engineering design phases. No matter how efficient or inefficient the construction or manufacturing phases are, the basic cost of the project has largely been determined by decisions taken in the preceding stages. The key decision-making phases of a project are the project evolution and the design phases. The 10 per cent — 15 per cent of the overall cost of the project expended in these phases basically determines the cost of the following stages. Control on the other phases of procurement and construction are more concerned with performance than with decision making. Figure 9.2 shows the relative influence of each phase on the basic cost of a project.

The importance of decisions taken in the early stages on the cost of the project cannot be exaggerated. The 2 per cent or so of the project cost spent on the preliminary design largely determines the cost of the remaining 98 per cent of the work, and tends to lock the firm into many of the essential cost elements of the project, which can then only be trimmed by further control effort. Similarly the 13 per cent or so spent in detailed design engineering can strongly influence the cost of the remaining 85 per cent of the project. Thus great emphasis must be given to cost control, or to give it a more meaningful definition, cost minimisation, in the early stages and this involves four factors, namely

1. Cost consciousness of all those concerned.
2. Company standards.
3. Design optimisation — 'design to cost'.
4. The early implementation of an effective change control system.

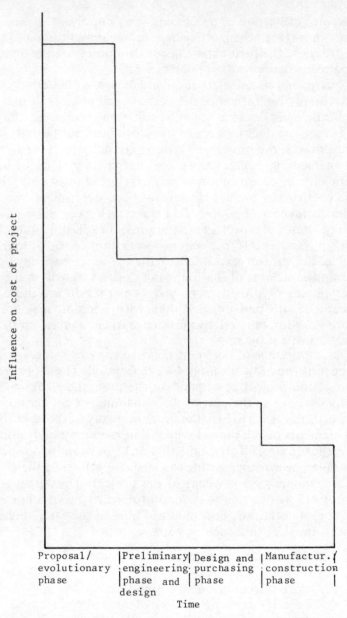

Figure 9.2   Relative influence of each phase on basic cost
             of the project

236

Cost consciousness

The preliminary and over-riding need is for the introduction and maintenance of cost consciousness throughout the project, but principally for the motivation of the engineering designers and draughtsmen. The many daily decisions they make, both large and small, are all reflected in the final cost. The company's management in general, and the project manager in particular, have to ensure the training and motivation of all the personnel involved in a project is directed towards cost limitation. This is essentially a general management function to ensure that all personnel involved, have as one of their objectives, not only satisfactory technical and schedule performance, but also the minimising of the cost of the project. In project work there is always a definite objective, with defined technical requirements, desired completion dates and maximum economic costs, all of which are influenced or controlled by outside market requirements. In these three objectives there is room for trade off and compromise; there are minimum technical requirements and desirable ones, in which if there is a saving in time and money, there may be some reduction. Similarly, it may be possible to allow more time, if it saves money, or conversely, it may be worthwhile to spend more money to gain time. These factors should be known by the project manager and communicated to all the personnel involved. It should be used by him to effect compromises to gain the overall balanced success of the project. Thus, the project team should know the money value of time and technical performance.

However, one difficulty in control is that the motivation of most functional personnel is the technical success of their part of the project. If they have to take a decision between a design with some element of risk, or a more expensive safe one, they will inevitably choose the safer unless some other influence is involved; they will tend to add a little bit here, a little bit there, a spare pump, a larger pipe size, a higher quality design, etc. There must be a balanced attitude between time, cost and technical performance. This attitude of mind is one of the best cost control tools and cost control engineers, systems, etc., can only supplement the efforts of all the personnel involved with the project and design, purchasing, construction and contractors, and if cost consciousness is not part of their philosophy then cost control will be ineffective.

Contractors designing a fixed cost turn-key plant with control over design and specification, have most experience of cost minimisation design. Normally a client, or his agent has produced a preliminary design, or perhaps a full design and a set of working specifications, which 'set' the cost of a project. These, in many cases, tend to produce a 'gold plate' design. An engineer's whole philosophy is against producing a minimum design and specification, that is, a 'poor boy' design. However, the difference in cost between a 'normal' design and a minimum design can be 15–30 per cent of the overall cost.

Company standards

Influencing the cost of many projects is the high standards, specifications or policies used by many large companies. Though the project design team may avoid many factors which lead to over-design, or a gold plated plant, they may also use without a second thought books of standard specifications for detailed work which, more or less, lay down the law 'thou shalt use. . .'.

More often than not these specifications have been established by design engineers with a view to having a high quality project or product. These standards can adversely affect the cost of the project, with sometimes no real advantage in quality. Standards, specification and policies should be questioned from time to time as to whether some cheaper alternatives would not be adequate for the job in hand and value analysis applied whenever possible.

Very often firms that manufacture for the nuclear industry, or the military, find it very difficult to compete for commercial contracts, because a philosophy of high quality has been accepted as a norm from the managing director to welders on the shop floor. Contractors very often complain of client companies who insist on certain policies or standards, when the contractor points out cheaper satisfactory alternatives. For example, one contractor commented that his client insisted on a certain type of large centrifugal compressor and its housing in a specific way, when he had pointed out that they had just installed a cheaper, perfectly satisfactory alternative for another firm which cost 20 per cent less.

This emphasis on cost control as applied to cost consciousness, standards and specifications should also be extended to the drawing office. Through force of habit many draughtsmen use details that lead to high material, construction and manufacturing labour costs without often being aware of the cost effect of their methods or the alternatives available to them. It is often ironic that a stroke of a draughtsman's pen, symbolically speaking, can add as much to the cost of the project as a main design decision or poor management performance. If the cost conscious draughtsman is given the job to review finished drawings to look for possible cost savings, he can normally always find areas in which substantial savings, or minor savings which repeated many times can lead to major savings, can be found.

Thus there is the need to review the firm's policies, standards and specifications, together with its drawing office practices from a point of view of cost minimisation; that is, a value analysis approach. This is not to pare specifications to the bone, such that operating costs and plant life are affected, though this has been done in the past, but more to establish what are satisfactory cost conscious specifications and practices, which are adequate for the job, but not over adequate.

Design optimisation/design to cost

It is generally possible to carry out a cost review of a completed design and/or set of drawings and find many savings. Familiarity with a design, plus the motivation of looking at it from a cost point of view, instead of principally a technical point of view, can generally identify areas where money can be saved by simple changes. This is carried out by some contractors and clients, but is more generally found when 'design to cost' principles are used. There is a growing tendency both in the construction and manufacturing industries to specify a cost for a project, or product, prior to starting work on it. Design to cost can be formally defined as:

'The practice of pre-determining the project, or product, cost necessary to achieve a profitable business venture, and then designing the project or product to achieve the required schedule and performance objectives at or below this cost.'

Essentially the main tool in designed cost (DTC) practice is the 'iteration' of the design. Once the first attempt at design is completed, it is reviewed for likely areas of cost saving. Generally it is not possible to save money on all areas, and attention should be placed on those parts of the design with high cost implications, that is, Pareto analysis; 20 per cent of the design may account for 80 per cent of the cost. Design teams can then review or revise the design of these high cost areas to try to reduce the cost by some target figure, say 10 per cent. This exercise can be repeated one or more times, usually with real but diminishing returns at each design iteration. Of course, this takes time, money and delays the project completion and normally one or two iterations are all that are generally possible, but they can save money by this optimisation of the design. Spending one or two per cent more of the project cost on the preliminary and basic design phases can often save 10 per cent on the total project cost. In particular if life cycle cost (LCC) is taken into account, that is, the cost of long production runs in manufacturing products, or operation and maintenance in plant projects, the expenditure of more time and money in the initial design stage can be well worthwhile, that is, trading recurring costs for non-recurring cost.

Often if savings on DTC are critical, that is, in tendering and competitive conditions to ensure competitive product prices, or because of budget limitations, changes in project scope or product specifications may have to be made during these iterations. For example, in military contracts the last 10 per cent of performance may or may not be critical, but it can account for 50 per cent of the cost. If these can be relaxed, substantial savings can often be made.

Control of changes to a project

One of the identifiable common causes of delay, cost escalation and low labour productivity are changes to the project. Many, many projects take longer and cost more than necessary because of changes and additions to the original scope. It is quite common for changes to a project to add anything up to 50 per cent to the project cost and not unusual for them to add more. Thus one of the most important and, unfortunately, unpleasant and troublesome functions of a project manager is to control the changes to the project. Changes have the following detrimental effect on performance in project work, namely

1. They increase the cost.
2. They cause delay.
3. They reduce morale and productivity.
4. They worsen relationships among those involved.

Changes in design in project work normally lead to additional cost and time to completion. In addition to this extra cost and time, which may or may not be justified, design changes during the engineering and construction phases cost more and the work takes longer than the same work would have if it had been included in the original project specification. This is because, in addition to work having to be redone, the sequence of work is disrupted; not only must the design of the particular item concerned be changed, but all those items interrelated to it be changed too. At the construction stage, changes are more costly still, because work, materials and equipment may have to be scrapped and design, materials purchasing and construction work must often also be done on a rush basis.

Though changes have a detrimental effect on morale and efficiency in general, this effect is multiplied in the manufacturing and construction phases. Whenever work has to be torn down or scrapped and repeated, labour morale and productivity is affected and this can lead to long-term effects not the least in the area of industrial relations.

One of the worse effects of changes is their effect on relationships between the project manager or managers, and other managers on the project. It is the project manager's responsibility to resist changes unless they are absolutely essential to the objectives of the projects and in the company's interests. This forces him into conflict in two ways. If the project manager is in the owner company, he must resist changes arising from his own company's managers, and also negotiate changes with any contractors involved. Changes, as mentioned previously, disrupt the design and construction work and are more costly than just the work directly involved. Thus the actual cost of changes is much higher than the work itself would make them, and they are a very difficult thing to estimate accurately and to negotiate. In addition, there are often legitimate differences of opinion as to what is actually a change to the contract, or what the cause and effect are. Some contractors also tend to over charge for extras, and make a significant percentage of their profits in this way. It is therefore often very difficult to disentangle these factors, and this uncertainty can cause differences of opinion and hence conflict. Probably the worst of these effects is on the project manager's relationship with other managers in his own company, be it client or contractor. The differences of opinion and conflict that occur have often to be resolved at a very senior level in the companies involved.

Changes may occur at any stage during the project and can arise for several reasons, namely

1. Changes in the specifications or scope of the project during the development stages. Changes to design occur legitimately in these stages, but often complex changes in scope or specification are proposed and accepted implicitly without adequate evaluation of the consequences in terms of time and money. Once the project specification and cost have been approved, changes in scope are very expensive and have a questionable value.
2. Late design changes are the most troublesome and

expensive changes of all. They normally arise out of errors and omissions in the original design work, afterthoughts, and from the client company attempting to keep up to date and incorporating the latest developments in technology. There is little alternative to incorporating changes to correct errors and omissions, but afterthoughts and changes to keep up to date are a bone of contention in project work.

3. Changes due to safety or legal requirements — here again there is little alternative but to include these changes in the project.

4. Changes which are justified or appear to be justified to improve the rate of return. The advisability of these kinds of changes is debatable. The fact that a certain addition to a project is estimated to give a 30 per cent internal rate of return may not be sufficient justification to include it. Whether or not to accept this type of change should be a matter of top company policy. One view is that they are not acceptable because this type of forecast rate of return is often inaccurate and biased; estimates of the cost of changes are very difficult to make, as discussed previously, and thus the rate of return is also difficult to estimate. More importantly, if the project is, say, to build an oil refinery at a certain capacity, changes of this kind do not usually add any overall significant advantage on a company or market basis, and the objective should always be to carry out the company's top level objectives as cheaply as possible, consistent with satisfactory time and technical performance. Many worthwhile projects have been failures because of additions of this nature. If spare capacity is worthwhile, this should be a top level management decision and not some design engineer adding a slightly larger size of equipment.

5. Changes which are thought desirable. This is a real area of conflict, particularly within companies. Operating managers would like certain additions for various reasons, sometimes worthwhile, sometimes simply luxuries; design engineers would like to add

243

certain features, upgrade others or increase some equipment sizes. The project manager has to resist this type of change and he must establish a clear definition between 'musts' and 'wants', and only accept changes that must be made to meet the original scope and safety standards, that is, 'musts'.

In order to control change, and reduce the conflict within and between companies, the project manager should endeavour to achieve the following

1. Implicit backing up by senior management of his efforts to resist non-essential changes. The policies on changes to increase the rate of return on projects should be spelt out by senior management. If this is permitted, the rate of return used should be significantly higher than that used as a cut-off point for normal company projects. As far as is possible a policy should be established and communicated by senior management on musts and wants. In other words, senior management must back up the project manager by saying 'no' to changes which are desirable, but not essential.

2. The original scope and specifications of the project should be as clear as possible. Factors like the policy of whether or not to allow for some spare capacity to allow for expansion should be spelled out by senior management.

3. At some clearly defined stage, no further changes must be permitted, excepting those that are absolutely essential for the success or safety of a project; that is, the project must be 'frozen' at some stage. The project manager would like this to be frozen at the development stage, but other managers would prefer it to be frozen at the construction or manufacturing stage. The earlier it is frozen, the lower the cost and the delay to the project caused by changes.

4. Finally, a change control system must be set up.

Change control systems

In order to identify, analyse and control changes to a project, the project manager must set up a system to handle these changes. This sytem must

1. Identify changes from the original scope.
2. Forecast their cost and their effect on other work and the time required for them.
3. Subject them to managerial analysis and decision.
4. Record actual figures on them.
5. Highlight them to senior management.
6. Set up a system for solving disputes with the minimum of conflict.
7. See that the changes are implemented.

The implementation of a change control system, sometimes termed 'trend forecasting', 'deviation control' or 'configuration control' early in the project life is critical. Such systems must emphasise periodic weekly or monthly reviews during the formative design and procurement stages of a project. Control is made effective during these phases by frequent reporting of changes and by the communication of change notices to key people, so that full consideration can be given to the necessity of the requested changes and their effect on cost and time.

This system must be a dynamic technique of estimate and specification revision, by which the effect of departures from the basis of the estimate and specifications are identified as they occur, and adjustments are made to the control estimate being used at that particular stage of the project. This enables those in control of the project not only to see the effect of change on schedules and cost much more quickly than previous techniques allowed, but also it enables them to consider corrective action, and in many cases to take such action at a time when alternative courses of action are still feasible to counter the effects of adverse variations. Thus a change control system must be considered to be a system of continually identifying changes, or deviations as they occur, from the conditions or facts assumed in the project estimate and specification baselines and of taking corrective action where applicable to counter the effect of adverse change on the cost or schedule.

Change control systems have evolved in different ways with different jargon in industrial projects and in advanced technology industries, primarily the aerospace weapons industry. In this industry change control is called 'configuration control' and is just one part of what is termed 'configuration management'. Although this is an esoteric term for construction projects, it is widely used in advanced technology projects and implies a formalised discipline for providing uniform product descriptions, status records and reports. Configuration management is essentially the formalisation of a discipline which integrates the technical and administrative actions of identifying, documenting, controlling and reporting the functional and physical characteristics of a product or project during its life cycle and of controlling changes to these characteristics. Thus configuration management is a more embracing term than change control system and has more emphasis on the initial structuring of a project and on an engineering change control system to ensure the product produced is the product desired. However, configuration control and change control systems are more or less identical processes involving the following steps

1. Establishing a baseline scope, specification, estimate, and schedule for the project.
2. Identifying changes to this baseline, communicating them to all concerned and determining their consequences.
3. Reviewing, approving or rejecting these changes.
4. Implementing these changes.

Establishing a baseline

A change control system should be implemented as soon as the initial scope, specification and estimate of cost has been defined. It does not matter how preliminary this scope and estimate are, they must be used as a basis for identifying changes, evaluating their consequences and controlling them. As more information becomes available, as previously described, the project scope, specifications, plan and estimate will become more refined and at each stage will form a baseline for the future control of changes.

The change control system should enable management to trace the reasons for the differences in estimates made at varying stages in the project. Often the question is asked by a client or contractor's management 'How did a £10M estimate at an earlier stage come to be a £15M estimate at this stage?' As described in the chapter on estimating, the quality of an estimate depends to a large extent on the amount of engineering that forms the basis for that estimate. As engineering progresses, better quality estimates can be made. A change control system bridges the time gap between a lower quality of estimate, based on less well-defined engineering, and the higher quality of estimate that results from more detailed engineering. Typically on important projects, a design specification is written at a relatively early stage, to define the particular design that had to be used in the project. An estimate is made of the cost of this plant and approvals are sought and obtained. Let us assume that this point in time is point A. Additional engineering must be put into the project. The detailed process design is developed and mechanical specifications are completed to the point where a fixed price competitive bid can be requested. A new estimate, on the basis of this greater engineering definition, is made at point B in time.

A–B thus represents the time interval during which the detailed design was carried out and could represent anything from several months to several years. Unless there is a good estimating technique, combined with a change control system, the project could easily get out of control. The change control system prevents this happening and makes it possible to trace the reasons for the differences in the two estimates.

Identifying changes

Before changes to the project can be controlled they first must be recognised. A change or deviation is identified as a noticeable departure from the control estimate, specification or schedule. It may be favourable or unfavourable. A change

247

occurs when any factor including design, but not limited to design, varies appreciably from the control. Thus a change in process sequence or addition of an extra pump or deletion of a pump, or an increase in the price of materials, or delay in construction, all represent changes. Similarly, a more complex design than that estimated for, represents a change.

Recognition of deviations can best be made by those parties directly connected with the details of the project. An estimator can notice a change from the assumptions he originally made. A design engineer knows when the scope is changed, or when he has to add equipment not originally felt necessary. The project manager is not only constantly aware of pressure for change, but should be aware also of general price increases. The important point is that everyone must conscientiously be on the lookout for deviations to the project and that it must be a co-operative endeavour since no one person can identify all the changes that can occur. Thus it is the responsibility of everyone involved in the project to bring to the project management's attention any change from the accepted baseline of the project. This must be done by the individual who first becomes aware of any change, as soon as he becomes aware of it, by making up a Change Request form and submitting it to a Change Control Group meeting for approval and further action. One example of such a Change Request form is shown in Figure 9.3. This form

Identifies the change, describes it and gives the cost account, work package or cost control number it affects.
Gives the reason for the change.
Identifies who is initiating or requesting the change and provides for his signature.
Gives a first descriptive appreciation of the consequences of the change and the segments of the project it affects.
Gives a rough estimate of the effect on the project schedule.
Gives an order of cost estimate of its effect on cost.
Can optionally give a code number to identify the base cause of the change for post-project analysis, for example, customer request, late design change, error/omission in design, legal, environmental reasons, increase in economic return.

248

```
                        CHANGE REQUEST      Number: ................
                                            Revision: ..............
PROJECT:                                    Date: ..................


ITEM AFFECTED:    Name:
                  Work package:
                  Item No(s):
                  Change requested by:


DESCRIPTION OF CHANGE:



REASON FOR CHANGE:

                                                  Code:

ITEMS/AREAS AFFECTED BY CHANGE



INITIAL ESTIMATE OF COST/SAVING*              FIRM ESTIMATE:

EFFECT ON SCHEDULE:



REMARKS:



CHANGE APPROVED/REJECTED* - CONTRACTOR'S SIGNATURE: ..................

                                            DATE:

                               CLIENT'S SIGNATURE: ..................
      *delete one                           DATE:
```

Figure 9.3   Change request form

Additionally, it provides space for

A firmer estimate of cost and time.
A record of approval or rejection of the change.

Change control board meeting

All the above change request forms would be submitted to a change control board chaired by the project manager and made up of key managers on the project. This should meet frequently, at least once a week in the formative stages of the project, and be a limited attendance 'stand-up' meeting concerned more with communicating changes rather than problem-solving.

At this meeting, which should not take more than a half hour, those parties working directly on the design, estimating and control, table anticipated and potential changes known to them, by using the change request form, that have not previously been tabled, or that they have changed since last being tabled.

Subsequent to this meeting, the cost control or estimating representative assesses the guestimated costs, properly estimates the changes having a significant effect, allocates a serial number to the change and passes the form to the project manager. He also prepares a summary report showing the effect on the estimate of all probable and potential changes to that date. The base estimate as revised by the changes can be considered to be the current most probable cost of the project.

Thereafter it is the project manager's responsibility to ensure that all groups affected by the change know about it. More importantly, he must review the change in conjunction with only the relevant people concerned and come to a joint decision on the acceptance or rejection of the change, or send it back for consideration of other alternatives. The project monthly report should then include

1. A list of changes arising in that month with their probable cost.
2. A summary of changes to date on the project.

Such a system has been found to have the following benefits.

It provides a realistic and current most probable cost and schedule for the project and thus avoids periodic drastically changed forecasts.

It identifies potential changes of questionable value, which in turn can be eliminated by good control procedures.

It identifies areas where corrective action should be initiated to counter adverse changes.

It establishes a disciplined approach to change in cost factors.

It makes all personnel more aware of the effect of change and its economic impact on the project.

It provides a means of subsequently analysing all changes as to cause and effect, so that future projects can be better planned and estimated.

It stops the acceptance of changes requested verbally and requires those requesting a change to make it legal and official by signing for it. If they are reluctant to do so then the need for the change is highly questionable. This removes a common cause of conflict in project work, as very often over the long life of a project, even with no intention of deception, memories fade and people forget about changes they requested informally.

Productivity

Another vital factor influencing the success or failure of a project is the level of productivity obtained in the manufacturing and/or construction phases of the project. In manufacturing projects this is a relatively stable factor, but in construction projects, site productivity is much more volatile and has been an important factor in cost escalation and delays in the completion of large projects. Management must be constantly on the alert to correct any factor leading to low productivity, as one truism about project work that exists is that 'once productivity is reduced, it can rarely be recovered.' Thus any one incident, leading to low productivity, not only reduces labour productivity directly, but its effects may be multiplied for the life of the project.

Though the management of site productivity falls mainly into the realm of construction management, project management does influence it strongly, and thus the factors which determine site productivity in construction work must be understood by project managers. There are three groups of factors which influence labour productivity in construction work and which interact with each other.

1. A basic attitude to work held by the workforce.
2. Industrial relations.
3. Construction and project management competence.

All too often the total blame for low labour productivity is given to industrial relations. For example, the UK Central Electricity Generating Board (CEGB) 1979 Annual Report blames the delays on their eight large power stations under construction on low labour productivity on site, poor industrial relations and squabbles over leap-frogging of pay rates.

This is a simplification of the problem and managerial competence also has an influence over site productivity. To put these factors into perspective, the CEGB also reports that in one of their power stations 23 months delay was attributed to labour and productivity problems and 47 months delay to technical design and safety difficulties.

Basic attitude to work

The initial attitude to work, essentially the base level of productivity of the worker on a construction site, is determined by many factors outside any individual project manager's influence. There is an accepted 'fair day's work', which is a norm which varies with time and the region, or country, the construction site is located in. It is difficult to improve on this norm, but very easy to reduce it by managerial incompetence and industrial relations problems. This basic level of productivity will also vary with the life cycle of the construction phase of the project, being higher at the start, when fewer men are employed, declining to a 'standard' level for the major phase of the construction and declining to a lower level near the end, when men are looking over their shoulders for the next job and pacing this one out as long as possible.

Industrial relations

The state of industrial relations at national, industry and regional level, and specific to the individual construction site, is a crucial factor influencing productivity. Given today's state of industrial relations, good management cannot guarantee good industrial relations, but on the other hand poor management whether it be construction or project management, does more or less guarantee bad industrial relations and low labour productivity. In general, management is in competition for the loyalty of its work force with militant elements, and all too often seems to drive its labour force into the arms of these militants. This is particularly so when the labour force loses its respect for the competence of its management.

One critical factor leading to industrial unrest on large multi-contractor construction sites is that very often earnings, conditions and fringe benefits are subject to wide disparities. Though incentive payments can marginally improve the basic level of productivity, they are a source of conflict as highlighted in the UK experience on the Isle of Grain power station contract. Different levels of incentive payments for employees of different contractors on the same site leads to leap-frogging pay claims, haphazard local bargaining and much ill-feeling. This topic in itself could justify a separate book, without coming up with any specific solutions.

Attempts to overcome this problem involve both individual site and national negotiations. On some sites, attempts are made to establish a 'federal site based understanding between the principal contractors' designed to ensure that disparities in pay and conditions do not occur. At national level, negotiations between employers' organisations, the principal unions involved in construction work and important clients with an interest in large sites, are attempting to produce national agreements covering wages and conditions.

253

National and local agreements, or accepted practices, that is, working 'rules' also affect productivity, e.g. the proportion of supporting labourers to craftsmen required, demarcation rules, breaks and number of foremen. This problem exists just as acutely in the USA as in the UK, with the difference that in the USA the rule book tends to be more clearly specified and disputes are usually resolved by semi-legal arbitration, rather than prolonged strikes.

The size of a project can also influence the base level of productivity, primarily through the limits of managerial competence in handling large projects, but also due to the large number of men employed. The more men employed, the more likelihood of industrial relations troubles, perhaps coming from one small group of men, but due to the interaction between groups and competitive factors between them, spreading throughout the site. Productivity also varies on large sites extending over a wide area, where it is difficult to supervise groups of men in widely spread out situations. It also varies with whether the labour force is permanently employed by the contractors involved, or is transient.

Productivity and industrial relations are also affected by the level of activity for the men employed. If there is plenty of work about for the craftsmen on other projects, labour turnover, wage demands and attitudes to work will be affected detrimentally. If there is high unemployment in the construction industry, workers will be reluctant to finish the project and productivity will suffer.

The geographic situation of a site will also have an effect on productivity with different base levels, attitudes to work and potential for industrial relations troubles being influenced by whether the site is in a foreign country, an industrialised area, in a remote area necessitating a site camp, or on a North Sea oil platform. All these factors must be taken into account in the actions of construction and project management, and the level of productivity must be estimated for effective planning and budgeting of the project. However, the actions of both construction and project management have a supreme influence over productivity directly and indirectly through their effects on industrial relations.

Managerial competence of construction management is important and often limits the size of contracts awarded on large projects. There are varying limits to the number of men and complexity of work that many contractors' management and supervisors can effectively handle. Thus often a large number of individual contracts are awarded on one large site, each with a manageable size of labour force, but this leads to problems of leap-frogging payment claims and overall co-ordination. When few contractors are involved on a large site, overall co-ordination is easier, but this puts a premium on good site management by the individual contractors. Unfortunately, experience to date is that the site management of many contracting firms have difficulty in handling the size of work force necessary. In addition, this small group of prime contractors often has to employ large numbers of subcontractors and this gives the same problems as before.

Thus good construction management is essential to ensuring satisfactory labour productivity on site, but unfortunately project management very often does not give construction management a fair chance to achieve good performance. Many of the pertinent decisions are taken before construction management becomes involved, and effective construction management is heavily influenced by the work done before the construction stage and by the overall planning, control and co-ordination of project management. Very often great pressure is put on construction management to increase the intensity of work and the length of the standard work week on a construction site to catch up lost time. It is very difficult to expedite a well-run construction site, but it is very easy to reduce productivity to abysmal levels by trying to. The intensity of work has an influence on construction productivity in several ways. There is a limit to the number of men who can work on any specific area without congestion leading to a reduction in productivity. Probably more important is that there is a limit to the number of men and intensity of work that management and supervisors can effectively handle.

For any size of job, measured in terms of total manhours, there is a characteristic standard job duration with which the base level of productivity is achievable. Attempting to employ more men to expedite the construction phase will reduce productivity and may or may not actually shorten the duration, but will certainly increase its cost. Manpower planning must take this into account, together with the rate of build up and run down of manpower, as discussed in Chapter 4, and the ratio of peak to average manpower. Attempts to build up men more quickly than the management and supervision can handle or having a high temporary peak of manpower, will reduce labour productivity and once lost, it is extremely difficult, if not impossible, to regain.

Similarly, working regular overtime, or going to shift working also reduces productivity and each contractor should have characteristic figures based on experience, showing loss of productivity against length of working week, for example, Figure 4.3. Very often overtime has to be worked because it is accepted practice, or is required to attract labour, but work gains from it have to be closely monitored and it is an expensive and often useless way of trying to expedite a project. Irregular overtime on the other hand, for specific objectives, does not have this same loss of productivity effect.

Site conditions can also have a significant impact on labour productivity. Although the weather is not under management control, good site conditions are. Off site, this implies good transport arrangements to and from site, and/or good jam-free access roads. On site it may include temporary enclosing of working areas to protect them from the weather, laying out permanent or temporary site roads for all weather access for the bulk of the main construction site, adequate free protective clothing and adequate break and lunch facilities, which do not involve long walks to reach them. All these factors are within management control and deficiencies in them have led to low productivity in the past.

However, given these factors, the general efficiency of project planning, co-ordination and control is all important. Each of the following problems influences productivity adversely, leads to a loss of confidence in project and construction management competence and in turn leads to a permanent reduction in productivity and industrial relations trouble. The old proposition that idle hands give trouble is very true in construction work.

Drawings unavailable when required.
Different versions of the same drawing being used by different people.
Frequent changes in instructions.
Delays due to delivery of materials and equipment.
Work being torn down and repeated because of changes.

Delays due to late deliveries of material and equipment together with changes imposed by the client, or design contractor, are one of the main causes of low productivity and are something which effective project management can influence, as discussed in the previous sections.

Notwithstanding these factors, one decision of project and construction management interacts with them, namely, the time to start construction work. In many projects, particularly in the civil engineering industry, design work is completed before construction work starts, but in many others, design, procurement and manufacturing or construction work overlaps to minimise the total project time, as in most cases time is money. In fact, it is questionable whether in today's conditions money and time are saved by overlapping these stages. If the project design stage is completed, and thus the likelihood of design changes reduced, all drawings are to hand and all material and equipment are delivered before field work starts, then construction management will not be adversely affected by these factors. Thus if site start up is delayed until this is achieved, construction management have the opportunity of achieving satisfactory productivity. If work on site starts early in the project life cycle, all the factors outlined above will almost inevitably occur and site productivity will be affected. In practice, a minimum overlap should be aimed for, rather than a major overlap and project management should attempt to shield construction management from these factors by good planning, co-ordination and control.

Thus even though labour productivity and industrial relations are normally thought to be problems in construction management, good project management is necessary to achieve satisfactory productivity, though it may not be sufficient in today's conditions. Management must at all times endeavour to maintain the respect of the work force for its competence, as when this is lost due to any reason whatsoever, whether it be within management's control or not, industrial relations problems and low productivity will almost inevitably follow.

10 Planning and Control of Procurement

Innumerable projects are delayed due to late delivery of materials or equipment, and yet many project plans only show a single arrow or bar entitled 'delivery of equipment and materials'. It cannot be emphasised strongly enough that the management, planning and control of this phase of a project is as important and should take as much effort as that of design and construction no matter the size of the project. Project management must extend to cover the firms supplying material and equipment to the project to include them in the global project control system. Essentially they are no different to other contractors, subcontractors or departments working on the project, and are part of the overall project organisation. Delays in deliveries can be kept to a minimum by effective, organised, planned reporting and expediting and unpleasant surprises can be avoided. Thus the project manager must be aware of the factors that go into an efficient procurement system, as follows.

The procurement personnel on a project have the responsibility for procuring all equipment and materials required for that particular project. This procurement service not only includes purchasing, but includes a complete follow up of every item to make sure that all materials and equipment are in accordance with job specification, and are delivered to the construction site on schedule. The procurement function can be considered to be made up of four subfunctions, namely

1. Project liaison.
2. Buying.
3. Inspection.
4. Progressing and expediting.

Project liaison

This should involve the following functions:

1. To advise interested company functions as to current commodity lead times, so that future requirements can be identified and incorporated into the company's overall plan, and engineering drawings and specifications are raised in sufficient time, as will enable procurement to be achieved in a timely manner.
2. To maintain a register of potential suppliers of equipment which may be required in the course of the company's business, and to seek out new sources of supply, processes and techniques, which may enable the company to fulfil its obligations, more profitably and quickly.
3. To assess in company with interested functions, the suitability of potential suppliers as approved company sources of supply.
4. To regularly advise interested functions as to current commodity prices, thus ensuring that accurate information is used in the preparation of tenders.
5. To advise tendering departments as to suitable commercial conditions to be included in purchase enquiries, to ensure that suppliers offers are compatible with the company's and their clients' contractual requirements.
6. To commercially assess and adjust as necessary, project tenders which have met the company's engineering requirements, and to recommend which offers should be incorporated in the overall tender.
7. To maintain such offers in a viable form, until such time as it is established that a formal contract will ensure and they are passed to the buyer to formalise.
8. To co-operate with engineering in the preparation of technical specifications and requisitions for all materials and equipment; that is, the technical preparation of orders. When bids are received this function also involves the preparation of bid summaries, analysis and purchase recommendations,

and is normally carried out by either or both the engineering design groups and project staff.

Buying

The buying group is responsible for the obtaining of bids from suppliers and the placing of orders. There are basically four types of purchase involved.

1. Equipment which is designed by a supplier, for example, such things as pumps or heat exchangers.
2. Equipment which is designed by either the contractor or made in the company, for example, pressure vessel.
3. Bulk materials such as piping, concrete, sand, reinforcing steel.
4. Services such as consultants, subcontractors or inspectors.

The purchasing department can be organised in two ways. It can either be set up that a group of buyers are assigned to a particular project, or it can be set up such that specialists concentrate on their own particular type of equipment, material or service, and one buyer serves all the projects for one particular type of service. The functions of the buying group are thus

1. To determine, in conjunction with engineering, suitable suppliers of material or equipment not established during the project stage.
2. To incorporate into formal purchase enquiries, all engineering quality control and commercial specifications, and to issue these enquiries to the selected potential suppliers.
3. To receive and commercially evaluate offers made by suppliers, which meet the company's engineering requirements.
4. To check the offers received against the purchase allowance, and to negotiate, where necessary with the supplier, to ensure that the offer accepted represents the best buy obtainable by the company. Where the

best offer exceeds the purchase allowance, the buyer must advise interested functions as to the reasons for the excess, and either obtain modification of the company's requirement, or obtain authorisation to overspend.

5. To prepare and issue suitable purchase orders embodying the company's requirements in respect of delivery or completion, engineering planning, quality control, inspection and commercial aspects of the offers selected, either during the tendering and negotiating, or contract stages of the project.

6. To ensure that the number of informal instructions to proceed are kept to a minimum, and that when used, are properly authorised and formalised as quickly as possible by the issue of an official order.

7. To off-load to suitable suppliers, work which the company finds it is unable to complete through its normal resources, including where appropriate, the provision of the material necessary to complete this work.

8. To ensure that the obligations accepted by suppliers are correctly fulfilled, including those requiring execution of work on sites removed from their normal places of business.

9. To resolve delays involving the manufacture and delivery of supplier's equipment beyond the scope of the expediting functions terms of reference, including negotiating and authorising payment of premium time or bonuses.

10. To determine and negotiate where necessary, appropriate rates of pay and material costs to be paid for additional work carried out at the company's request, where it is not possible to assess costs prior to work commencing.

11. To impose on defaulting suppliers, the fiscal commercial conditions of the order such as liquidated damages for late delivery, or penalties in respect of deficiencies in the guaranteed performance.

Inspection

This involves the physical inspection of equipment and materials to ensure that they comply with the purchase orders, the company's specifications and statutory regulations. The inspection department may be a separate department, part of purchasing or engineering design, but however it is organised it must work closely with these areas and the project staff.

Progressing and expediting

This function involves the continuous review of the performance of suppliers and relevant subcontractors. It involves the reporting of the status of all orders, from order placement to delivery and the exerting of pressure, as necessary, to ensure the maintenance of planned performance. This normally comes under the supervision of the purchasing department, although project management often get involved. The functions of progressing and expediting include

1. To determine whether the purchase order should be subjected to routine progressing from within the company, or to visits by expediting staff. This decision will normally be reached after consideration of the complexity, value and importance of the order and will take into account the supplier's past delivery record.
2. To obtain from the supplier a formal delivery commitment.
3. To obtain where required, details of the supplier's manufacturing plans to supplement the company's overall plan, and to monitor the progress of the work during manufacture.
4. To monitor suppliers during the life of the order, and to eliminate or minimise, in conjunction with the supplier, any disruptions or delays to their acknowledged commitment.
5. To determine any restraints attributable to the company or its client, and to assist the supplier in removing same.

6. To issue delivery instructions to suppliers when orders are complete.
7. To advise interested parties regularly, as to the status of orders, to ensure that where necessary remedial action is promptly taken.

The basic information which should be available for the procurement control cycle is:

1. Delivery dates quoted on orders.
2. Schedules or manufacturer's plans for fabrication and delivery.
3. Periodic progress reports.

Unfortunately, experience has proved that all these factors can be very unreliable. The normal pattern of a delivery delay is for reports on progress to be satisfactory until, as the delivery date approaches, it becomes obvious it is not going to be met. It is generally not possible to avoid all delays in deliveries, but they can be kept to a minimum. Almost as important, is the fact that, if possible, there should be a realistic forecast of all deliveries. In many cases delivery dates are quoted optimistically, or are based upon inadequate estimates: many manufacturers do not produce shop schedules, and progress reports are often obtained without the actual work being observed.

It is difficult enough to get the project manager's own organisation to plan and control effectively, but it is much more difficult to get realistic plans and reports from some manufacturers and subcontractors who are separate companies over which the project manager has no direct control.

The procurement control process must start when the list of suppliers for bidding purposes is made up. The project manager and other in-company groups involved should use up to date assessments of the previous and current performance of suppliers, and select, as far as possible, those who have a reliable performance.

Thus the procurement or purchasing department must continually examine both existing and potential sources of supply to ensure that they are

1. Technically competent.

2. Have adequate facilities and capacity, consistent with carrying out the company's requirements.
3. Have sufficient inspection and quality control personnel, to ensure that the required specification is adhered to, and that no extensive acceptance of corrective procedures would be required by the company.
4. Financially sound.

To ensure that these principles are fulfilled usually entails visiting the supplier's premises to interview key personnel and examine the facilities offered; a process which can range from visits by a commercially oriented engineer in the case of small firms, to visits by teams of qualified personnel in the case of large manufacturers. This process is sometimes known as Vendor Auditing or Supplier Evaluation and normally involves examination of the following areas.

1. Organisation and finance.
2. Sales.
3. Engineering/drawing office control.
4. Purchasing/stores management control.
5. Production control.
6. Production facilities.
7. Quality control and inspection facilities.

The full scale examination of suppliers usually involves personnel from purchasing, engineering, quality control and inspection. To ensure that such examinations are consistent in the results they achieve, most companies examine against a pro-forma schedule, which lists the points on which it requires assurance and which are laid out in such a manner, as will enable the team to complete it as the examination proceeds. Such forms vary from company to company, but normally cover such areas as:

1 *General information*

   (a) Services offered.
   (b) Facilities available, for example, heat treatment, research and development, non-destructive testing.
   (c) Subcontractors utilised and the principal operations

carried out by them.
(d) Recent major customers.
(e) Labour relations.

2 *Organisation and finance*

(a) Organisation structure and personnel.
(b) Finance, company accounts and ability to finance orders.

3 *Sales*

(a) Personnel.
(b) Points of contact.
(c) Quotation procedures.
(d) Standard conditions of sale.
(e) Willingness and ability to comply with purchase conditions.
(f) Receipt of order procedure.

4 *Engineering/drawing office procedure*

(a) Organisation structure and personnel.
(b) Engineering/drawing control, how are client's requirements passed to production and purchasing, and how are revisions to these requirements handled.

5 *Purchasing/stores management control*

(a) Organisation structure and personnel.
(b) Purchasing, how are suppliers selected and requirements made known, how are materials accepted and what inspections are carried out?
(c) Stores management, who controls, how are stock levels monitored and allocated?
(d) Stores control, how laid out, how are special materials and welding consumables stored, what quality control provisions are taken, is any equipment used to verify raw materials, how are stores records maintained, what procedures are used for issue and receipt of materials?

6 Production Control

(a) Organisation structure and personnel
(b) Order information, what information is received by production control about orders received?
(c) Factory loading, how assessed and what are key resources?
(d) Scheduling, how is delivery confirmed, are orders scheduled on each resource, how is process recorded.
(e) Progressing, how is progress monitored and who should be contacted, what remedial measures are used?

7 Production facilities

(a) Organisation structure and personnel.
(b) Facilities, details of bays, cranage and equipment, heat treatment and hydraulic test.

Following an examination, the supplier should always be advised of the team's findings and conclusions to enable him either to correct deficiencies found, or to contest the findings reached. Although initially it is necessary to seek permission to carry out a quality examination and to ensure that kcy personnel will be available for interview, ideally suppliers should be asked to accept the principle of random checks to ensure that no special precautions are taken.

Audit examinations provide purchasing with the basic information regarding a supplier's performance, but there are other ways by which the company updates its information, a few of which are

1. Information gleaned from visiting salesmen regarding new products, processes, orders received and changes in lead times.
2. Reports in technical and national press.
3. Research and technical information passed to learned societies.

Exchange of information

Once the order is placed it is often overlooked that there is generally the necessity of an exchange of information between the ordering company and supplier. Equipment drawings are often required from the supplier before some of the design work can continue. Also further design data is usually required by the vendor before work on the order can actually start. This exchange of information is required quickly to avoid delays on both sides. One of the first jobs of the expeditor may be to expedite his drawings. Similarly the information required by the vendor often needs to be expedited by the project staff. When criticised for late delivery a supplier will often point out that delivery was quoted as 'after all information has been supplied' and that the ordering company was lackadaisical in supplying it.

Effective expediting

The function of progressing and expediting, is to achieve planned deliveries, to give reassurance, that deliveries will be met, and if not, to say why not and when they will be achieved. It begins work when the formal order is placed and only ceases, when the supplier has completed all deliveries. Effective expediting requires considerable effort and must be a positive, aggressive function. To achieve results it must recognise the beginning of slippages in suppliers' programmes, anticipate problems and take evasive action before delays occur. It should influence decisions before orders are placed and start immediately afterwards, and should only finish when every item has been delivered including spare parts.

It is very desirable that the expeditors should be experienced or technically qualified in the areas they are working in, and have knowledge of production techniques involved. Otherwise it is not possible for them to make their own judgement and evaluate the estimates and promises given by the suppliers. This desirable state of affairs is very difficult to achieve, because of the availability of this kind of personnel, and many expeditors are simply clerks, who are not able to make their own estimates from their observations on the shop floor. They do their expediting by phone or letter, and when they do visit a supplier, they find it difficult to judge his statements. This concentration on the use of the telephone or letters for expediting must be avoided, if expediting is to be effective. It can be used to supplement visits to suppliers, but if used by itself it will often lead to delays and broken delivery promises. Suppliers, if not deliberately misleading, will always tend to be optimistic about meeting delivery dates, and there is no substitute for intelligent, objective observations on the shop floor. Thus the decision whether to progress from 'in company' or to expedite by 'visit' is reached, after considering the following factors.

1. The order value.
2. The complexity of the order.
3. How critical its delivery is to the overall programme.
4. The supplier's past delivery record.

In practice, orders normally fall into the following categories

1. Those progressed by telephone or letter;
   (a) uncomplicated orders, (b) medium to low priority orders, and (c) orders with reliable suppliers.
2. Those expedited by visits; (a) complex or high value orders, (b) orders with critical deliveries or penalties for late delivery, (c) orders subject to progress payment by result, and (d) orders on suppliers with a poor delivery record.

One of the advantages of using both progressing and expediting, is that the manner in which orders are monitored, can be altered at any time up to completion to accommodate changing circumstances such as sudden unreliability. Progressing and expediting orders involves the following procedures.

1 *Progressing*

Having taken the decision to progress, the order is passed to the progress clerk responsible for that supplier under the direction of a section leader whose duties are:

(a) to familiarise himself with the order and its requirement;
(b) to commit the supplier if not already committed, to a specific delivery;
(c) to set up lines of communication with the supplier, and obtain and pass to interested parties at the specified

times, reports of the order's progress;

(d)   to identify restraints and discrepancies and initiate remedial action;

(e)   to receive sub-orders, test certificates and advice notes and pass these to planning, engineering, inspection and shipping;

(f)   to advise the supplier of the address to which the material or equipment should be sent.

2 *Expediting*

Once the decision to expedite has been taken, the expeditor must:

(a)   understand the requirement, the supplier's structure and organisation and his past delivery record;

(b)   make arrangements to visit the supplier to set up the procedures to be used to monitor completion;

(c)   on visiting the supplier, set out to generate a relationship of mutual respect, establish points of routine and emergency contact and decide, in conjunction with the supplier, how his manufacturing programme should best be monitored;

(d)   on subsequent visits the expeditor must visit the shop floor to check progress, identify restraints and aid the supplier to mount any recovery plan agreed as being required;

(e)   having visited the supplier, the expeditor must promptly submit his visit report, showing restraints and reasons for delays. As most suppliers have a mixture of routine and special orders in hand at any time, reports need not always be required in the same detail.

As will be apparent from the above, the basic requirements of both progressing and expediting are the earliest possible identification and notification of restraints and the initiation of remedial action. Remedial action can vary from assisting a supplier to plan recovery, to clearing restraints within the company, so it is essential that its 'in company' lines of communication are as good as those established with the supplier. Progress and expediting should not, however, appear internally to identify itself solely with suppliers, but should also project the image that it is willing and able to assist company personnel in resolving problems they are experiencing with suppliers.

One of the problems which a progressing and expediting organisation in heavy engineering must meet and overcome is that, while reporting by supplier, they must translate the information gleaned into contract reports, involving many different suppliers and differing types of materials and equipment. To achieve this, it is becoming commonplace for progressing and expediting organisations to include a section responsible for the compilation and transmission of contract reports from the information passed to them by both progress clerks and expeditors.

Supplier's plans

Many of the problems of effective progressing and expediting can be overcome if realistic plans can be obtained from the supplier. Then all that is required on a visit is to compare progress against plan. If a slippage is evident then expediting can be carried out directly or it can be brought to the attention of the project manager for him to apply pressure at a more senior level. These plans, job or shop schedules as they are sometimes called, should be part of the job order or subcontract. When an order is placed it should be possible for every supplier to produce a plan with key data on it as to when and how he intends to produce the item ordered. Many firms include this request in their order specifications. Unfortunately, there is often great difficulty in achieving this state. Planning is an area of weakness in many firms – some will not and others cannot – but the net result is often that plans are not supplied, or they are extremely rudimentary, or they bear no relation to how the job will be carried out. To avoid delays in delivery becoming apparent only near to delivery date, a minimum form of plan must be obtained for all important items, materials and subcontracts so that a control system can be set up.

It is at this stage that, if satisfactory plans are not forthcoming, the project manager or one of his staff should intervene. Obtaining satisfactory manufacturing plans is as much part of the project manager's function as planning design and construction. There are normally only between ten and twenty critical suppliers, even on large projects, and the problem is not as big as it first seems. The project manager, or his deputy, should establish personal contact by visiting the suppliers with the purchasing officer or expeditor. On this visit it is usually possible for him to get or put in hand the preparation of a minimum satisfactory plan. Often it is worthwhile for the project manager to provide assistance or guidance to the supplier in producing this plan. Two of the planning techniques covered are very appropriate to this stage of procurement and they both produce meaningful job plans, which can be used for monitoring purposes.

The first of these is milestone reporting, where, as stated before, several significant dates or milestones are established with the supplier. These are points of significant and observable accomplishment in his shop, such as the start or completion of various parts of the job. They may include such things as lead time before actual work starts; when drawings are ready; when critical materials such as castings are received; when various parts of the manufacturing process are complete and so on. Thereafter progress between milestones, and when milestones are due to be reached, can be reported by anyone visiting, either expeditor, inspector or project engineer. In addition, telephone calls to report progress between visits tend to give much more reliable information when they are based upon actual milestones being reached. The big advantage of this method is its simplicity, especially where suppliers are unwilling to plan or commit themselves. Any job can be split into a minimum of four parts and delays in manufacture can be picked up on any one part and action taken. This avoids delays not being picked up on the overall job, and delays can only occur on a quarter of the job before pressure can be brought to bear.

The other form of planning that can be used is to use standard job plans, either separately or with milestone reporting. The manufacture of most items is usually done in a repeatable way and an arrow diagram or bar chart for each class can be a standard sub-plan or module. Once made up, they can be used on many suppliers for many projects, as a basis for discussion and preparation of their plan or establishment of milestones.

It must be emphasised that this planning, reporting and expediting system must also be carried out with the supplier's subcontractors and material suppliers. In many cases suppliers give as a reason for delay the late delivery of equipment or materials to them. Thus, to completely control the project at procurement stage, the control system must be extended to cover these firms.

Analysis and reports

Once the planning and control system plans are established, reports on work progress start coming in from firms, expeditors, inspectors and others. Progress is compared to plan and any deivations brought to the attention of the project manager or his staff for action. These reports are formed into the monthly status report covering all orders; in cases of projects with short life spans, very critical items or items on which delivery date is slipping; these reports are often produced bi-weekly. The report in itself serves no purpose and is only a link in the control cycle. The same elements are present in this cycle as in the project planning and cost cycle, namely plan, report, forecast, analysis, control action and check the effect of control action. The analysis of the order status report and the forecasting of possible delays are thus of extreme importance, and must include a critical questioning of the reliability of the data that went into the report. It must not only look for delays but, more importantly, look for the first signs of delays and take action to minimise or stop them.

On large projects this order status or report is often produced by a computer, and can be several inches thick. In these cases reporting by exception is normally used, and a summary sheet shows the position of those items on the critical path, and those with delays forecast. Unfortunately experience has shown that reporting by exception must be treated with caution, as often it is the unexpected that causes trouble.

In the busy life of a project manager reviews in depth are generally not carried out each month, but just as in planning and control of other work, there has proved to be a danger in only following critical paths or items. Inevitably it seems some items, thought non-critical, eventually become critical and affect the whole project unless they are given some management attention. Thus, in addition to a normal monthly review, major reviews of procurement should be carried out at logical intervals in long time scale projects, in the same way progress and cost reviews are carried out. These major reviews go over every order, examine the facts, and determine if any further follow up or action is required. The object is to catch those items off the critical path which may cause trouble, and to ensure that the normal expediting process is working.

In the normal monthly review, the additional technique of sampling can be used with advantage, just as with progress and cost analysis. Each month, in addition to the summary sheet, a number of orders are examined in depth on a random basis to ensure that the overall system is working correctly. This would involve not only a sample from each type of order, but each month examining one type of order in depth. These techniques of exception reporting, major review and sampling are necessary, due to the complexity and size of projects, and the information explosion. Unless critical human analysis and judgement are used a computer can simply be a big typewriter which makes unreliable information look impressive.

If a procurement system, such as outlined here, is carried out, it should not only have the direct effect of minimising delays and giving accurate reporting, but it will also have indirect advantages. Once it is seen that an interest is being taken in procurement plans and reports, personnel involved will give them more weight and attention. When an efficient system is being used, suppliers will tend to co-operate; they will tend to perform planning and reporting better than average on the order placed, either because they see it as worthwhile, or know that any neglect will be picked up.

11 Human Behaviour in the Project Setting

The bulk of this book up to now has been concerned with project management systems. There is one system which has not been covered and without it being effective, all the other systems will not work; that is the 'People System' or the human relations system. Effective project systems and good human relations systems are both necessary for good performance on projects, but neither is sufficient on its own. However, if one has good human relations on a project reasonable performance can be obtained, whereas if people are forever antagonising each other good project performance will never be achieved, no matter how good the project systems are.

Technical problems on a project can always be solved given time and money, but people problems are much more difficult if not impossible to 'solve' in the short life span of a project. Thus in addition to his professional skill in planning and control, a project manager must develop his skills in managing people if he is to be successful, as these are critical to project performance, which in reality is actually people performance. In this he can learn a lot from the work done in the field of the Behavioural Sciences and also in its particular application to the project setting. This is because project management is an area of management where an individual can quickly develop and learn human relation skills, as the normal patterns of human behaviour in management are both accelerated and accentuated in the management of projects. If an individual is aware of the modern human relations concepts, more can be learned in two years of project management experience than in ten years of normal management experience.

This is because the project manager has a very difficult task and more problems in human relations than the normal manager. He has problems arising out of the complexities and ambiguities of the matrix organisation, such as dual subordination and uncertain authority, and any interpersonnel, group and intergroup problems are accentuated by the temporary nature of the project and the fact that many organisations are involved in one endeavour.

The project manager has to manage a complex organisation requiring the work and contribution of many people from different professional backgrounds, different trades, different departments and different companies. Therefore even in the best of circumstances, the management of a project is a difficult problem. It is a very difficult task to co-ordinate, communicate, provide leadership, motivate all the personnel involved, provide the necessary drive to achieve success, to plan, organise and control, that is, to manage a project.

A project manager's task is made more difficult by the fact that he acts as a junior general manager with normally ill-defined authority limited to that project. His lines of authority or influence are grafted on to the existing pyramid structure, cutting across the normal vertical lines of command and departmental boundaries. He does not work in the normal superior-subordinate relationships but must manage his peers, juniors and superiors in other departments and companies contributing to his project. Personnel in these departments work for two managers, namely the project manager and their own departmental or company manager.

Thus in the normal project organisation, personnel and groups from several different functional departments, contractors and subcontractors must work together, but are generally not responsible to the project manager for pay rises, promotions or performance assessments and other line relationships. They have different loyalties and objectives, and have probably never worked together before and may never do so again. The only thing that binds them together is the project and the project organisation. The project manager must therefore deal with the managerial problems of developing a project team out of these diverse groups working on a project. This involves complex relationships with many other managers in these departments and companies.

The temporary nature of the project group means also that members of the project group work together for a limited period of time and there is no time for interpersonnel relationships to develop into a static state as in normal line management. Group performance is necessary from the very beginning of a project as mistakes made and time lost at the start can never be recovered. In addition the composition of the total management group on a project is constantly changing with new members joining it and the role of some older members diminishing in importance. It is further complicated by the fact that project managers must work under pressure to achieve cost, time and technical targets and their functions include applying pressure on the people and groups involved in the project.

Two principal characteristics of project management are the existence of dual responsibility and split authority. These characteristics are not new, but are more clearly recognised in the project concept. Most complex industrial organisations recognise that the classical unity of command concept, with authority and responsibility packaged in neat boundaries on a traditionally organisational chart, do not portray the actual organisational reality. Most managers in any organisation are subject to several sources of power or influence.

Dual subordination may not be a good thing, but as long as instructions are non-conflicting, there is no reason why a subordinate should not receive instructions from two people. The project manager determining what is to be done and by when, and the functional manager controlling how and by whom. The project manager is primarily concerned with time, cost and coordination, and the functional manager primarily concerned with technical performance decisions. When there is conflict, one superior either the project manager or functional departmental manager, must clearly be recognised as the one who must be initially obeyed. Any conflict must be resolved by these managers.

The problems and challenges of achieving effective human relations in the project setting could be the subject of a complete book or books, and all that this chapter can achieve is to introduce the reader to some of the main factors involved.

These are

1. The authority problem in project management.
2. The engineer as a manager.
3. Interpersonal problems in the project setting.
4. Group behaviour in the project setting.
5. Conflict and its resolution in the project setting.

The authority problem in project management

The principle of organisation from which project management varies most is that responsibility should always be coupled to corresponding authority. The project manager is responsible for the success or failure of his project but has only limited authority over the personnel in his own company and others who are contributing to his project. Yet if he is to manage or co-ordinate effectively he must have some authority over them all.

The project manager must manage across functional lines of command in his own company, and across organisational lines of command in other companies to bring together the activities required to accomplish the objectives of his project. In a traditional bureaucratic organisation, business is conducted up and down the vertical hierarchy. The project manager on the other hand is more concerned with the lateral flow of work in horizontal and diagonal directions, than he is with flows in the vertical direction. Problems of motivation exist for the traditional manager but these problems are compounded for the project manager, because the traditional leverages of hierarchical authority are not at his disposal. However, he must act as a focal point for making project decisions, and if he is to manage his projects and not be simply a co-ordinator, he must be given adequate power to accomplish these objectives, but often this power is not the formal authority of superior-subordinate relationship.

Except in the divisional project concept, no project manager whose activities cut across functional lines, or companies can have complete authority. Authority is granted relative to many considerations. The project manager normally has written contractual relationships with other companies and these companies generally want to maintain goodwill to ensure future business. Therefore he does have a formal basis of authority which exists in contracts or purchase agreements. The personnel working for these other companies can never be fully integrated into the one project organisation, but for all practical purposes in a healthy situation they can work together in an overall project team.

In his own company the project manager's position is usually one of getting the job done without the line of authority or binding contractual arrangements for controlling this in-house work. Thus it is often more difficult for the project manager to exert authority over his own company departments than it is for him with outside firms. Although a considerable amount of a project manager's authority must depend on sources of authority other than that formally given, his position will be strengthened in his own company by the publication of documentation to establish his position and what his legal authority and responsibilities are. This will include identifying his role in managing, organising, planning and controlling the project, and the explicit recognition of the project organisation form used.

Project managers in the matrix form of project management are thus faced with the difficult task of obtaining performance from others not under their direct control. To accomplish this they must often rely on sources of power or influence other than formal authority. The more limited the formal authority, the greater the pressure on a project manager to employ other means of obtaining authority.

Authority is difficult to define and words like 'authority', 'influence', 'leadership' and 'power' tend to be used interchangeably and in a rather loose association. It is therefore useful to establish an understanding of what is meant by these words, at least in the context of this book.

Authority is usually defined as the formal, legal or rightful power to command or act. As applied to the manager, authority is the power to command others to act or not to act, and in the traditional theory of management authority is a right granted from the superior to the subordinate. Authority, at least, formal authority, is a right of a person to be listened to and obeyed. It is delegated through the media of position descriptions, organisational titles, standard operating procedures and related policy, and is sometimes termed position power. Such a duly appointed superior will have power over his subordinates in matters involving pay, promotion and performance reports.

Influence on the other hand may be assumed by an individual without legitimacy or an organisational position, and is often termed informal authority. An individual may exercise influence in his environment because he has knowledge and expertise, without the documentation of formal authority. It can thus be based on an individual's competence and reputation, and on his or her personality.

Leadership is a particular form of influence. It is often associated with attempts of a superior to influence the attitudes or behaviour of his subordinate, but it can also apply to someone other than the formal superior, who attempts to significantly influence the behaviour of others with whom he is involved. The distinction between influencing and leading is that the exercise of leadership will almost always involve an attempt to influence attitudes and behaviour, whereas not all attempts at influence involve leadership.

Power is a concept frequently associated with authority and is defined on the ability to unilaterally determine the behaviour of others regardless of the basis of that ability. The simplest way of looking at it is to consider it on the sum total of a person's authority and influence, that is

Power = Formal authority plus influence

As power and authority tend to be interchangeable terms in practice, this can also be expressed for any individual as

Total authority = Formal authority plus informal authority

A manager's power or total authority is a combination of his formal authority and his influence, such that subordinates, peers and superiors alike accept his judgement. Thus authority is made up not only of the formal authority granted to an individual but also from his personal effectiveness. This can be obvious when two people who have differing amounts of influence occupy the same position in succession. Though this formal authority is identical, their power or total authority can vary considerably.

The project manager accomplishes his objectives through working with personnel who are largely professional. Consequently his use of authority must be different from what one would expect in the simple superior-subordinate relationships. For professional people project leadership must include explaining the rationale of the effort as well as the more obvious functions of planning, organising, directing and controlling.

Unilateral decisions, dogmatic attitudes and the resort to the authority of a hierarchical position are inconsistent with the project environment. The project manager's job is to search for points of agreement, to examine the situation critically and to think reflectively and only then to take a decision based on the superiority of his knowledge. This rather than his organisational position is the basis for his authority.

The effective authority of the project manager is thus seldom autocratic. His most meaningful authority may be based on his ability to build alliances with the other managers involved in the project and in resolving conflict between the various managers involved. One asset of a good project manager is that people from different departments and companies who work with him on a project should regard him in their own specialised way as an asset. The technical, engineering or scientific people may think of him as a buffer between them and the irresponsible demands of other people, the finance people may think of him as a businessman, the computer people may view him as someone who can understand them and communicate with operations people.

The project manager must thus earn the respect, and gain authority over elements of the proejct which are not under his direct formal authority. Although the project manager may or may not have legal authority, he gets most of his work done through influence and authority other than that legally extended. The successful project manager gets things done through co-operation of others gained in many different ways. This may be a combination of forces such as his status and respect enjoyed both within and outside his organisation, his persuasive abilities, his reputation and capability in resolving opposing views, the priority of his project within and outside the organisation, his specialised knowledge and his rank in the organisation. Voluntary co-operation is more effective than that forced by legal power but if informal authority does not work then formal authority is needed. Nevertheless in the project setting, the naked use of authority is one of the least effective ways of obtaining commitment and performance.

The project manager by virtue of his position and his function has tools which he can use to establish his authority over those involved in the project. Among the most important of these are the plan and budget. Provided they are constructed with the involvement of all those concerned, then they commit the individuals and groups involved to specific allocations of resources and performance. The project manager then has the authority to hold them to this commitment. Similarly, the use of psuedo subcontracts for organisational cost accounts and work packages also obtains commitment and establishes the project manager's authority.

The project manager is also at the centre of the information system and this in itself can be a means of obtaining influence. When combined with responsibility for control analysis and reporting, it enhances the positional power of the project manager. In addition the ability to call meetings, to chair them and to minute them, gives the project manager a measure of informal and formal authority. Finally, if the project manager is involved in the formal performance assessment of people from other functions involved in his project, he has in effect achieved some measure of formal authority over them.

Authority, organisation and managerial philosophy

The extent of the project manager's authority in his own company is thus the deciding factor in the form of organisation actually used. As a staff co-ordinator he has very little authority; as a divisional project manager, he has complete line authority over his own company personnel; and in the matrix organisation he shares it to varying degrees with the departmental heads.

In the case where the project manager acts as co-ordinator, that is, basically a staff function although given line responsibilities, the project manager must pursue performance objectives with a great deal of skill and persuasiveness and must constantly refer back to his line manager for authority. The situation is not inheritantly incorrect provided all concerned are aware of the project manager's lack of authority and are willing occasionally to allow delay in lack of achievement in pursuing project goals. This is not to say that the manager with greater authority should not use skill and persuasiveness in his operations. However, when a crisis arises, speed in the implementation of instructions or corrective action is required, sometimes on the inconclusive early evidence of advance trends. The manager with some real authority has a much better chance of success because he can redirect personnel and money and make decisions with the minimum of consultation. With limited authority the project manager who is a co-ordinator must take some considerable time to consult with supervisory authority and must attempt to persuade other personnel on the basis of inconclusive information.

In the normal matrix organisation, the project manager is working with shared or indefinite legal authority and thus he depends a great deal on his unofficial authority. The actual working form of matrix management depends on the respect and loyalty held for the individual project manager by his colleagues. Before the matrix form of project organisation is introduced, it must be preceded by a careful analysis of the projects to be handled, the existing organisation both unofficial and official, the personalities involved and the managerial philosophies of the firm. The extent of the project manager's authority will vary with each organisation and with each project manager. Experienced departmental managers cannot be expected to share authority with a lesser executive who is appointed as a project manager. Therefore project managers must have the respect of their fellow executives and the degree of authority together with relationship to functional departments spelled out. Where there is mutual respect and confidence in each other, the functional managers will accept a project manager's decision as a generalist and a manager, and he must accept their technical recommendations. The basis for this healthy situation is the appointment of project managers who have their fellow executives' respect and confidence and a logical division of authority based on a careful analysis of the situation.

Thus one factor which determines which is the most applicable form of project organisation for any individual company is the managerial philosophy of that company. Each individual organisation is as distinctive and unique as the people in it, and each has its own personality and character. Thus the form of project organisation which works for one firm will not necessarily work for a seemingly similar firm, as a company's organisation and philosophy of management must be compatible.

Any company's management philosophy evolves over several years and reflects the personal convictions of the senior management of the company. Therefore any changes in organisation which are not compatible with the deeply held views of the top men will fail. For example, the following points will illustrate a few aspects which affect the success or failure of any new organisational form and which cannot be changed overnight.

1. The prevalent managerial style is historically either autocratic, or alternatively participative.
2. Is the company conservative or will it try out new ideas?
3. Does it encourage delegation of decision making to lower levels of management, or persist in having every decision referred to senior management?
4. Is personal accountability emphasised, or must all important decisions be taken by a committee?

These factors generally represent deeply held beliefs and convictions of senior management and are very difficult to change. Therefore whatever type of project organisation is used, it must not only reflect the needs of any particular project but also the 'givens' of the situation. If powerful functional departments or individuals are dominant, conflict and frustration will certainly arise if a strong project organisation is attempted. A weak project organisation emphasising communication, co-ordination, planning and monitoring of progress may be the best solution for such a situation. Where a company's philosophy is participative and encourages delegation, a strong or fully mixed matrix organisation will achieve better results on project work. It can lead to effective team building and the generation of a project attitude of mind with good human relations.

The engineer as a manager

Much has been written and many studies carried out relating to the engineer's success and failure in the field of management. It is generally recognised that many engineers encounter problems when they reach the stage in their career that marks the transition from engineer to manager. They often find difficulty in overcoming problems caused by the lack of compatibility between the purely technical role of the engineer and the non-technical requirements of the managerial role. This can lead to engineers as managers having difficulties in communicating with people, having a lack of knowledge of other disciplines because of their narrow technical interests and feeling conflict between their role as an engineer and their role as a manager. These problems can often arise out of the change of working environment from one of precision and predictability of physical problems to one of uncertainty and rapid change of conditions. This presents serious problems to both the engineer and the organisation in which he is employed, and can materially affect project performance.

As the majority of managers working on a project are engineers, the project manager must understand the problems facing engineers when they perform the role of managers. It is useful in this context to examine the task, role and character of an engineer in relation to the organization and to compare the task, role and character of the manager with those of the engineer. This can give the project manager a greater understanding of the interpersonal conflicts arising from these aspects of the essentially two different professions.

The engineer

The engineer works in an environment where physical rules and laws are his tools. His designs are based on these laws and consequently a high degree of physical certainty is attached to the solution of his problems. His world is one of black and white, right or wrong, clear decisions with clear outcomes. He generally performs tasks of a technical nature, calling for precision, mathematical ability, the application of well-proven, precise theory, the mechanical approach to problem solving and the need to seek a single, lasting solution in an environment of high certainty and little change. The engineer's role thus requires an attitude of precision, a mechanistic approach to problem solving and a bias towards technical factors.

Thus the general conception of an engineer is that he is unemotional, prefers to deal with things rather than people, has narrow technical interests and chooses to specialise in physical sciences. As a result, studies of the personality of the engineer identify some of the engineer's typical personality traits which are symptomatic of the problems encountered by an engineer in his transition to management. Traits such as difficulty in dealing with people, procrastination in decision making, fear of being proved wrong, a resistance to change, maintenance of the self-image as an engineer and not a manager, sensitivity to criticism, a bias towards short-term rather than long-term planning and a distinctly task-orientated behaviour.

The manager

The manager on the other hand performs the task of planning, organising, directing and controlling the resources of his firm, principally men, money and materials, in a world of uncertainty, intangibles and constant change. These tasks call for a much broader, creative approach, and ability to diverge and search for many alternative solutions to a problem and to then choose the best solution applicable at that particular time. The manager's role in contrast to that of the engineer, thus requires an attitude of precision only in so far as its usefulness is justified for the goal to be achieved and the time available to reach that goal. It requires a non-mechanistic approach to problem solving and a bias towards efficient resource utilisation and more people orientation.

The engineer's career path

If an engineer's career path is traced through his organisation, he will start his career usually, at a point part-way into the task-orientated portion of the engineering function. As his career develops he will become less technically-orientated as he is given more and more responsibility for staff and other resources. He will become progressively more managerially orientated in his role until, he crosses the boundary into functional management. At this stage in his career he is concerned with managing engineers in the function or discipline in which he has worked for a number of years, but he needs to recognise that he is now predominantly a manager, and not an engineer. Not all engineers who have made this transition recognise this factor.

In the traditional non-project organisation, the next stage of promotion is for a functional manager to move into a general management position, where he is responsible for the management of resources for the complete organisation. At this stage he is concerned with multi-disciplinary management, and thus has moved almost completely away from his technical role. This is a very demanding task for someone who started out as a technical specialist, but a limited number of people of any discipline reach the top position of general management.

However, in project management an engineer can reach a position of general management at essentially the level of function manager, that is, middle manager or lower and thus is faced with the problems of multi-disciplinary management at a much earlier stage in his career development.

The engineer as a functional manager

When an engineer first becomes a functional manager he runs up against the first problems facing an engineer as a manager, namely, role identity and conflict. The engineer although in management, tends to still identify himself more closely with the role of an engineer, rather than that of a manager.

The above attitude can lead to internal stress and can impair the performance of the functional manager, if he continues to bias his role backwards to the task-orientated engineering role, leaving less time to perform his prescribed role as a manager. This can lead to interpersonal conflict with both project management and the engineers under the functional manager, with both parties recognising that he is not performing his role as a functional manager.

Similar symptoms of intergroup conflict occur between the engineer as a functional manager and other departments or segments of the organisation. The boundaries between the engineering segment and all other segments are essentially potential points of conflict and give rise to such problems as territorial jealousy, role conflict (due often to role overlap), withholding or distorting information and poor interdepartmental communication.

The engineer as a general or project manager

When an engineer moves into the general or project management area he is faced with several problems. He has to lose the greater part of his identity as an engineer and has to acquire an understanding of and sympathy with the needs of the total role comprising all parts and functions of the organisation. He has to obtain, or already possess the skills needed for this new role. It is here that the engineer may find his problems are at their greatest, due possibly to the lack of management education and training, and the incompatibility of his personality with the requirement of his role.

Symptoms such as differences of perception and orientation of the different departments and organisations contributing to the project, time needed for the task, interpersonal orientation and environmental needs arise. The general or project manager must master these skills and understand these needs in order to effectively carry out the task of managing and resolving the inter-group conflicts arising.

Engineers in general thus tend to be tremendously conscientious and work orientated. Their loyalty or commitment is very often to the plant, equipment or project they are working on rather than to the overall company. They have a great deal of pride in their work, but this can often be a disadvantage to the project manager. This pride leads to the engineer being very sensitive to criticism and having an enormous need to be right. He is more concerned with being technically correct than with time and cost objectives, or with people. Promotion to managerial position often depends on the engineer's technical ability, rather than the ability to manage people, and thus the engineering manager often takes with him this emphasis on technical perfection, pride in his work or group, and sensitivity to criticism.

When this is combined with the fact that in many organisations the level of interpersonal trust, support and co-operation is low, it means that the project manager has a very difficult task in managing the many people and organisations involved in his project.

Interpersonal behaviour in the project setting

The project manager has the task of overcoming the many problems involved in obtaining his personal and group performance from individuals and organisations in achieving the project's objectives, within the 'givens' of the managerial, organisational and technical systems they work in, that is, the sociotechnical system. Any individual's performance on his job is a function of this sociotechnical system, his or her ability and motivation. Given that many of these factors are not under the project manager's control, the main behavioural factor he can influence is the motivation of the personnel working on his project. The skills of the project manager in dealing with people can make a significant difference to performance on his project, and in this an understanding of the work of the many people who have studied the problems of human behaviour in managment is well worthwhile.

Very few organisations are ideal and a person's management history can lead to attitudes, which can perhaps in the short term of a typical project life be modified, but rarely can be changed. Man is a complex being, highly variable, but capable of changing. The same manager may perform poorly in one part of the organisation, where he feels alienated, but perform satisfactorily in another part. Managerial styles may be required to be different for different individuals and different groups. Human beings are complex and no one set of assumptions is generally applicable; different people and different groups of people will show behaviour that can be accounted for satisfactorily by several different sets of assumptions about people. Thus each manager in each situation must avoid making assumptions too soon and must draw on a range of models of human behaviour to see which one suits the behaviour he observes around him at work.

The classic assumptions about human behaviour have been crystallised by McGregor in his Theory X and Theory Y, and both may be appropriate at the same time in any one project organisation. Theory X postulates that man is a rational economic being with the following characteristics

1. The average human being has an inherent dislike of work and will avoid it if he can.
2. Because of this characteristic, most people must be coerced, controlled, directed and threatened with punishment to get them to put forth adequate effort towards the achievement of organisational objectives.
3. The average human being prefers to be directed, wishes to avoid responsibility, has relatively little ambition and wants security above all.

Theory Y, on the other hand, postulates that

1. The expenditure of physical and mental effort in work is as natural as play and rest.
2. External control and the threat of punishment are not the only means of bringing about effort towards organisational objectives. A man will exercise self-direction and self-control in the service of objectives to which he is committed.
3. Commitment to an objective is a function of the rewards associated with their achievement.
4. The average human being learns, under proper conditions, not only to accept but to seek responsibility.

5. The capacity to exercise a relatively high degree of imagination, ingenuity and creativity in solving organisational problems is widely, not narrowly distributed in the population.
6. Under the conditions of modern industrial life, the intellectual potentialities of the average human being are only partly utilised.

In the project setting, the project manager does not normally manage workers at shop floor level but is involved with other managers and professional people and this concept of a self-actualising man outlined in Theory Y is probably more realistic, given a healthy sociotechnical system. The problems of motivating professional people has been studied by Herzberg and others who found that accomplishment and a feeling of job growth are genuine motivators for people like accountants and engineers. He found that what they call hygiene factors such as pay, working conditions and canteens could cause dissatisfaction, but their improvement did not lead to satisfaction, merely to the elimination of dissatisfaction. They were essentially prequisites for motivation but did not motivate by themselves, just making it possible for motivation to operate. Motivating factors are more associated with the job itself. Thus self-actualising man had a range of motives ordered in a hierarchy of importance depending on how they contributed to his survival. Given that his basic body and safety needs, and his desire for fellowship are met, his desire for autonomy in the work he does and fulfilment of himself in his work are such that a suitably designed job will enable him to engage himself fully in it and so satisfy himself and the needs of the organisation. In the project environment where hygiene factors are generally reasonably well cared for, the personnel can be assumed primarily concerned with a search for fulfilment of their self-esteem needs. In this the characteristics of an engineer may be both a disadvantage and an advantage to the project manager.

The project manager can in this environment benefit from the use of participative methods of management. In fact in the matrix set-up he is always forced to use participative methods to varying extents with other functional managers and other company's managers. Participation means a willingness of the project manager to consult with his fellow managers and other personnel working on the project, to acquaint them with the project's problems and to involve them in the decision making. The participative project manager does not abdicate his organisational responsibilities. He is still responsible for his project, but he has learned to delegate and share operating responsibility with those who actually perform the work. Participation increases this opportunity for those working on the project to develop increased ability, satisfaction and thus motivation from the project. It can lead to the removal of conditions which set the personnel and groups apart.

However, each individual and group involved in a project may differ widely in their human relation problems, and in how much they may be trusted to achieve sub-goals on their own, or how much they require to be closely monitored. The project manager has to quickly analyse the individuals and groups working upon his project, and ascertain specifically what are the best methods of dealing with them and what motivating factors are most important to them.

He must be a good human observer and be looking for signs and symptoms of what makes them tick right through the life of the project. The abilities and motivations of the people in the various sub-organisations are so variable, that he must have the sensitivity and diagnostic ability to be able to quickly appreciate any differences.

It may be necessary to be detailed and autocratic with one individual, delegate with mild control with another group, or individual and be fully participative with others. Each management style or strategy will be the correct one for each individual or group. The project manager should become skilful in several different kinds of managerial styles, each consistent with the particular situation. The authoritarian style is more consistent with many traditional organisational forms, whereas participative management can work well in a matrix organisation. To do this the project manager must be aware of his actual managerial style and consciously switch styles when required.

The temporary nature of the project group means the members of the project group work together for a limited period and there is no time for interpersonal relationships to develop into a static state, as in normal line management. Group performance is also necessary from the very beginning of a project, as mistakes made and time lost at the start can never be recovered. In addition, the composition of the group is constantly changing with new members joining it and the role of some older members diminishing in importance.

He must be able to quickly size up people, and be aware of the electricity in the air depicting tension between groups. It is a fact that in the temporary nature of the project setting, attitudes and relationships are 'set' very quickly. The position is made more complex as project managers must work under pressure to achieve cost and time objectives, and their function includes keeping the pressure on the personnel involved in the project. They have to gain a feel for how much pressure can be usefully applied. Most personnel work better under a certain amount of pressure, and indeed accept and welcome it in the project setting in order to achieve reasonable objectives. This comes from accepting the new challenge and taking risks and increasing their abilities, but too much pressure leads to resistance, conflict and unproductive tension.

Therefore, the project manager must be sensitive to the reactions of people and endeavour to act supportively instead of threateningly. He must be perceptive to the reaction of people to him, and the interactions between people, and this involves such factors as being aware of body language, and of the factors that indicate threatening behaviour or supportive behaviour. For example, the first word chosen, tones of voice, points omitted, can tend to increase defensive reaction, restrict communication and impair the persons commitment and motivation to the project. Supportive behaviour from the project manager or other people can tend to reduce defensive behaviour and lead to greater project commitment. The project manager does have one important factor going for him in obtaining good personal performance. Project work by its very nature can be very stimulating, satisfying and give to those involved a real sense of achievement. Many professional and supervisory people feel alienated by the nature of their work and their failure to see how it fits in the overall company picture. The many layers of management in a large organisation leave those at the lower levels feeling a sense of powerlessness and remoteness from decision making, and it is difficult for them to equate their own personal needs with that of the organisation. This leads to a loss of involvement and commitment to their work and the objective of the groups they belong to.

Project work with its definite visible goals can lead to a high level of personal commitment and satisfaction. Everyone on a project can become associated with its success or failure. For example, the objectives of a project group may be to design and build the physical plant required by the company to fulfil certain market demands. With this objective in mind, the personnel involved can readily visualise and adopt the companies objectives for their own. Projects can be extremely frustrating for a project manager caught in a power complex with little authority, but more often, people in all kinds of occupations involved in a project comment on the pleasure they had working on it. They can see how their contribution fits in to the overall picture, and if they work a little harder, they can see what effect it has on the progress of a job. This kind of feedback leads to a greater interest and motivation in the job. It leads to the development of the project attitude of mind, in which peoples' interests are subordinated to the overall project and they associate themselves with the project.

In addition the concept of cost accounts and work packages as pseudo subcontracts may be partially threatening in a control sense, but in fact give people clear objectives and clearly delegated responsibility. This gives them personal targets and essentially is equivalent to the methods used in Management by Objectives, and can lead to a greater commitment to the overall project and their part of it, which is clearly defined.

The project manager must thus make use of this unique motivational opportunity to obtain personal, group and global organisation performance. He must deal with people, with the assumption that most individuals have drives towards personal growth and development, and these are most likely to be actualised in an environment which is both supportive and challenging. Most people desire to make and are capable of making, a much higher level of contribution to the attainment of organisation goals than most organisational environments will permit. However, he is working with many different people from many different organisations, and therefore with the 'givens' of any situation he may have to treat different individuals and different groups in entirely different ways to achieve the best performance for his project.

Groups in the project setting

The great majority of human beings have a natural desire to seek the companionship of other human beings in informal or social groups. They seek this for basic personal and psychological reasons such as satisfying human needs for friendship, for association with others, for a sense of increased security and as a home base. Thus most people wish to be accepted and to interact co-operatively with at least one small reference group, and usually with more than one group. One of the most psychologically relevant reference groups for most people is the work group which includes peers, superiors, and subordinates.

These groups can make a considerable contribution to achieving an organisation's objectives in that they can give a member of a group a feeling of security and of belonging, can maximise the contribution of each individual involved, lead to a greater participation in decision making and problem solving, and result in a greater commitment of the individual to the group's and hopefully the organisation's objectives. On the other hand, if the group is unhealthy, it can lead to internal bickering within groups, the group's objectives not being the organisation's objectives and to serious conflict between groups, all of which are detrimental to achieving the organisation's and the project's objectives. The project manager must therefore be aware of the characteristics of groups and of intergroup behaviour and of the factors which can lead to the evolution of effective groups.

Principal factors contributing to the formation of a group are

1. They are engaged together in a task or operation.
2. They come into day-to-day contact with each other.
3. They are interdependent.
4. They have the same backgrounds, skills and sense of values.
5. Leadership and management.

Several different types of groups have been classified and all exist in the project setting, namely

1. Vertical groups
2. Horizontal groups
3. Mixed groups

A vertical work group consists of people from different levels in the same company, department or function. Formal, permanent, vertical work groups form part of the organisation of most companies, and provide a home base for the majority of people involved in a project. They are normally created to carry out or perform one specific function and are made up of people with the same background, skills and values, and can be considered as a uniform group.

A horizontal group in a project is a group of managers or technologists at the same hierarchical level or status, often, but not necessarily so, in the same profession. For example, the project managers of the owner, the principal contractor and main subcontractors may form a group by themselves, or may form a group with the heads of the various functional groups contributing to a project, all more or less at the same hierarchical level. The mixed group is one which includes people from different levels from different companies or departments involved in the project.

Groups are very necessary in the project setting because a project is never a one-man or one-manager task. The complexity of a project, the contributions required from the many different specialised skills which no one man can have, the amount of work involved, the large number of activities that require to be managed, organised, planned and controlled, the mass of information necessary and normally the number of companies involved, all necessitate the involvement of a number of managers and specialised technologists from different functions. Thus in a large project there is not one group but many formal and informal groups. Likert in his book *New Patterns of Management* states that organisations can be considered as systems of interlocking groups. The typical project organisation is thus not just a set of relationships between individuals, but between sets of interlocking and interdependent groups. These interlocking groups are connected by individuals who occupy key positions of dual membership of groups and serve as links between these groups. In the typical project organisation there are many groups of all three types: each individual department or section will tend to form a vertical group, the people in each company working on the project will tend to form a mixed group, and ideally, all the people working on the project will form another mixed group. These groups may lead to greater effectiveness, but they can also lead to a consolidation of a 'we/they' attitude.

The vertical group, consisting of people from different levels in the same company or department, is probably the group that forms most naturally in the project setting, but it may be the least desirable from the project manager's point of view. It can be a healthy group, with great cohesion and team spirit, and can lead to greater effectiveness within the company or department on internal matters. The great danger is that a 'we/they' attitude can be established between this group and other functions, departments and companies working on the project. That can lead to complex intergroup resentment and conflict, and as all groups in a project must work together, this in turn leads to a less effective overall project group.

The senior members of the departments, functions and companies in the project are usually involved on a day-to-day basis and form a horizontal group which can link the overall organisation of the project together. They occupy key roles in the project organisation and serve as channels of communication, influence and policy integration from one group to another. The personnel in the various groups may not all be aware of each other, but if the horizontal linking group is effective this will set the whole tone of the organisation and tend to lead to the other groups becoming effective teams. It is possible for a project group involving several sub-organisations with different management philosophies to work effectively together provided that the linking members of this horizontal subgroup form an effective team. They can be bound together by mutual respect and an over-riding commitment to the project.

Horizontal groups may tend to form in each function, for example, the construction staff of the contractor will come into contact on a day-to-day basis with the client company construction staff. This may lead to conflict if each forms a separate group with the 'we/they' attitude, but if they can combine to form one group, this will lead to greater overall effectiveness. This does not mean that there will not be conflict, but can mean that conflict can be resolved by the logic of the situation. It involves mutual respect of both ability and commitment to their common objectives. Among the factors affecting the chance of achieving this type of group is the simple one of physical contact. Take the construction group, if each has a separate site office the tendency is to form separate groups. If they share the same building, have day-to-day contact, have lunch and coffee together, there is a much greater likelihood of their forming one effective group.

The principal group the project manager must endeavour to establish is a mixed group, which includes people from different levels and different functions of the departments and companies involved in the project. This kind of group leads to greater cohesion of the total project group and a commitment to the total project objectives. However, this is probably the most difficult group to create as the project group is a temporary formal group created to carry out a specific project, and when the project is finished, the group is broken up. The group may exist for several years, but the fact that it is temporary has an influence on each member. They may feel the group may be broken up at any time, and are more or less looking over their shoulders all the time to their parent company or department.

The members of this formal project group carry out the formal tasks necessary for the completion of the project and this can be regarded as the basic function of the group. If this is the only function of the project group then it will not develop into an effective team. Hand in hand with the formal functions must go the informal functions of satisfying the behavioural, personal or psychological needs of the group members. The objectives of the project manager is to get the aims of the informal groups and formal groups in the project committed to the same objectives. If he fails on this, the informal groups may be hostile or apathetic to the formal project goals and waste time and energy on intergroup conflict. If he succeeds, the project is on the road to success if it is humanly possible.

There is a great difference between a number of individuals working together and an effective group or managerial team. One needs only to note some of the observable signs of an effective team namely, team spirit, enthusiasm for the project; the members are supportive of one another and use the term 'we' instead of 'I'; they manifest towards one another, if not friendliness, at least respect for other members' competence and points of view; they show staying qualities when things get rough and a resistance to frustration; there is a minimum of bickering and members do things because they want to, rather than because they have to. An ineffective group will have apathy, jealousy, bickering, disjointed effort and pessimism about the project. Instead of saying 'we will have a go and make it', members will point out all the difficulties involved and will be negative about achievement.

If the co-operative relationships and interdependence of teamwork can be achieved, the interest and enthusiasm of all concerned, regardless of their organisational responsibilities will be committed to the project. The great advantage of an effective group in project organisation is that greater emphasis is given to the total organisational effectiveness than to that of the departmental or individual companies contributing to the project. Objectives between companies will differ, but all will have a commitment to the success of the project.

Team development

Effective groups or teams do not just coalesce as soon as

299

people are brought together. Groups are dynamic entities which are not static and unchanging. Studies of groups have shown four stages in the process of formation of an effective group. Effective in this instance means working towards project objectives, without interpersonal or intergroup conflict, and with satisfied and involved members. These stages are

1. The development of mutual acceptance and trust leading to a diminishing of defensive behaviour
2. Open communication
3. Co-operation and sustained productivity
4. Resolving of problems and control by mutual agreement.

Thus an effective group takes time to develop and at any stage in process can go in reverse. That is, an effective team can be destroyed by many factors; unsupportive management philosophy of any contributing company, a rogue key member, or failure of the project. Once a team has reached full effectiveness, however, it is reasonably resilient to minor factors affecting it. Such a team is a good training group for new staff and has also been used to endeavour to correct the behavioural practices of problem members of staff, provided that they are not key linking members.

Thus for a project to be successful, the project manager must provide the leadership necessary to develop a managerial team and the organisational environment must be favourable to his work. Where a company's philosophy is participative, a strong or fully mixed matrix organisation will achieve good results. It can lead to effective team building and generation of a 'project attitude' with wide behavioural consequences. This project attitude is a way of thinking that penetrates throughout the organisation and unifies all activities towards accomplishment of the project's common goals. It will become no longer enough to say 'that our department's effort was satisfactory but that the project was held up because of someone else'. No single organization effort is satisfactory in a project unless the project is a success, and every effort should be made to assist other organizations to carry out their tasks successfully. It involves taking off departmental 'blinkers' and co-operating by helping one another to successfully complete the project in terms of all its objectives.

In order to build an effective team and generate this project attitude, the company's managerial philosophy must permit the project manager to use participative management with its emphasis on creativity, open communication and participation. The project manager has also thus to be more aware of human relations and personal sensitivity than the normal functional manager.

The leadership capabilities of the project manager are essential to the growth of an effective group, that is, the personal qualifications, skill role and strategy of the project manager. The development of mutual acceptance, trust, co-operation and open communication can be helped or hindered by the project manager, but cannot be brought about by him alone. Nevertheless an essential factor leading to an effective group is the perceptiveness and the ability of the project manager to recognise and resolve group problems. The sort of signs the group manager must be on the lookout for are, for example, members of a group at a project meeting who fail to pay attention to each other and show lack of respect, members preoccupied with their own personal objectives, the existence of threatening attitudes, etc.

For a group to optimise its effectiveness, the project manager cannot perform all of the leadership functions in all circumstances at all times, and all group members must assist each other with effective leadership and member behaviour. Thus the behaviour of the group is not only influenced by the project manager's leadership qualities, but by attitude, knowledge, skills and capabilities of the individual members and the characteristics of the companies and departments involved in the project.

Thus the project manager must deal with the managerial problems of developing a project team out of these different groups working on a project. In this he is helped by the fact that the main advantage of project-type work is that there are clearly definable goals of schedules, cost and performance, which are ideal for managerial team building. If the co-operative relationships and interdependence of teamwork can be achieved then the associated intrinsic rewards associated with a successful project can generate the interest and enthusiasm of all concerned, regardless of their organisational responsibilities. In achieving a project attitude of mind the project manager has one distinct advantage in that the project is a discrete entity in itself. Thus the group has one primary task, which is the completion of a clearly defined project, within a specified time span, to a technical specification and within a budgeted cost. People working on the project are associated with something concrete, not something intangible, and a successfully completed project is obvious to everyone and people even remotely connected with it can draw satisfaction from this. The project manager has to use these advantages to establish effective team work and all that arises from it.

The project also has the advantage that all contributors to it must work together in establishing plans and budget and in carrying out the work. The project manager cannot arbitrarily set time limits and budgets; he must negotiate what is reasonable with the various functional managers and companies involved, making trade-offs between time and money in the light of the overall situation which only he knows, but which he must communicate. There is also the opportunity for intrinsic rewards which are so important to professional people and which exist in the clear and unclouded achievement of the project. The complaint of members of functional groups is often that they never see the overall picture but only their small task. It is possible in project work to communicate the whole picture and for the individual members to share in the success or perhaps the failure of the project. Extrinsic salary increases and promotions can then be fairly based on project contribution and achievement with the assessment of personnel normally being carried out both by the functional department head and the project manager. Co-operative relationships and interdependence thus must exist between all those working on a project or the organisation would grind to a halt. This in itself can lead to effective teamwork.

Finally, the more successful the management of a project is, the more obvious is the attitude of mind of those involved. They have a very real confidence in themselves and in each

302

other. This creates an atmosphere of mutual respect and collaboration, which is essential when a large group of people must work together towards a common objective.

Thus, though the project manager is faced with the problem of welding together people from various backgrounds and organisations into one, effective mixed project team, he does have certain advantages which can help him overcome the disadvantages of the matrix organisation. It is up to him to make use of these to achieve the project's objectives. Unfortunately because of the existence of different objectives and the fact that many groups are involved in a typical project, he must also have great skill in overcoming or preventing intergroup conflict.

Intergroup conflict in the project setting

It is an unfortunate fact that in many medium to large firms, even with the normal functional and hierarchical organisation, there tends to be intergroup conflict or hostility. It is almost impossible to have a project without differences between people; differences of opinion, values, objectives, etc. These differences can lead to discussion, argument, competition and conflict. Discussion and argument are constructive, whereas competition can be both constructive and destructive, but conflict is always destructive. It would be foolish to imagine that groups can work together on a project without disagreement and some conflict. Disagreement between people is almost inevitable in the project setting, and indeed, to a certain extent, it would be undesirable if this were not so. There is bound to be some disagreement in a healthy organisation, and it is often essential for efficiency and effective decision making.

One of the most important functions of the project manager is thus the solution of intergroup conflicts occurring among groups involved in his project. If he is to maintain an effective mixed team comprising all the groups working on his project, he must constructively prevent and overcome this destructive intergroup conflict. If he does not, the project performance will almost certainly be seriously affected.

303

Conflict in a project arising between

1. Individuals in the same group.
2. Individuals in different groups and companies.
3. Groups in the same company.
4. Groups in different companies.
5. Between companies, that is, between sets of groups.

In particular there is the great likelihood of conflict between

1. Project and functional groups.
2. Engineering and operations groups.
3. Owner and contractor groups.

Consequences of conflict

Where there is hostility or conflict between key linking members of groups, or between groups, it breaks up, or makes impossible to form a healthy effective team out of all those working on a project. It leads to a lack of respect and trust between groups, a lack of harmony and co-operation, and a breakdown in communication, with information being distorted, censored or held back. Each group will tend to reject ideas, opinions and suggestions arising from the other groups, and feelings or emotion will run high with a greater chance of mistakes being made by people under stress with clouded judgement. Groups will tend to have unspoken objectives, different from those of the project, such as to 'get' the other group, block anything they propose, achieve dominance over them and show them in a poor light to senior management. Project objectives will be subordinated to the group goals which concentrate on achieving dominance or victory over other groups. This accelerates the breakdown in communication between groups, and creates unfavourable attitudes and images of other groups.

There will be a polarisation into a 'we/they' attitude, instead of 'all for one and one for all'. Decision making and problem solving will be slow and difficult, differences will not be worked through in an open manner and you will have win/lose situations leading to more conflict and hostility, lowest common denominator compromises, or submission of disputes to higher levels of management for arbitration. In general conflict is detrimental to overall project performance and will make it almost impossible for a project attitude to develop.

On the other hand, conflict between groups can actually enhance the cohesion and team spirit of the individual group. Competition does stimulate individuals and groups to greater performance in a similar way that it stimulates an athlete to give of his best. Group loyalty will increase, differences will be buried within the group and there will be a greater commitment to the groups objective, but not necessarily to the project objectives. They will tend to close ranks against a common enemy, that is the other groups. Within these groups there is thus a more purposeful atmosphere, and probably more autocratic leadership patterns, more structuring and organisation, more in-group loyalty and conformity for a solid front to the 'enemy'. The group within itself tends to be more effective in achieving its own objectives where co-ordination and interaction with other groups is not required. Though this may be advantageous for the individual group, it will prevent the formation of horizontal and mixed groups and lead to poorer overall project performance.

Reasons for conflict

It is probable that whenever individuals are involved together in any undertaking or operation that, given the variations that exist in human nature, there will always be differences and thus a potential for conflict. One of the basic reasons for this in a company is that there is a division of labour, that is, functionalisation, and this inherently creates groups with different sets of values and objectives. In almost every medium sized and large company there tends to be to a greater or lesser extent, antipathy or conflict between line and staff, and between different functions, for example, marketing and production, operations and engineering.

Each group will have a different set of values and given the same information, even with goodwill between groups, they will often come up with different points of view, or decisions based on these values. For example, the design engineering groups will want to design the project to the

305

highest technical standards, whereas the project group will want to compromise between time, cost and technical standards. This will influence their points of view on many decisions and problems and will inevitably lead to disagreement with a potential for conflict. It will also lead to differences between objectives between groups in the same company. For example, the operations people will want a production plant which is easy to operate, has many installed spare pieces of equipment, capacity for expansion and possibly some items which would be classified as luxuries by the project staff. The project group will want to balance time to completion and overall cost against performance standards, and thus they will have different points of view, values and objectives, and inevitably there will be differences and thus a potential for conflict. Request for changes to design, as discussed previously, are also a source of conflict between the design, project, construction, manufacturing and operations groups within a company.

There will also tend to be competition between these divisions of labour, that is, groups, in the same company for dominance within the company, (for example, production is the prime department and 'what they say goes') and for resources of men, money and promotion. There is also the problem of priorities and competition between projects for scarce resources. Certain groups involved in a project may be handling several projects at the same time, and their managers may have to allocate their resources to the various projects in a way that the project managers of the individual projects may not like. This leads to differences, and hence conflict between the project manager and the managers of these functional groups, and also between project managers in the company for these scarce resources.

This difference in values and objectives will also extend to the owner and contractor company groups working on a project. The contractor is in business to make a profit and he can only do this at the expense of the owner, or so the owner thinks. The owner wants to minimise the cost of the contract, which he can partially do at the expense of a contractor, or so the contractor thinks. The extreme expression of this is in the cost plus contract. In the worst situation the contractor, or so the owner's staff consciously or subconsciously believes, wants to maximise the cost of the project, at the expense of the owner, to maximise his profit. Thus the owner's staff will tend to supervise the contractor closely, question his decisions and performance, and from the contractor's point of view, interfere far too much. In a fixed price contract, the extra cost of changes will be a source of friction as discussed previously.

The problems arising from the division of labour in the normal firm are increased when the matrix organisation is used. There tend to be many groups involved in the typical project and there is thus the potential for conflict at each group interface. The project management group needs to be involved in the planning and control of the work of all groups in the project and this can be resented. Where responsibility and authority are unclear, there is always the potential for conflict. Defence of territory is one of the prime sources of conflict, and functional managers and contractors' managers will always tend to believe that the project manager is impinging on their territory or authority, but he must do to do his job effectively. The dual subordination of a functional group member to the project manager and functional manager can lead him to feel insecure in his position, and the functional manager may also resent the project manager's interference or, as he believes, reduction of his authority. With a contractor, contractual relationships may be unclear and this will always tend to cause conflict.

In a project, people are always working under pressure, and the project manager must always be a hustler, and thus will be applying more pressure to people to meet time and cost objectives, and this in itself can lead to conflict. When added to the role and territory uncertainties, it will enhance the personal stress that people are working under, emotions will be raised, tempers will be short and conflict can easily arise.

When groups or companies have different managerial philosophies, there will inevitably be differences. There will also be personality clashes in any organisation. There also tend to be problems with defensive behaviour by managers whereby they are reluctant to implement change, act on their own, delegate, take risks and make decisions. This can arise

307

when a manager is promoted beyond his abilities, where a technologist has been promoted to a managerial position and either has not adjusted to the managerial requirements, or is now out of touch with the technology he came from and he feels insecure. There is also occasionally a rogue manager involved who is determined to succeed at the expense of everyone else. He may be autocratic, ruthless and willing to stab other managers in the back to get on. Not only does this in itself cause conflict, but the other managers involved will probably react to defend themselves, and teamwork will be lost.

There are also problems which by themselves in a healthy team would not create conflict, but when coupled with one or more of the other problems described will cause conflict. These include differences in technical opinion, differences in time, cost and technical standards and strong personal commitment to one line of action.

The methods used to resolve conflict can often in themselves cause resentment and thus lead to further conflict. In resolving differences there are several strategies a manager or group can follow. For example

1. Forcing through their point of view by the use of formal or informal authority. The naked use of over-riding power may gain the point in question, but it will probably ensure a lack of commitment to carry it out and increased feelings of resentment and hostility.
2. Submission of the differences to a high authority, which will lead to the same result for the loser.
3. Withdrawal from the confrontation and sulk, with the same result.
4. Compromise at a low level of agreement with the probable result that both groups will lose and feel resentment.
5. Work through the differences in a frank and honest way with mutual trust and respect. This is essentially the ideal response from an effective team and the principal way of diminishing hostility and conflict, but unless one has trust and respect it is difficult to implement; which comes first the chicken or the egg?

308

Finally, one of the principal reasons for conflict is a history of previous hostility and conflict. At any one point in time there may be ill feeling between groups in a company which has built up over the years and which is very difficult to resolve within the temporary lifespan of a project. This may be the project manager's own company or it may be one company in the global organisation. There is generally a new global organisation for every project, and any one of the companies involved may have this situation, which if not resolved for the individual project, can spread through the total organisation like a disease.

The resolution of conflict

One of the project manager's principal tasks is that of an integrator and as such, the management, prevention and resolution of conflict is his responsibility. It is often impossible to completely eliminate differences, disagreements and competition, and it is questionable if it is advisable to do so. An organisation without visible signs of these natural human traits is normally mediocre, overly conformist and a dull place to work in. These factors contribute to better performance, problem solving, innovation, decision making and commitment to objectives, provided they are constructive. If they are about how best to carry out the project, then they are beneficial to the project. It is when they degenerate, and the project is not so important as scoring over the opposition, that conflict is harmful to achieving the project objectives.

A method of resolving differences, without creating conflict, is not to deny that they exist, but to accept that they occur naturally and to endeavour to resolve them by the logic of the situation. This is not just appealing to the groups to be objective, but also to take into account the more non-tangible contributors to conflict. If there can be frank and open discussion, that is, levelling, and a mutual analysis of the problem and the solution with respect for the other's point of view, then differences can be worked through and resolved without adverse conflict. This can lead to a greater understanding and commitment to the outcome, and if successful contributes to the growth of an effective team.

309

Unfortunately the working through of differences in this manner is one of the attributes of an effective team, and without having the makings of an effective team it is difficult to achieve; a chicken and egg problem again. Thus the problem the project manager is faced with is how to create the conditions, and how to provide the leadership and management that will increase the chances of an effective team evolving and prevent or reduce the likelihood of adverse conflict arising.

The various steps he can take can be classified into three sets, namely

1. Formal organisational steps
2. Informal organizational steps
3. Managerial or personal behaviour steps

The biggest advantage the project manager has is, as before, that there exist what the behavioural scientists call a superordinate objective, that is, the project itself. It has been shown that the biggest factor leading to a reduction of conflict is for all the groups to have a common objective to which they are committed and that requires them to interact with each other. Thus if the project attitude can be established, the project manager is half way or more to defusing adverse conflict. In addition, project work is normally challenging work, and when individuals are involved in challenging work there is less likelihood of conflict.

To encourage the establishment of this superordinate objective, all the organisations involved must emphasise that the criteria of individual and group performance is the total project organisation's effectiveness, and not that of the individual or single group. This involves such factors as performance assessments and salary increases and promotions being based on overall project performance, and thus the project manager having a say in these factors. It also involves the companies concerned recognising that the global project organisation is an entity which exists, and giving it due recognition.

To ensure that commitment to the project is built up and maintained the project manager must have a formal and informal information system that keeps everyone involved informed of progress and permits open communication. The project objectives, progress, problems and success must be communicated to everyone involved. There must also be as clear a definition as is possible of the responsibilities of those involved. The use of the work breakdown structure, cost accounts, work packages and matrix of organisation charts enables individuals right down the line to know what these responsibilities are, who they must interact with and the role of the project manager.

Not only must formal organisational factors be used to encourage the formation of an effective mixed project group, but so should informal factors. This implies encouraging the formation of informal group and social interaction between groups, for example, involvement in sports, having dinners together, dances, cocktail parties and having coffee and lunch in the same group. Physical factors should be used to stimulate project groups; for example, a common office for those involved, partitioned areas instead of a large 'bull-pen', visits to each other's companies. It is not generally possible to form an effective team with people you don't know fairly well, and thus both the owner and contractor should encourage prolonged visits of key personnel to each other's offices. Once people have had face to face contact and know each other, physical proximity is not essential in the long term. Without this, communication will be limited to formal channels, and without informal information channels, effective communication between groups will be greatly handicapped.

In dealing with the people and groups involved in his project, the project manager must be aware of the likelihood and hazards of conflict, and use tact in his dealings. Though he must of necessity use pressure, he must be aware that if pushed too hard into a corner, an individual can only resist, and the harder the project manager pushes, the harder the individual will push back. Therefore he must show respect for and listen to opposing points of view, and on occasions he may have to compromise and back down on a point, in a conscious effort to manage conflict. He cannot afford to become too emotionally involved and he must at all times keep calm. One of the basic lessons of management is that if you cannot manage your own emotions in the workplace, you cannot manage other people.

The project manager must be aware of the problems involved in the other functions involved in the project, and this often involves rotation of personnel among the basic functions. The project manager who has worked for both an owner and a contractor company will be in a better position to appreciate the other 'side's' problems and position. Finally, the project manager must be aware that in a matrix organisation he is impinging on other managers' roles, authority and territory, and he must do so with caution, respect and tact. Given all that, he must still attempt to minimise time and cost on his project and he is not in a popularity contest. At times he must throw caution to the winds and go 'bull headed' for what he believes to be necessary, but he must also be aware of the consequences and the alternatives. An effective team will respond to a greater challenge with more commitment to succeed, and he may be able to achieve his objectives without creating conflict.

Bibliography

Proceedings of Internet 76, *Project Implementation and Management: Bridging the Gap*, 5th Internet World Conference, Vols. 1-5

Proceedings of the 6th Internet Congress, 1979, Vols. 1-4

The Project Manager, Journal of the Association of Project Managers

Cost/Schedule Control Systems Criteria, Joint Implementation Guide, (1976), Departments of the Air Force, the Army, the Navy and the Defense Supply Agency, USA

Military Standard Work Breakdown Structures for Defense Material Items, (1975), Department of Defense, USA

North Sea Costs Escalation Study, (1976), Department of Energy, Peat Marwick Mitchell & Co., and Atkins Planning, HMSO

Avot, I. 'Why does Project Management fail?', *Management Review*, Jan. 1970, pp 36-41

Baumgartner, J. S., (1964), *Project Management*, Irwin

Baumgartner, J. S., (1979), Systems Management, The Bureau of National Affairs, USA

Cleland, D. I., 'Organisational Dynamics of Project Management', *IEEE Transactions in Engineering Management*, Feb. 1969, pp 96-106

Cleland, D. I. and King W. R., (1968), *Systems Management and Project Management*, McGraw-Hill

Hackney, J. W., (1977), *Control and Management of Capital Projects*, McGraw-Hill

Handy, C. B., (1979), *Understanding Organisations*, Penguin Books

Hanson, J. T., 'The Case of the Precarious Program', *Harvard Business Review*, Jan-Feb 1968, pp 14-34, 170

Jack, A. B., *Purchasing in a Heavy Engineering Industry*, Anderson Strathclyde Ltd., an internal report

Jennet, E., 'Experience with an Evaluation of Critical Path Methods', *Chemical Engineering*, Feb. 1969, pp 46-106

Kharabanda, O. P., et al (1980), *Project Cost Control in Action*, Gower Publishing Co. Ltd.

Knight, K., (1978), *Matrix Management*, Gower Publishing Co. Ltd.

Krause, W. A., 'Cost Control: A Contractor's Viewpoint', *Chemical Engineering Progress*, Dec. 1968, pp 15-19

Lock, D., (1977), *Project Management*, 2nd ed. Gower Publishing Co. Ltd.

Lockyer, K. G., (1975), *An Introduction to Critical Path Analysis*, Pitman

Lockyer, K. G., (1966), *Critical Path Analysis: Problems and Solutions*, Pitman

McGregor, D., (1960), *The Human Side of Enterprise*, McGraw-Hill

McGregor, D., (1967), *The Professional Manager*, McGraw-Hill

McPhail, N. A., (1980), *The Engineer as a Manager*, Unpublished M. Eng. Dissertation, University of Glasgow

Marciariello, J. A., (1978), *Program Management Control Systems*, J. Wiley and Sons

Middleton, C. J., 'How to Set up a Project Organisation', *Harvard Business Review*, Mar-Apr. 1967. pp 73-82

McNeil, J. F., Program Control Systems, *IEEE Transactions in Engineering Management*, March 1964

O'Brien, J. (ed.)., (1969), *Scheduling Handbook*, McGraw-Hill

Peart, A. T., (1971), Design of Project Management Systems and Records, Gower Publishing Co. Ltd.

Pilcher, R., (1973), *Appraisal and Control of Project Costs*, McGraw-Hill

Schein, E., (1970), *Organisational Psychology*, Prentice Hall

Taylor, W. J. and Watling, T. K., (1979), *Successful Project Management*, Business Books

'Time and Resource Aspects of Project Management in the Construction of Chemical Plants', *The Chemical Engineer*, June 1967

Index

Inflation
consequences of, 148
effect on escalation of costs, 150-2
forecasting, 149-50
project costs, 148-54
Influence, 280
Interpersonal behaviour, 289

Level of detail planning, 38-41
Levels in planning, 63, 66
Line and staff form of project
organisation, 12
Line of balance, 137-43
LOB, 137-43

Management information systems, 190,
222-7
Management philosophy of planning,
35-8
Matrix of responsibilities, 20-1
Matrix organisation, 14, 18
authority problems of, 283
complexities of, 276
Milestones, 110-11

Network analysis *see* CPM/PERT

Operational planning,
problems with, 83
modern methods of, 114
Organisation
co-ordination form of, 12, 283
divisional, 13
global, 18
company, 11
matrix, 7, 14-17
of projects, 11
temporary nature of, 277, 293
Overheads, 195

Participation, 293
Performance analysis, 192, 197, 202
Performance report, 211-12, 220-2
PERT *see* CPM/PERT
Plan as management tool, 43
Plan as a tool to achieve authority, 282
Planning
art of, 31
completion and commissioning, 58-60
computer based systems, 87
data base for, 96
design, 53, 58

detail, level of, 38-41
development stage,
difficulties with, 32-6
functions of, 42-3
human factors in, 32
hierarchy of plans, 60, 66
levels of planning, 63-6
library modules, 124-31
line of balance, 137-43
LOB, 137-43
managerial philosophy of, 35
manpower,
milestones, 110-11
modern methods of, 95
multi-project planning, 131-4
operational, 83, 114
planning the planning process, 44
real time, 41
rolling wave concept, 66
reports, 95, 97, 100
resistance to, 35
resources, 117-24
S curves, 101, 110
sorted output, 95-101
specialist, 36-8
very large projects, 134-7
power, 280
attitude, 294
complexity of, 4
definition of, 1
objectives, 46
strategy, 46
Procurement
buying, 261
planning and control of, 259-74
project liaison, 260
suppliers' plans, 264, 271-3
Productivity, 251

Real time planning, 35
Reports
monthly, 227-30
performance, 212, 220-2
Resistance to planning, 117-24
Role of staff planner, 36-8

Schedule performance index, 203,
214-16
Schedule variance, 214-16
S curves, 101, 110, 203, 209-10
Shortcomings of project management, 10

317